Expecto Patronum:
Using the Lessons from Harry Potter to Recover From Abuse

By Matt Atkinson

RAR Books

Ordering Information:
Special discounts are available on quantity purchases within the USA by non-profit corporations, agencies, associations, and others. For details, contact the publisher at the email above.

Printed in the United States of America

First Edition

14 13 12 11 10 / 10 9 8 7 6 5 4 3 2 1

"Harry felt a great leap of excitement. He didn't know what he was going to — but it had to be better than what he was leaving behind."

Contents

PREFACE

In my years of work with the issues of domestic and sexual violence, I have formed many close friendships with survivors of childhood abuse, rape, trafficking, emotional abuse, and other traumas. I first encountered many of them through my therapy practice, and then from my previous book, *Resurrection After Rape*. Some of them even contributed their own writings to my second book, *Letters To Survivors*. My clinical work, which included occasional full-day training seminars and conference workshops for mental health therapists, tended to be heavy on the academic basis for treatment of post-traumatic stress disorder arising from abuse.

This book, though, is for the "Potter-struck" reader. It is the book that may have been the most fun to write, because it combines two topics that are so dear to me: academically-sound evidence-based methods of recovery from trauma, and Harry Potter. My goal in writing it is to go further than merely commenting on basic parables and inspirational analogies drawn from the Potter series; it's not enough, for example, to say "Dementors represent depression!" and leave it at that. Nor is my purpose to draw parallels between trauma recovery and Harry's personal journey, which could be done in a pamphlet. Rather, I hope to take complex psychological topics and give the reader a novel way to examine them through the familiarity of Harry Potter symbolism. It's one thing to talk about "stuck points" and "dissociation" and "internalized shame," but when those dry psychological concepts are presented through the lessons of the Harry Potter mythos, my hope is that the reader can say to themselves, "Oh, so *that's* what that means! I get it so much clearer now! The Horcrux imagery to describe PTSD makes sense!"

Millions of people have grown up with the Harry Potter books; in the United States an estimated 20 million children read them, and of the 400 million books sold we have no data about how many adults have also read them. Those who read them as children and teens are now adults, and many are passing the experience on to their own children. Because statistics also reliably show that about one in five children will experience some form of abuse in their lives, the overlap between people who grew up with Harry, Hermione and Ron and those who grew up with the pain of personal trauma is significant. I wrote this book in a style that does not talk down to the reader, or which makes assumptions about the reader's age, experiences, or capabilities; Potter fans I have met tend to be intellectual, sophisticated, and capable of unfolding nuanced ideas. Those who have lived through torment and abuse *and* who grew up with dreams of Hogwarts are now at a point where they are prepared to confront the pain in their pasts, and to apply the wisdom of the *Harry Potter* books in an even deeper way than they could in childhood.

For that reason, I have not shied from addressing complex psychological topics. For example, explanations of how the amygdala's function in the brain relates to trauma triggers is not a simple matter, as it involves brain chemistry, neurology, and an understanding of what triggers actually are—and all of those are in this book. Touchy subjects like forgiveness, progressive concepts of equality, and challenging topics such as self-harm are all part of this book's breadth. Additionally, I examine not just the personal journey of Harry himself, but also of Ron, Hermione, Dobby, Winky, and other characters as well.

I have written to the reader as either male or female, varying the pronouns I use and carefully selecting anecdotes from both male and female clients in my past work. My hope is that the writing itself will find its way into the hearts of readers of any age, male or female, straight or LGBT, and who have endured any type of trauma. Unlike *Resurrection After Rape,* which was written specifically for female rape survivors, I try to incorporate information about many types of trauma for the benefit of both male and female readers, and with an awareness that abusers can also be either gender. The clients I have worked with have survived such traumas as physical abuse, sexual molestation, rape, human trafficking, antigay violence, verbal and psychological abuse, and other forms of exploitation, all of which I combine into the category of "betrayal trauma." The betrayal of the human relationship is often the heart of the pain.

To address pronouns and syntax just a bit further, the reader will occasionally find instance where I refer to "your abuse" or "your rape." This wording has been the topic of much discussion on internet forums

I help moderate. I want to assure the reader that such wording is simply in deference to proper grammar rules, and there should be no deeper inference in the wording "your rape." I am absolutely mindful of the possible implication that the descriptive word "your"can be misinterpreted by some as an ascription of responsibility or ownership, and want to offer readers assurance that this is not the case. Therefore, phrases like "…your abuse" or "…your trauma" are merely standard English, and have no deeper significance.

I also make occasional references to the "soul" or "spirit", such as the description of a trauma's effects on "your body, mind, and soul." I have avoided overtly religious wording in this book, other than those words of poetic imagery. While the *Harry Potter* books carry obvious religious parallels, they speak for themselves and don't need me to impose a particular theology on the reader. This book, then, offers an interpretation of *Harry Potter* that is both secular but respectful of the spiritual themes that J.K. Rowling has written.

This book was written with the assumption that the reader is seeing a therapist to help with trauma healing. I realize that assumption will not always be true, and I do not want the reader to be put off with me over my references to therapy and therapists. I have kept in mind that many readers will not be clients of a therapist at all, and have tried to provide content that will be helpful nonetheless. I do recommend the guidance of a qualified, licensed mental health therapist, though, and in some sections I will even explain why this is more helpful than a go-it-alone approach. For example, a clinical therapist is particular helpful during the process of writing and reading your memories of your traumas, and the subsequent emotional triage after you have gone through such an agonizing rite of passage in your recovery work. Therapists will also find this book useful, as it will provide them with a new vocabulary with which to help clients who might not respond to conventional "therapy lingo," but excitedly assimilate the same concepts when processed through *Harry Potter*.

Quotes from the *Harry Potter* books are cited from their American sources, are limited to the briefest possible excerpts that demonstrate a point, and are used in compliance with Fair Use protections for the purpose of academic/commentary use.

CHAPTER ONE

Harry Potter and the Hero's Journey

Harry Potter had no idea that he would one day transform the world—even the Muggle world. As a small child, cowering under the stairs in an abusive home where he was commanded to remain silent, subservient, and free of any hopes or dreams, there is no way he could have known that years later, children and adults would use words like "Qiuidditch" and "Horcrux" in normal conversations. Nor could he have known that scholars, therapists, and professors would ever take the books about his life seriously.

Of course, Harry could not have known this; he's fictional, after all, right? The mind behind Harry, though, J.K. Rowling, has given us truths in parable form, which have kept the book series alive in our hearts to the point that even many of us adults are shamelessly in love with the tales. These books are not special merely because the stories are "cool," or because billion-dollar merchandising has made eternal customers out of us. They are special because they stir something inside us that runs deep. Deeper than the angst of mere supernatural teen love or mere action and strife, Harry Potter's story stirs us because it brings truths that are both sad and hopeful together in ways that we often recognize in our own lives.

Many of us crave the adventure of a life lived for heroism, but that's not actually what elevates the Harry Potter series for us. Many of us recognize the tale of a young hero plucked from a modest life and sent on a quest to change the world; we have Luke Skywalker, Katniss Everdeen, and Frodo Baggins to take us on such quests. Many of us love stories that remind us what it was like to be a wide-eyed child, excitedly taking in the world of adventure that lay at the end of an unpaved bike trail or in the heights of a tree house. But even that's not quite it.

In my work as a therapist with both teens and adults, I began to notice that the Harry Potter stories held an even more reverenced place among those who had lived through suffering, than they did for perhaps any other mega-fan. My relationships with wounded people—those who had been abused, neglected, raped, rejected—revealed to me that Harry's heroic journey touched their hearts just a little bit deeper, and seemed to offer a special sort of hope to the sadness they had carried inside. These were not just the stories of a boy from a dull life who had become a hero; these were the stories of an abused boy who had wrestled with his own traumas, learned what it takes to overcome them, and replaced his grief with joy. Harry's battles were both external and internal; his fought not only Voldemort who pursued and attacked him at every chance, but he fought the remnants of Voldemort's horrors that had been left embedded within Harry himself. These are not just stories of a hero winning over an enemy, they are stories of a wounded person overcoming his own trauma and becoming healed.

The significance of J.K. Rowling's seven-book parable is not lost on wounded people, although sometimes we might not even realize why we are responding so strongly to her writing. I think we recognize in Harry a kindred spirit, a fellow wounded person, a survivor of trauma, who has embarked on a hero's journey that reminds us of what we face in our own healing. While many readers see trolls and Dementors as just fantastic monsters, an abused person recognizes symbols for real truths about fear, the torment of depression, and what it takes to heal our spirits from pain. People who have lived with trauma know how it feels to be lonely, rejected, treated as if your life and your soul don't matter. When Harry struggles with those same feelings, they ring true. What Harry wants most in the world isn't fame or glory, it's simply to be connected to others who love him. When he finds that in Hermione, Ron, Neville, and Luna, he begins to heal.

"But I'm not like Harry Potter!" you might be saying. People relate to Harry as a hero and beloved literary character, but may have trouble identifying with him as an abuse victim like themselves. In some cases, readers may feel that their own abuse is worse than Harry's, so offering Harry as a model for overcoming abuse isn't accurate: "I was beaten, raped, molested, tortured; Harry was kept under the stairs. How can you possibly make a case that he's a role model for my situation?" Others may see Harry as more of a role model than they deserve: "I was abused, but only verbally. Harry went through so much; how can I possibly aspire to relate to someone like him?"

In order to apply Harry's journey to your own life, it may be important to take a step back and look at the bigger picture of abuse, so that the details that vary between your own life and Harry's don't get in the way. It would be a shame if Harry had achieved something wonderful that could inspire you, too, but a dissimilarity between your story and his kept you from absorbing the lesson. To do this, let's first be clear that Abuse is any behavior through which another person uses power to control you in ways that cause humiliation, shame, pain, and trauma. Trauma is the inner psychological wound that results from being abused. In my work as a therapist, I have seen people in group treatment "rank" themselves by comparing their abuse to everyone else's, based on what they thought were the worst kinds of abuse, and which kinds were the least serious. But in reality, any abuse that causes trauma is as serious as any other, and pain is pain.

Some of my clients had endured years of emotional abuse, constantly being told they were ugly, unloved, failures, worthless, and at fault for everything. Because they thought "abuse" meant being beaten, they would say to me, "…but at least I wasn't abused!" Meanwhile, they had the same feelings of shame, the nightmares, headaches, muscle pain, anxiety, depression, substance abuse, self-injury, mistrust of others, panic attacks, and startle reflexes as my clients who had also been beaten, raped, and tortured. I also worked with people who had been raped, but because they had always thought of rape as something that happens when psychos in the bushes attack in the dead of night, they had not been able to name their own traumas when they had been raped by someone they knew, even in a relationship. All they knew was that they felt they had done something wrong.

Research into the effects of abuse has found that all types of abuse result in very similar psychological and emotional stress.[1] Dumbledore knew this, too, when he explained to Harry, "there are much more terrible things than physical injury."[2] Harry may not have endured all the same traumas as some—he was never raped or molested, for example, while as many as one in five people have endured sexual assault in their lifetimes—but he has been through the traumas of physical violence, neglect, verbal

1 "Childhood Psychological Abuse as Harmful as Sexual or Physical Abuse." American Psychological Association, Oct. 8, 2014, http://www.apa.org/news/press/releases/2014/10/psychological-abuse.aspx
2 *Harry Potter and the Half-Blood Prince*, p.559

abuse, torture, and bereavement. From a clinical point of view, it is actually remarkable he can form as deep and meaningful attachment with others as he does, let alone becoming an example of the abused person's journey to recovery. Harry Potter is, in every way, a suitable role model for you, even though your life experiences are so different than his.

Harry also finds mentors who can help guide him. Despite sometimes feeling lost and alone on his journey, he learns that becoming strong is not something he can do on his own. There is no spell, no self-help book, no pill that will cleanse trauma from your life, and abuse is not the kind of injury that heals simply by passing time. Abuse hurts you emotionally and spiritually by severing your sense of belonging and connection to others, so trying to recover in isolation without help is the opposite of the cure. Harry may occasionally feud with his mentors, as we all do, but he is able to finally accept that they truly care for him.

Many heroes experience an intense disillusionment toward their mentors/counselors/ministers at some point in their journey. Some feel abandoned when the mentor compels the hero to step forward on their own (like Harry Potter becoming furious with Dumbledore in The Deathly Hallows), and others feel disillusioned when the human fallibility of their mentor becomes apparent (like when Harry becomes disgusted with Remus Lupin when Lupin makes a poor decision about his own family). The mentor is no longer idealized as perfect. When you have been abused, it can be difficult to accept that people have the potential to be both good and flawed, and feeling frustrated by a mentor, guide, or therapist is very normal. Trying to find others who will never fail will leave you more depressed from the false belief that nobody in the world is actually dependable. But connecting with others who can understand and help share your pain is very healing. Harry doesn't always get it right, and neither will you, but he doesn't give up. You may even find that as you turn to therapists, friends, and other mentors for support, the people who abused you may intentionally try to damage those relationships. The scandal-mongering gossip Rita Skeeter nastily casts aspersions on the Harry-Dumbledore relationship, implying that it is pathological, sick, and even dangerous, and people believe her, including, at times, Harry himself.

One tragic example of a failed potential hero involved a middle-aged woman who came into my office for group therapy. She regarded herself as exceptionally flawed, alone and unique in her experiences of pain. She believed she had been hurt in ways so extraordinary that she would boast that she was an elite sort of abuse victim. It was as if she thought of herself as special by having endured traumas that exceeded the mundane understandings of the rest of us ordinary folks. She was the "Gilderoy

Lockhart" of abuse victims. When we tried to connect with her, to know her at any level, she rejected our efforts like marshmallows thrown at a wall: "you wouldn't understand me. You've never faced anything like what I am facing." Sure enough, after just a few sessions of this, she announced she was leaving therapy. Her reason: "I don't feel like I fit in here. You all are so warm and accepting to each other, but it's as if you don't care about me, so I won't be taking any more of your precious time." She had fulfilled her own prophecy of being grandly unknowable. She put her own wounds between herself and the rest of us who wanted to help, and then felt rejected when we couldn't reach through to her.

That's not how Harry would have done it. Harry admits that he can't succeed without his friends, and depends on them at every turn. His worst emotional pain during his quest is any time he and a friend feud and become separated. When they reconcile and mend the friendship, he becomes strong again. Like you, Harry knows that loneliness is an emotional echo of abuse, and any time he feels rejected his heart returns to those feelings of being a bullied, beaten little kid kept in a closet. The only time Harry intentionally separates himself from his friends is when he goes to face Voldemort alone. This is a perfect symbol for how you can handle trauma, too. We can depend on friends for strength and understanding, but it is not everyone else's job to fix your issues for you. You can't simply tell them what triggers you, and expect them to make every trigger go away. This is your work to do, even though it's unfair that you carry those traumas in the first place. Harry can't stand the thought that anyone else would suffer for him, to the point that he willingly walks toward Voldemort to give up his own life. At the time, Harry doesn't know that facing Voldemort in that way will actually be the solution for how to defeat Voldemort; likewise, facing your traumatic memories and feelings is what will finally help you release them from inside your heart. Others can help by loving you, listening to you, being patient with you, and mentoring you, but they cannot do that work for you. It's yours to do.

In real life, you will have to pass through a dark time as a crucial step toward healing. For Harry, it means having one last vision of his family before forever relinquishing the resurrection stone and entering the forest to face Voldemort. For you, it might mean finally declaring yourself to be an abuse victim, and becoming able to name your trauma to others. It can mean pouring out a final drink and giving up the stress comforts of alcohol or drugs, and becoming sober. It could mean self-injuring for the last time and covenanting with yourself or another person that it is finished. For trauma victims in therapy, it might mean finally hand-writing the complete narrative of your abuse and then reading it aloud. All of these are forms of becoming vulnerable, so that you can finally face your traumas without layers of denial to protect you, just like Harry had to face his worst fear without defenses. Many victims halt their journey right here, refusing this agonizing-and-life-saving step. But Harry takes that final step in order to purge himself of his own trauma.

Harry does what he knows it will take to confront Voldemort for the final time, and he does it honestly and without tricks. He doesn't realize at the time that walking defenselessly to face Voldemort is actually what will really cleanse him of Voldemort's possession of him. He simply knows it's time to face his worst enemy. What Harry does in that moment teaches us something else about coping with trauma: there are no shortcuts or tricks to get out of it.

You may have been abused or raped years ago, and perhaps you're wondering why now, after so long, the feelings from it are becoming unbearable again. I've learned from working with victims of trauma that if you are not ready to cope with it yet, there's nothing you or a therapist can do to force the process of healing. But if you are ready, there's nothing you can do to stop it from coming up in your mind again; your soul will force you to confront your trauma when it's time. You'll have to walk into that dark forest like Harry did, and have a showdown with your own inner pain.

That means wasting no more time on fake coping methods. No more getting high to wall off anxiety or nightmares. No more cutting yourself to change the emotional pain through a release of physical pain. No more trite inspirational slogans, positive thinking mantras, "balancing your energies" with crystals, and no more telling your therapist you're fine when you're shaking inside with grief and rage because of your abuse. You have to face every part of your trauma to get through to the other side of it. Too often, I have seen people succeed at every stage of this journey, and then give up at the last step.

A young man I counseled, Tyler[3], had grown up in a violent family, pushed around by an older brother, yelled at by his affair-having, wife-threatening father (from whom Tyler often hid in closets and bathrooms), and was made to feel invisible. Tyler's father bullied the family, even resorting to kicking and strangling pets, while feigning pompous Christian morality in public. Tyler had emerged from a life of adolescent binge-drinking, drugs, violence, and suicide attempts to become a vibrant, creative, and promising voice for other men who had endured similar struggles—something much needed in this world! But alas, he chose the road most traveled, returning home to a life much smaller than his dreams and a family that darkened the fire from his eyes. Nothing is quite as sad

3 A pseudonym

as a person who once lived with fire and power, resuming their crouched place inside a cage.

I actually genuinely liked and admired Tyler, but Tyler was often difficult to be around; he would often lapse into sour and hostile moods. When this happened, Tyler would lash out at people, including those who cared for him and sincerely wanted to help him. In his mind, people who expressed affection or admiration for him were really just a bunch of phonies who were only trying to scam him with their flattery. To him, the more that a person expressed their regard for him, the more convinced he became that they were secretly obsessed with devising ways to exploit him. Each act of kindness shown to him became, in his damaged imagination, more evidence for his conspiracy theory; "I think the world of you, and you're pretty awesome" became, in his mind, "See? This person is trying to force their way into my life to trick me, to take advantage of me like they always do; someone who claims to love or care for me is just trying to thieve from me yet again!" As a result, he kept people at a distance, was often short-tempered, only offered vague hints of how he really felt, and the faulted people for not supporting him adequately. If you had asked him, Tyler would have said that he craved being loved and cared for, but then he rejected efforts from friends, loved ones, and myself as his therapist. All of these traits are common symptoms of unhealed trauma.

When Harry, Hermione, and Ron are carrying the locket Horcrux together, its effects on them become dreadful. Each of them who carries the Horcrux became very Tyler-like, suspicious of the motives of the others, argumentative, and surly. Each of them soaks in and reflects the toxic emotions of the Horcrux, almost as if it was radioactive and they were absorbing its poisonous energy. Carrying the Horcrux locket had very similar effects to carrying the deep, hidden inner wound of trauma, and they nearly lose each other's friendship because of it. When the locket finally opens, the evil voice within it attacks Ron with all of Ron's insecurities, taunting him that those who claim to love him really don't want him around, that they're happier without him, that he has failed them, and that they are laughing at him while pretending to care about him: who could look at you? Who would every truly care about you? What have you ever really accomplished? Everyone knows you're nothing compared to all the people around you who are better and more deserving…the words issued from the Horcrux are the same as those your trauma still says to you from deep within, too. Ron nearly succumbs to the dread of those inner fears, but he is able to muster the strength to face and destroy the source of those fears and resurrecting the friendships it had nearly cost him.

Harry Potter and the Hero's Journey

If a victim of trauma disengages from their support system, or rejects help, or perceives deceptive motives in every offer of help, or tries to "go it alone," they will also become lost and wander for years. The hero's journey is a bloody, sweaty climb.

If it were any other way, it wouldn't take a hero to complete it.

CHAPTER TWO

Recovery and the Triwizard Championship

We therapists can be a boring lot of people. We tend to put things into dry, academic language: internalized shame, processing your stuck points, countertransference and projection, self-actualization, and worst of all, "how does that make you feel?" Ugh. But behind all the stale vocabulary, there really are some important, well-developed concepts about therapy that we use to help partner with you through the healing process. Whether you work with a therapist or not, the concepts can still be helpful. However, nobody wants to read a book about "initial acute crisis management, strengths-based dialetics, and stuck point processing." I could write that book, and it would sell maybe five copies.

Cleverly, though, that is exactly the book that J.K. Rowling has already written, only she disguised all three of those concepts as the tests in the Triwizard Championship in *Harry Potter and the Goblet of Fire*.

When you first begin to deal with your trauma—and I mean *really* deal with it, without denying it, suppressing it, medicating it with alcohol, or feeling helpless about it—you may feel worse rather than better. The clients I worked with were tempted to drop out of therapy, convinced it had been a mistake to even begin, because rather than going home feeling better, all their worst emotions were gushing up now. It was as if everything they had ever feared about their pasts was now right in front of them, snarling at them, making them feel helpless and overwhelmed. They were sure there was no way they could survive! Their nightmares became worse, their headaches got worse, they were tempted to get drunk or high to cope, they would often self-injure more than usual, and all of their buried shame was erupting up again.

All of that is completely normal, and it does pass. But at first, it's horrible. One reason I liked group therapy for trauma work was so that newcomers in this "going through hell" stage could hear from others who had already beaten it, and who had words of encouragement. They could know for a fact that others had been through this test and also survived, and they could too.

Once you begin to open up about your trauma and start talking about it, reading and writing about it, and remembering it, you are facing the worst thing you can imagine. The childhood violence, or the rape, or the molestation, or the verbal abuse—whatever it was you lived through—is the dragon you have to come face-to-face with now. This is your first test, and it's horrible. You may even be afraid that you can't survive it. Like Harry facing the Hungarian Horntail, you are putting yourself directly in front of the most vicious, most fiery part of your past, confronting it, and just trying to get through with this. Cedric, Viktor, and Fleur have all gone before and succeeded, so Harry knows there is a way to triumph, but it's no less terrifying when he has to do this on his own, relying only on his inner strength.

Therapists call this "acute crisis management," and it describes the flood of turmoil you will probably go through when you first begin dealing with your traumas. This is the "it gets worse before it gets better" stage, and it's where people are most likely to drop out. In my own work experiences, this is where people were suddenly afraid that I was out of my league as a therapist because their traumas are *too* severe to be healed, or they start wishfully thinking that perhaps some Trelawny-like mystical energy will heal them without them having to endure all this struggle (one client of mine abandoned therapy because, as she explained to me, a shaman she had met online told her to simply put her face into a pan of water, speak the names of her traumas into the water, and then boil it—presto!). Facing the dragon is the "acute crisis management" of the Harry Potter parables, and there's no way to fake it or skip around it, and Harry had to rely on his own strength to succeed. Dropping out of this test only means you'll have to face it again, but after it's had time to grow even stronger. Triwizard lesson #1: Face your dragon when it's time. Hate it, but do it anyway.

Once he had succeeded, Harry felt relief and a newfound sense of strength and confidence. Others celebrated his progress, and he could continue without quite as much frenzy and crisis. His next task was to decipher the mystery of the dragon's golden egg. After he had been helped by Cedric Diggery to learn the solution, the egg revealed its clue in the form of a song:

Come seek us where our voices sound,
We cannot sing above the ground,
And while you're searching ponder this;
We've taken what you'll sorely miss,
An hour long you'll have to look,
And to recover what we took,
But past an hour, the prospect's black,
Too late, it's gone, it won't come back.[1]

Harry, knowing only the words of the song itself, has to deduce that the voices which "cannot sing above the ground" are from beneath the surface of water. The song refers to the holding of his best friend, Ron, by the Merpeople at the bottom of Hogwart's lake, and the challenge is to rescue him.

When you first begin to deal with your traumas directly, the feeling can be overwhelming, but as you make progress the crisis will subside, like Harry facing the dragon. Once that happens, you will feel drained and weak but hopeful, because you've just endured the psychological fight of your life. It is at this point that you will need to gather back what you've lost to your trauma. This is the time to rebuild your strength, your knowledge of how trauma works (and how to overcome it), and the relationships you need in order to continue onward.

Think of the song from the golden egg as being the voices of your traumas speaking to you; the abuse, the rape, the neglect might be over and in the past now, but the effects are still under the surface. They still affect you, perhaps not through here-and-now abuse that still happens, but under the surface they still tell you that you are unworthy, weak, and broken. They are not voices "above the ground," but rather voices that are buried deep within you now. Each time you experience a flashback, a panic attack, or a nightmare, it feels like the abuse from your past is "speaking" to you all over again from below, making you feel pushed back into those old emotions. Over and over in survivors' discussion groups that I help moderate, people in this stage of healing pose the same questions: "Does this ever end? Will I ever be over it?" They hear those voices from beneath the surface, telling them again that they're not good enough.

Trauma does take things from you. In my training seminars, one point I try to make is that abuse should be seen as a form of theft, a betrayal that takes something from someone else. Too often, people have simplistic views about why abuse happens: abusers get drunk and can't control themselves (false), abusers have anger management problems and

1 *Harry Potter and the Goblet of Fire*, p.463

21

they can't help it (false), rapists are perverts who can't get sex any other way (false), or abusers don't realize what they're doing is wrong (false). To pick an example from these, consider how often rape is treated as a form of coerced sex, or worse, *misguided* sex (for instance, a news article reports, "Teacher has sexual affair with 14-year-old student," or the myth that "women can't rape men" (and if they do, the males are simply lucky, not victims!)). The notion of rape being a form of corrupted sex is wrong, but it's what many people think. That is why I try to help people reframe the issue as a form of theft instead. I would have my clients write a journal, "If rape is a form of theft, what did it steal from me? And what did it *not* steal from me?" Both questions are important, and this exercise can apply to all forms of abuse, not just one.

Like the egg song says to Harry, "while you're searching, ponder this; we've taken what you'll sorely miss…" What did your abuse take from you? Begin a new tradition of avoiding cataclysmic phrases like "it took all of me/my soul/my worth as a person." Abuse took NONE of those things from you; you still have them. Work toward a new way of seeing: "It stole my night times. It stole the dreams I used to look forward to at night. It stole the safety I once felt at hearing footsteps. It stole the excitement and pleasure I felt in the touch of another person. It stole countless hundreds of hugs I would have given my family if I had not loathed my own body instead."

The egg song continues with a warning that now is the time to recover what was lost before it's gone forever; if you face the dragon and then stop working, the achievement will not last, and the traumatic symptoms will return. Fighting onward is what you are doing in this phase of healing. What have you *not* lost? What things can you recover as you heal? Which parts of you do you REFUSE to give away, no matter what? What do you hold for yourself as a treasure within? The idea is to begin to change the language you use when you talk about abuse. You need to see it as a hurt done to you, not a permanent stain of filth and badness about you. The first part – "what did my abuse steal?" – does invite a darker way of thinking because it asks you to focus on losses. It is common that this part of the two-part question can bring up anger and grief. But the work does not stop there. You are to take one more step toward reclaiming some of these stolen gifts. A survivor must avoid "all-or-none" words such as "always, never, everything, nothing" when she thinks about herself, and begin to realize that her entire self-worth is not lost.

You are going deeper beneath the surface now. Facing the dragon is all about overcoming the palpable here-and-now, in-your-face crises that your trauma causes when you first start to deal with it: the panic attacks, the substance use, the self-harm, the anger. But this second trial is about dealing with the voices beneath the surface, and beginning to gather back the things that have been stolen. One client of mine wrote this in her journal for this step in her work:

> What parts of me am I not giving to you—
> You'll never have the joy I feel when I look at my little girls, knowing that they will never be hurt by you, or a man like you. The peace I feel at night when I lay my head on my pillow, knowing I've made the world a better place. It gives me great joy to know that you don't have that peace.
> You'll never be able to see the love and compassion that I have for humanity. I would never want you to think I'd give up either one. There is the amazing person I've become. Smart, funny, caring, loving – that, you'll never see. You will never have the woman that I've become.
> You can never touch my healed woman. Never hear her words, live in her world – a world that still hopes, that is committed to keeping children safe from people like you.
> You found me when I was alone and abandoned. You should be ashamed. My pride for all I've survived will never be taken by you!

Like Harry Potter, she is diving beneath the surface of her pain to find what she could have lost, what her traumas could have taken from her, and she is claiming those things back again. They are *hers*, not her trauma's, and she is refusing to give in to the voices beneath the surface or abandon her strengths and her loved ones. She is not letting her traumas cost her her love of family and self. Like Harry expending himself to save his best friend Ron, she is using her energy to rescue the things she knows she will need to remain strong.

Rather than isolating and becoming morose and frail, this stage is when you will need to find your strengths and preserve the parts of your life that your trauma has begun to erode. Remember that Harry had no idea how to do this, and was convinced he would fail at it. He believed that everyone but him had the ability to succeed at this trial, and that he alone was too unlearned, too inexperienced, too young, to do what others could. But the support and advice he was able to find from someone else (Dobby, in this case) helped him succeed. In fact, his love for so many other people and his sense of mercy led him to not only rescue Ron from the Merpeople, but to also help with the rescues of Hermione, Cho, and Gabrielle as well. Although you may feel weak and hopeless at times, others who are struggling can sometimes find strength in seeing your efforts, and you could be helping to save more than just yourself during this trial.

Some people have difficulty with this stage because it compels them to consider positive things about themselves—"These are the good things I still have." This is an uncomfortable way for some to think, because the negative voices from beneath the surface are still so strong. A person who is accustomed to feeling hollow, worthless, and ugly either resists the assignment, or feels he is being arrogant if he does think about his positives. That is why it's a good idea to actually sit and write these answers out—"what did my abuse steal from me? What has it *not* taken; what do I still have? What can I recover?"—rather than just sort of tumbling the answers around in your mind like a lump of candy in your mouth. It's important to really plunge deep here. Write with intensity. Write like you're doing homework like Hermione would, not like Ron would. Two feet of parchment! This isn't the time for superficial pseudo-inspirational positive thinking stuff; treat this as a serious step in your self-rescue. Contemplating what you have left after your abuse, and which parts of you were stolen and need to be claimed back, is not a trivial matter. It is at the heart of what it means to heal, so go deep.

As one client of mine realized in therapy, "There are some pieces of me I just won't ever get back. I have to accept that they are gone. And for years I felt hopeless because of that, as if the core of me was stolen and I had to live out my days like a hollow tin man with no heart inside. But what I realize now is that I don't need those old pieces to re-grow. Those were pieces of a person I'm not like anymore. They were pieces of a hurt and broken me, and they can have 'em. I'm growing someone new." She had gone beneath the surface, terrifying as it was, to reclaim what she had lost. Triwizard lesson #2: realize that trauma has stolen from you, but you can reclaim those things if you are willing to go deep.

Finally, Harry had to face the maze. Fans of the *Harry Potter* books know that the maze turned out to be a rigged gambit to trick Harry into touching a portkey that transported Harry to a confrontation with Voldemort, but that is an adventure plot point, and not quite what I'm getting at here. For this analogy, take the final maze at face value in terms of the third trial: this is the part where Harry has to find his own way, confused and sometimes lost, but carrying all his prior learning with him.

When Harry reaches this stage of the trials, he has actually begun to feel confident in himself. He knows the maze will be challenging, but he is not as scared as he was during the previous tests he'd endured. He knows the maze lies ahead (it's been shown to him in advance), so he has time to prepare. He uses that time to learn specific skills that will help him, such as a spell that will point his wand north, the Impediment Curse to slow down attackers, a Shield Charm, and more. He is learning to anticipate what challenges might come, and to know what his own weaknesses are so that he can specifically strengthen them. He is also learning that while he is going through the trials, he does not have to take care of everything and every need around him: "[Sirius] reminded Harry in every letter that whatever might be going on outside the walls of Hogwarts was not Harry's responsibility, nor was it within his power to influence it." (Many abuse victims become people-pleasers who are afraid to say "no" to others, who fear confrontation, and who exhaust themselves by deferring their own needs for the needs of others; Harry is learning to not be like that, because right now he needs to focus on building up his own strength.)

This third trial is less about confronting the issues of the past, and more about preparing yourself for what comes ahead in your life. Harry learns spells that he thinks will be most important, based on what he expects to face in the trials ahead. Having faced your dragon and reclaimed your strength in the previous stages, you might begin to think about what aspects of your trauma could still be troublesome for you: are you prone to panic attacks? Are you occasionally attracted to relationship partners who are controlling or unkind? Is addiction an issue? Whatever your personal weaknesses are, this is the stage where you can begin to learn specific coping skills for each of them. It is also where you work your way through and out of the maze of confused thoughts that your past traumas have caused.

In therapist's terms, we call those confused thoughts "stuck points." Stuck points are the little fragments of broken, incorrect beliefs that still affect how you see yourself and your world. They are the rotten remnants of the ideas that your abuse and your abusers planted in your mind that still cause you to stumble, because they pull you back into accepting your abuser's beliefs:

- You are weak
- You did put yourself in that position
- People don't believe you after all
- Nobody will ever truly love you
- You did cause what happened
- You complied with your abuser's commands, which means it was partly your fault
- You should have been strong enough to stop it from happening
- You froze instead of fighting back, so it was your fault for being so weak

- As a child, you actually enjoyed the special gifts and attention your abuser also showed you, so maybe you are just as bad as he was
- You went back to your abuser after leaving them, so you're just as at fault as they are
- Maybe it wasn't rape, because what happened didn't seem like how rape is portrayed on TV
- If good things happen to good people, and bad things happen to bad people, but these bad things happened to you, that means you are a bad person

These are the mazes of damaged beliefs—stuck points—which you have to make your way through. The bad news is that they are incredibly tough, resilient thoughts, and not at all easy to overcome because they feel so true. They are the artifacts of your abuser's beliefs, implanted into your own mind, telling you to see yourself the way your abusers saw you. They lurk in wait, and then attack without warning, like the Boggarts and skrewts in the Triwizard maze. Any time you degrade and shame yourself, you are agreeing with your abuser, letting their remains come to life and control you, like Voldemort possessing Professor Quirrel. The good news is that stuck points tend to be the last difficult barriers between your traumatic past and your healed future, and you can prepare for them.[2]

Stuck points tend to be the things you are most ashamed of from your traumas, which is why they are so hard to face. For example, I once had a client who considered herself tough as nails, fierce, and smart, and she worked for her campus' rape prevention program. When she was raped on campus, she felt like an idiot. Her stuck points were: "I of all people ought to have known better! I should have been practically un-rapeable! Maybe I'm not tough…maybe I'm actually weak and stupid and easy prey!" That had become her "maze of thinking" that she had to get through, and no matter how often I or people in my therapy group tried to challenge her faulty beliefs, she would defend and reinforce them! In her mind, they felt so true, so they must *be* true, and anyone who challenged them was simply wrong. She had to work her own way through those beliefs, like Harry through the maze, facing the hidden traps of panic attacks and nightmares along the way, until she had truly, finally, really overcome those last stuck points.

Harry has to learn to accept help along the way through his maze. He has prepared for the maze challenge as if he has to work all on his own

---

2 Regehr, C., Cadell, S., and Jansen, K. "Perceptions of control and long-term recovery from rape." 1999 Am J Orthopsychiatry 69;1:110-5. Rape victims who had stronger beliefs in personal competence and control had less associated rates of depression and PTSD.

without guidance or company, but that turns out to not be true. Although he is skeptical of others, having been hurt and betrayed before, the support of Cedric Diggory becomes essential to Harry's own progress. In addition to the skills Harry has learned on his own, he also learns that other people are also part of his strength! He does not have to face his final test by himself, because there are others who are also going through the same things, and who are willing to accompany and defend him along the way.

Likewise, in your own journey there are so many other survivors of abuse, rape, molestation, and neglect who are worthy allies and friends. Sadly, I have also seen victims of abuse reject available support for the most pitiful of reasons: believing nobody else can truly understand them; refusing to accept the support of a fellow victim who is not their same gender; their abuse wasn't the same exact type, so they're not a suitable ally.[3] Not everyone who has gone through these traumas is automatically a capable supporter, but many are, and to this day some of my closest friends are people I've met through this work.

Advancing through the maze of stuck points becomes a new way of fighting back. Your journal is not an object of sadness; it is a weapon, a spell book, a scripture, that chases out the lies of abuse the way a Patronus makes Dementors scurry off. Approach your journaling with a sense of angry, courageous, determined strength; you are picking a fight against abuse itself every time you pick up your pen. If you choose to write endlessly about how empty, dark, broken, and ugly you are, you'll lose every battle. But when you call out the worst things abuse makes you think and feel, then challenge them, then shred and dispose of them with intelligence and insight and self-care, you will begin to kick trauma's ass.

Triwizard lesson #3: prepare for the things you'll still have to face, but realize you don't have to face them alone. Work your way through the maze, and accept help.

---

3 For example, I have a friend who is a male survivor of sexual assault, who has devoted his public life to advocacy for rape victims' rights. Unfortunately, he has also endured ridicule, hostility, and even outright rejection by some victims' groups, blogs, podcasts, and political organizations purely on the basis of his being male, with some opponents of his work flat-out denying that male abuser survivors' wounds and needs are as genuine as those of female victims.

CHAPTER THREE

Occlumency and Therapy

Repeatedly during therapy, I would be pressed by new clients with the simple challenge, "why do I even need to do this? What's the good in sitting there and spilling out your guts for someone else to listen to? Can't I just deal with this stuff on my own?" Those are fair questions. They seem even fairer when people often find that the early stages of therapy make them feel worse, not better.

Which brings up the question, why even do therapy at all? What's the point? Why can't someone recover from trauma all on their own without help…or can they? To answer these questions, we need to first uderstand what "recovery" from trauma even is, and if it's possible. I've worked with clients from ages 13 to 70, and many of them would insist to me that they were fine, they had recovered, they were "over it," while still cutting themselves, starving, drinking, getting high to deal with anxiety and flashbacks, and generally miserable. In fact, not a single client of mine ever began therapy because it just seems like a good idea at the time; in nearly every case, they had to attend therapy because they were dealing with problems at work, addiction, suicide attempts, and countless other problems. They had no intention of talking to me about their traumas. To them, that stuff was all in the past, and they just wanted to fix the here-and-now stuff and get the hell out of there. Seeing me for therapy was about as much fun as Harry being told he had to begin private lessons with Profesor Snape. Oh, joy.

Occlumency And Therapy

Frankly, many of them thought I was as mean as Snape, too. They couldn't believe I was actually trying to help them; they thought I was unfairly forcing them to think about their traumas, even when it hurt. As gentle as I was, taking care to go slowly and let them control the process (see? I'm not actually like Snape at all!), they still resented even being reminded of their personal pains. The reason I encouraged them to face their past traumas was the same reason Dumbledore needed Harry to learn Occlumency: those things can still invade our thoughts, taking us over, and bringing pain to us again and again until we learn how to guard ourselves.

Occlumency, in the *Harry Potter* books, is the learned ability to seal your mind shut as a way to protect yourself from malicious "mental spying" by an enemy. Mind-reading, or Legilimency, is a form of invasion into the thoughts of another person without their consent. If that sounds like psychological rape to you, you're reading it correctly. In Harry's case, Voldemort is able to sneak into Harry's mind to plant false images that manipulate Harry into traps, and to spy on Harry's activities and friends. Dumbledore realizes that Harry is susceptible to Legilimency, and arranges for Harry to learn Occlumency, the ability to block those invasions.

Again, reading and understanding *Harry Potter* can sharpen your understandings of trauma in real life. Experiences like sexual abuse, rape, and violence cause symptoms of depression in as many as 95% of victims, and this can last from childhood into adulthood. The physical effects of stress caused by trauma can cause physical aches and pains, such as joint pain, headaches, and digestive problems. Other effects of trauma include:

- Increased substance abuse
- Eating disorders, including overeating, food refusal, and bingeing,[1]
- Deliberate self-injury behaviors
- Onset or increase of smoking habits
- Fatigue and loss of energy
- "Anhedonia" – the loss of sensations of pleasure
- Exaggerated startle responses
- Loss of relationship quality
- Anger outbursts
- Retarded motor skills/response times
- Diminished ability to concentrate

These symptoms are caused by internal physical conditions that happen because of abuse trauma. Because they are physical conditions, they cannot be healed by sheer willpower, toughness, or ignoring memories of your

1 Zlotnick, C., et al. "The relationship between sexual abuse and eating pathology." 1996 Int J Eat Disord 20;2:129-34

trauma. They have to be fought directly and beaten, one-by-one, for them to fade away.

A good therapist is able to challenge your beliefs about yourself, your abuse, and the world you live in. Those challenges are not to put you down or discourage you, but to help you learn new ways of thinking about things so that your past abuse will lose its power to convince you that you're weak, ugly, unlovable, shameful, and that your abuse was your own fault. Since you might have very strong beliefs about those things, being challenged by a therapist can feel like Professor Snape just picking on you until you snap. That's not what's going on. "Thought challenging" cannot happen alone. It takes someone else suggesting other ways of looking at thing you may have never thought of before, and being willing to push you just a *little* farther in therapy than you are comfortable with, but still respecting your right to put the brakes on and stop the process when it becomes too tough. Like Snape and Harry, these sessions can feel brutal and exhausting, but as you become stronger in your "therapeutic Occlumency," you also become less vulnerable to the effects of those painful memories.

Occlumency cannot be self-taught; it is a skill that is passed on from one experienced wizard to another in a teacher-student relationship. The experience of learning Occlumency is never pleasant; it is miserable because the student must face repeated mental penetrations by the mind of the teacher in order to practice self-defense. This is why Snape warns that being the kind of person who "wallows in sad memories and allows themselves to be provoked easily" are defenseless. In order to become less wounded by sad memories and provocations, students of Occlumency must repeatedly and intentionally confront their own sad memories. They cannot simply try to avoid them, or distract themselves, or pretend that they are unbothered by them; they have to *face* them in their minds, and become a little bit stronger each time.

You can see why Occlumency lessons are brutal, and why they exhaust Harry. Therapy works the same way. The therapy you receive for your traumas will test you. At times, you will be furious with your therapist, and you will regard them as cruel and insensitive because they compel you to examine issues that are painful, and that you would rather leave in the vague realm of subconscious thought. Even though I was as compassionate as possible during therapy, clients of mine often told me later that they felt like therapy was punishment—"why is he doing this to me?" Dumbledore, of course, offered the answer: "It was important, Dumbledore said, to fight, and fight again, and keep fighting, for only then could evil be kept at bay, though never quite eradicated..."[2]

2 *Harry Potter and the Half-Blood Prince*, p.645

Occlumency And Therapy

It is possible to arm yourself to take on this struggle, though. You will be fighting Dementors in the weeks ahead, and every battle leaves its bruises and pains. If you go into battle unprepared with weak armor and useless weapons, you will not succeed. But if you regard yourself as a warrior, not a shrinking victim, you can see this process as a form of fighting back against rape itself. Here is a list of survival tips for managing your health during your treatment process:

- Eat. Do not starve yourself, and do not subsist on junk food and caffeine. Your brain requires protein and healthy fats to function, and foods rich in omega-3 fats (fish, or supplements) do an incredible job of stimulating the parts of the brain that manage stress and conflict. Consume plenty of these healthy sources of fat and protein.
- Sleep. Do not stay up late and wake up early. If you have dificuty sleeping because of stress, speak to a doctor who can prescribe some medical help for this problem. Don't lay in bed and text or surf the Internet "one last time" before sleep. Don't get into "internet argments."
- Manage your hygiene. It's hard to re-conceptualize yourself as a strong, capable person if you neglect your physical health, like Winky the house elf. Keep up with laundry, clean clothes, and grooming. Lack of care to these details is a common symptom of depression.
- Buy a journal and write as often as possible. Do the homework you are assigned by your therapist and this book. Actually hand-write your entries, rather than typing them at a computer.
- Prepare yourself mentally for therapy sessions. Therapy should not be an appointment you cram into your day. Consider what you would like to work on in each session, and rehearse talking about anything you need to reveal to your therapist. Don't wait until the last 10 miutes of therapy to bring up an issue.
- Do not listen to violent or abusive music. Trauma survivors can have an uncanny attraction to aggressive, abusive music because it creates a false sense of power. But this "power" comes from vicariously identifying with the singer, and if your music is abusive and violent you are teaching yourself to regard violence and abuse as forms of strength. This subconsciously reinforces your perception of yourself as weak.
- Listen to triumphant, empowered music. Intelligent singers and songs about positive choices are forms of medicine. When

you listen to love songs, you'll notice that they almost always obsess about another person: "I need you, you're my whole world, and I can't live without you." Instead of adopting the "love song" mindset that you need another person to complete you, begin to hear those as love songs to yourself.

- Don't try to take on the whole issue at once. Take on only a small bite of the issue a day. If you feel overwhelmed, slow down. If you experience panic, discuss it with your therapist and work on coping skills related to panic attacks.

- Don't skip sessions, or drop out, just because the work gets hard. A good therapist will understand how difficult this is for you. One of the symptoms of rape trauma is the urge to avoid any stress that is triggered by memories of your rape. If you succumb to the temptation to abandon therapy, recovery will become more difficult when you attempt it the next time. I like to compare this to a bacterial infection: if you partially treat the infection but stop the treatments too soon, the bacteria that survive become stronger and more resistant to medications. Subsequent attempts to treat the infection are less and less effective.

- Stay sober. If you're working in therapy sessions and then getting drunk or high at night, there's a problem. It actually increases your risk of problem drug use because it teaches you to associate both pain and recovery with substances.

- Find the right therapist for you. You are a person, not just a patient, and you have every right to search for the helper who fits. Don't just jump to a new therapist because you're ticked off at something your current therapist is coaxing you to work on, though! But if your therapist shows signs of not being skilled at trauma work (and not every therapist is!) feel free to continue services with a different person.

When Harry goes to enter the forest to face Voldemort, in what Harry thinks will be the end of his life, he suddenly realizes just how precious he actually is. He does not become prideful or see himself as superior to anyone else, but the miracle of his being alive at all becomes amazingly real to him: "he felt more alive and more aware of his own living body than ever before. Why had he never appreciated what a miracle he was, brain and nerve and bounding heart?"[3] Nobody tells Harry any of this, and he hasn't waited until praise and encouragement from others gives him his

3 *Harry Potter and the Deathly Hallows*, p.692

motivation; he comprehends that part of what will make him able to complete his task is an awareness of his *own* worth, in addition to his wish that nobody else had ever suffered. In essence, he is finally able to see that he is as worthy as those he loves, and that his protective feeling for others who have suffered and died is a feeling that he himself deserves to have, too. Many abuse survivors have a sense of compassion and esteem for other victims, extending understanding for them while still inwardly mistreating themselves as unworthy of the same grace.

Part of your healing is to find that grace for yourself, and to treat yourself as the same miracle that Harry finally realizes he is as well. That means treating your body with respect—the very same body you've perhaps called ugly, fat, broken, and disgusting for years. The same body you may have punished with drugs, with cuts, with countless forms of cruelty (one abuse victim I worked with had even tattooed the word "BROKEN" across her chest). It means taking care of your mind, filling it with wisdom and meaningful thoughts and images of beauty, rather than with "junk food" thoughts and entertainment. For example, one friend of mine decided to finally read as much classic literature as possible, since his abusers had denied him any intellectual nourishment during the years in which he was told how stupid and useless he was, going so far as to work in bookstores to be exposed to as much literature as possible. I became a western painter so that I could focus on what's beautiful in the world, as a way to re-balance my soul after absorbing trauma from hundreds of clients' accounts of sexual assault.

Common mistakes that happen during Occlumency/therapy

Trauma therapy never happens without hitting some bumps and snags, and I have never encountered a client whose recovery progressed flawlessly (in fact, I get concerned when anyone's recovery seems to be going too well, with no difficulty). It is essential that you keep in mind that therapists are not flawless people, and that you are the paying client. This means that there will be times when a therapist makes mistakes, just like you do, and will fail to correctly understand some things, just like you will. When that happens, try to resist the impulse to become frustrated, blame the therapist, or feel betrayed. Like in Quidditch, there are bludgers that will try to knock you off course.

Sometimes, clients have the best Occlumency skills toward their own therapists! What I mean is that sometimes we, the therapists, are blocked out from what a client *really* thinks, and the entire therapy process falls apart because the therapist did not realize something that was important to you. I have had clients who never spoke up about concerns or insights they wanted to address in sessions. Trying my best to intuitively direct sessions without that feedback meant that I made mistakes and operated under beliefs that were not always correct. I was not aware of these blunders until a client would suddenly drop out of therapy! Clients would assure me that I was being helpful and effective, but in my absence complain to others that their needs were not being met, or that they resented some aspect of our relationship. They would praise me in person and then blast me to others a month later. In defense of your therapist, it is unfair to withhold concerns from him or her, and yet hold your therapist responsible for issues you never expressed to them. You and your therapist are a team, and communication, not mind-reading, will keep the process running smoothly. If you become frustrated or concerned, discuss this with your therapist!

Honestly, I cannot claim that I have been a catalyst for full recovery in every client I have seen in therapy. I believe that in some way I have helped all of my clients, but there are some who simply have not yet achieved full recovery from rape. This does not mean that therapy, or I, or they, failed. It means that the process may not be complete, but it is as far along as it could be at this point. But I have also received clients into therapy who have come from treatment centers, drug rehab programs, hospitals, and other therapists, and did not receive beneficial therapy because of several common mistakes. You should be watchful for these mistakes and address them if you recognize them.

Perhaps the most common, and disastrous, mistake I have seen in therapy is to minimize the impact of trauma. I have seen two ways that this mistake happens. First, a therapist who is misinformed about trauma may believe that because your abuse might have taken place many years ago, it is no longer a relevant issue. Clients of mine have described being in therapy in which previous therapists failed to connect a rape from a decade ago to current symptoms of panic attacks, substance abuse, or depression. Because they were far apart in chronological time, the therapist assumed that they are separate matters. After all, the therapist concludes, if the trauma were really the core issue, you probably would have been in counseling back then instead of just now. So they regard the trauma as a background detail, but not part of your current needs.

The second way this mistake happens is that therapists are not the only ones who err in this way. Many clients of mine have come into therapy for addictions, panic attacks, meltdowns at work or school, self-injury, eating disorders, or general depression with sleep disturbances—yet they say "this isn't about my rape. That was so long ago; I've dealt with it, it's in the past!" These are the classic symptoms of rape trauma! Regardless of how long ago a trauma occurred, the symptoms can echo through time until they are addressed.

In fact, trauma that happened a longer time in the past can be a *more* powerful Dementor to you, because along with the trauma itself you've also got years of grief, bad habits, and faulty understandings about it that you've developed in efforts to cope with the pain. Trauma from ten years ago could have morphed into trauma *plus* self-harm *plus* alcohol abuse *plus* years of depression affecting your brain. J.K. Rowling even said that learning Occlumency was more difficult for Harry than for Draco because Harry had also stuffed years of pain into his mind after deeper traumas than Draco had ever endured:

> I think Draco would be very gifted in Occlumency, unlike Harry. Harry's problem with it was always that his emotions were too near the surface and that he is in some ways too damaged. But he's also very in touch with his feelings about what's happened to him. He's not repressed, he's quite honest about facing them, and he couldn't suppress them, he couldn't suppress these memories. But I thought of Draco as someone who is very capable of compartmentalising his life and his emotions, and always has done. So he's shut down his pity, enabling him to bully effectively. He's shut down compassion...[4]

The important lesson here is that putting off your "healing work" (therapy) for years makes the work more difficult. It does not make the trauma less painful. Take on your traumas when you are ready, and without spending years of your life suppressing them. Although Rowling says that Harry is more "damaged," resulting in emotions very near the surface, she also points out Harry's positive qualities, too: he's honest about his pain. He doesn't just stuff it down. Draco does, and that's something that separates Harry, who strives toward healing, and Draco, who loses his empathy and conscience, becoming a bully.

Finally, be curious about what is happening to you during your healing. One flaw in the wizarding world of Hogwarts is that there is very little curiosity about *how* things work; wizards simply take for granted that magic *does* work. Nobody ever wonders why people are magical, Muggles,

---

4 Anelli, Melissa and Emerson Spartz. "The Leaky Cauldron and MuggleNet interview Joanne Kathleen Rowling: Part Two," The Leaky Cauldron, 16 July 2005

or squibs, or how owls work, or why certain types of wands produce different effects, or why stirring a potion in one direction works but in the opposite direction it just smokes and stinks. Hermione is our one bastion of pure curiosity; she wants to understand why things happen, not just the words to say to make them happen. When Harry is unable to achieve a summoning charm she is teaching him, she backs up and has Harry read textbooks on the theory behind the charm. For her, reciting words is not enough; she wants to know why those words cause a certain change.

Likewise, being in therapy does not work if you are merely saying words that answer a therapist's questions. All the self-help books in the world won't work if they're just words you read. Journaling is nothing more than an annoying chore if it's nothing more than writing down words. It's important that you understand why talking about your abuse or your rape matters (it changes how your brain physically reacts to triggers). Reading books about abuse is important, even though it's not fun, because it can help you understand why people abuse, which alleviates feelings of self-blame, and why your brain responds to trauma the way it does. Avoiding reminders of your past is one of the symptoms of post-traumatic stress, but taking a cue from Hermione and actively seeking insight about trauma is self-strengthening.

What Occlumency Feels Like

When Harry begins his private lessons with Snape, he is flooded with misery and stress as soon as Snape begins testing him. As Snape challenges Harry's defenses with efforts to probe Harry's mind, Harry becomes overwhelmed with both physical and emotional pain, anger at Snape, flashes of terrifying images, and fury at even having to be put through this at all. Harry is left feeling "...as though someone had been trying to pull it from his skull."

In fact, although the books never say this directly, beginning to learn Occlumency feels like being attacked by Dementors all over again.

When you begin to confront your story[5], you are putting yourself in a face-to-face confrontation with your deepest shame and fear; in fact, that's the whole point, as Professor Lupin pointed out: "What you fear most of all is– fear. Very wise."[6] But connecting so strongly with these feelings can also trigger self-defeating habits and thoughts that you have linked

5 By "story," I mean the account of all the details and feelings you experienced during your traumas.
6 *Harry Potter and the Prisoner of Azkaban,* p.155

with shame and fear to this point. Until the sharing of your story feels like the victory it is, you may not be able to fully comprehend how it was helpful at all. Like Occlumency, beginning therapy for trauma can feel like someone is pulling out the worst memories and sensations you have ever felt, all over again. It can even feel cruel. Putting your pain into words is itself painful, but it allows you to begin expressing feelings, and expressing them helps you become free of them. Dumbledore taught this about the power of words when he said, "Words are, in my not so humble opinion, our most inexhaustible source of magic, capable of both influencing injury, and remedying it."[7]

For some people, the only feeling they have as they begin to open up in therapy is deeper shame, because their beliefs are screaming at them from inside, "Now I've gone and done it! Now someone else knows! They won't think about me the same way. They'll be imagining me being abused when they look at me. They might be nice for now, but it's pretend—they'll really turn on me because now they know how disgusting I am!" One client told me much later, "telling my story was the best thing I have ever done. You making me do that literally saved my life. But at the time, it didn't feel like therapy, it felt like punishment. I kept thinking, 'why is Matt doing this to me? Can't he see how much it hurts?'" Harry is so furious with Snape during Occlumency lessons that the hate feels like venom in his veins. He cannot see that this is helpful, or that Snape is guiding him toward new skills that will protect and heal Harry. To Harry, this is just pure torture, and being pressed onward by Snape feels unfairly cruel. Why would Snape be deliberately bringing such painful images back into Harry's mind? Why would Dumbledore make Harry reveal all of the horrors Harry had endured in the cemetery with Voldemort?

In the *Harry Potter* stories, one of the methods used by wizards to intentionally re-experience past events is the Pensieve, a basin into which a person immerses their face so that they can return to a selected past memory. In comparisons to real-life therapy, I remain skeptical about the so-called "recovered memory" phenomenon, and I do not suggest that there is a particular reliable method for recalling lost memories back into consciousness. But we can still draw a lesson from the Pensieve allegory; the very name of it is taken from the word "Pensive", which means to be deeply thoughtful. As you begin to face your story in order to cleanse it of its painfulness, your approach must be a pensive one; like Dumbledore entering the Pensieve, you are deliberately going back into your memories to examine them for details and unrecognized truths in order to learn what to do to heal past harms. Dumbledore repeatedly examines the

---

7 *Harry Potter and the Deathly Hallows Part II,* film adaptation

awful memories of Voldemort's origin in order to pluck every scrap of information from them, to discover how to overcome Voldemort's power. That means inspecting each act of violence committed by Tom Riddle, rather than avoiding those memories out of shock or horror.

Clients of mine have had to struggle through pain and exhaustion to pensively scrutinize their traumas rather than suppressing them, so that the compressed emotions from the times they were beaten, or molested, or raped, or humiliated, can be released. It is the Pensieve that leads Dumbledore to discover the Horcrux cave, into which he must venture, even suffering the worst agony of his life as he devours the potion of suffering that Voldemort has devised, in order to finally access the Horcrux at its heart so that it can be destroyed. Likewise, my clients learned to stop fleeing their feelings and sit alone, pen in hand, and write out their traumatic memories: how it felt when they were abused, what they remember hearing, what their abusers said to them, what they smelled, what they tasted, what they feared, what they did to cope, what they said to their abusers, what makes them feel ashamed or guilty to this day, *all* of it. They are returning to those memories in order to drain each one of them of its poison.

That is not something a person can do in trickles, or while intoxicated, or while avoiding the details, or by posting vague status updates on the internet; being pensive means to be serious, devoted to your thoughts, and willing to examine what comes forth from beginning to end. Using a Pensieve, then, is perhaps the counterpart of Occlumency: the Pensieve is meant to purposefully re-open thoughts that have been locked away, while Occlumency is meant to protect thoughts from being opened. Both have their use in your recovery.

The irony of Occlumency is that to learn how to protect yourself from painful and dangerous "thought intrusions," you have to first become willing to endure them. Your guide, such as Professor Snape, must be able to help those thoughts become present in your mind, seeking any details in them that cause you to become vulnerable to them, so that you can learn to overcome them. That means you must begin by facing what you most want to run from. Or to put it in therapy terms, whatever triggers you is what you must directly, intentionally, and bravely face in all its detail, rather than running from the trigger. Being "triggered" by your traumatic memories can not be seen as a sign of the stuff you should avoid. It's the opposite of that: whatever your triggers are, those are what you must consciously turn toward, face, and examine. That is what Snape is doing with Harry. Snape is intentionally putting Harry into contact with Harry's most dreadful experiences (and wow, does Harry hate him for it!), because

Occlumency And Therapy

Snape knows that traumatic pain is Harry's vulnerability. Unless Harry can overcome those traumas, he will forever have a mental "back door" for intrusive thoughts to continue to pierce him. Hiding from them won't keep you whole, it will keep you un-whole.

During your recovery work in therapy, you will have to come face-to-face with your deepest shames and expose them. You will bring things up into conscious thought and speak them out loud, taking them out of their hiding places in your mind. These are things you had buried and hidden because you had told yourself that they would cause you to be rejected, scorned, or abandoned if others knew them. That may have even been true in the past. And now they have to be revealed. As Dumbledore said, "Understanding is the first step to acceptance, and only with acceptance can there be recovery. He needs to know who has put him through the ordeal he has suffered tonight, and why."[8]

Ultimately, pulling your shames and fears out of hiding and revealing them is a very healing thing to do, and it begins the process of ridding yourself of those shameful thoughts. It's like cleansing your house of an infestation. But the positive results aren't immediate outcomes that will affect your emotional balance. Before the benefits show up, what impacts your emotions first are those fearful beliefs and self-talk about the shameful, embarrassing truths you have revealed. "I have exposed myself, and that exposure is going to cost me dearly. It is going to change what people think about me now." So the first reaction you have to deep therapy isn't always positive relief, a lifted weight, and freedom; it's terror and disgrace. As you go through this, you will feel resentment toward your therapist, like Harry felt toward Snape. Hopefully, your therapist won't scold you for it, like Snape does to Harry. But if it helps, instead of feeling like you are simply being peeled open and having your worst shames exposed, tell yourself that you are learning Occlumency just like Harry Potter did, and for many of the same reasons. One of my friends told me what it was like to take this step:

> For me, at least this week, it's breaking through the explicit and implicit rules that I was given which said don't talk, don't tell. It's shattering the shame that goes with those rules and know-ing that now that I have said the words, the earth did not shat-ter, my therapist did not dump me...and I can now work to rebuild new and better guides in their place. It's realizing and rewarding myself for hard work and believing that I deserve good things.

---

8 *Harry Potter and the Goblet of Fire*, p.680

Or as Dumbledore put it,

> If I thought I could help you by putting you into an enchanted sleep and allowing you to postpone the moment when you would have to think about what has happened [to you], I would do it. But I know better. Numbing the pain for a while will make it worse when you finally feel it. You have shown bravery beyond anything I could have expected of you. I ask you to demonstrate your courage one more time. I ask you to tell us what happened.[9]

---

9 *Harry Potter and the Goblet of Fire*, p.695

CHAPTER FOUR

Headmasters, Mentors, and Therapists

Trauma from abuse is something you cannot heal from in isolation, because loneliness is one of the wounds of that trauma. It takes guidance and support from others, including people who are able to challenge your own beliefs and feelings of shame. Harry, who has never thought of himself as important or loveable, needs to hear this from others. Heroes in fiction stories almost always have a special mentor, a guide who dispenses wisdom and advice that the hero later uses to become victorious. Mentors seldom intervene directly in the hero's battles, but the hero is able to draw upon the lessons they have received in order to personally overcome their struggles. In fiction, this might be a Dumbledore or Yoda/Obi Wan character, or Rupert Giles (*Buffy the Vampire Slayer*), Gandalf (*the Lord of the Rings*), Professor X (*The X-Men*), Mr. Miyagi (*The Karate* Kid), or Morpheus (*The Matrix*). In non-fiction, the mentor may be a therapist who takes a special interest in the client/hero, like Dr. Davenport to Antwone Fisher (who invites Antwone into his home, has dinners with Antwone, and continues to love Antwone even as Antwone rages hatefully against him at times). For Dr. Martin Luther King Jr., it was Gandhi (and for Gandhi it was Yofe).

Headmasters, Mentors, and Therapists

Harry, who had been neglected for the first ten years of his life, later had many mentors to help guide him, beginning with Hagrid, and then expanding to include Professor Lupin, Sirius Black, and his closest mentor of all, Dumbledore. It is Harry's neglect in childhood that gives him such a need to have mentors, because Harry has never been told that he is valued, or that his life has a purpose, or that he has qualities that can help him heal from what has been done to him.

Let me be careful here, because it is possible to learn the wrong lesson from the fact that Harry needs others to look up to, and to hear that they value him. It is absolutely important for you to know that you are worthy of being loved, and that much of your strength will come from your relationships with other people. But that does not mean that you are not valuable *until* someone else affirms that about you. If that were the case, it would mean that other people determine when you are worthy, rather than you having worth intrinsically. Harry's healing comes from within, rather than being handed down to him like a sock to Dobby. But when others recognize your worth, it strengthens you by strengthening your relationships, and in addition to coming form within, healing also comes from relating to others in healthy ways. The point is that others reflect your worth back to you, not that you get your worth from others.

Because trauma can cause you to feel rejected and disconnected from others, it is common that when you face your traumas, those feelings will temporarily surge again. Some heroes cannot believe they really possess the power and ability to succeed. Others are convinced they are too worthless to deserve the trek to victory. Many wounded people often see themselves as low and unworthy, and they discredit themselves; during group therapy, they will remain silent or apologize when they do speak for "taking time from everyone else." They feel guilty even receiving support from a mentor/counselor/healer because they tell themselves their problems are so trivial, so stupid, that they should just "get over it" and let the mentor use their time to help those who *do* deserve it. When they are told they are loved by a mentor or other supporter, they become upset by the internal tug-of-war between desperately *wanting* to be loved, yet feeling so unlovable that they become convinced this must be a trick, a form of manipulation, a way of "taking advantage." Sometimes, rather than doubting the affection they receive from others, survivors of trauma simply feel unworthy of it at all. In those cases, the isolation that arises from trauma is self-inflicted. Harry suffered from this form of loneliness as well, and avoided confiding in his friends even though they wanted to support him. Dumbledore advises Harry that this kind of self-seclusion is not wise:

"I think [your friends] ought to know. You do them a disservice by not confiding something this important to them."
"I didn't want —"
"— to worry or frighten them?" said Dumbledore, surveying Harry over the top of his half-moon spectacles. "Or perhaps, to confess that you yourself are worried and frightened? You need your friends, Harry. As you so rightly said, Sirius would not have wanted you to shut yourself away."[1]

Harry endures all of these feelings. As lonely as he's been for most of his life, he craves guidance and acceptance from role models and friends. In Dumbledore, he finds a mentor who helps protect Harry's life for as long as possible. But Harry does not realize at first that even the gentle, brilliant Dumbledore is a flawed mentor. One of the things Harry has to learn is that good people can have flaws. Accepting that Dumbledore is flawed actually helps Harry to accept himself, too, by realizing that he—Harry—can also be good, despite having flaws, too.

The Contradiction of Protective Love

At first, Harry's misbehavior at Hogwarts mostly takes the form of rules he breaks to protect his own pride, such as flying a broom to challenge Draco Malfoy. But as Harry's violations of the rules become more serious, Dumbledore has to eventually threaten to actually expel Harry if they continue. Dumbledore, while kind-hearted toward Harry, is able to maintain strictness with him too, in order to protect Harry. Yet while Dumbledore is able to hold Harry to certain standards to protect him, he is not always able to hold himself to the same standards, even when doing so would also protect Harry.

As an infant, Harry is placed with the Dursleys after the death of James and Lily Potter, so that Harry will be protected from Voldemort by the magical charm carried through the bloodline shared between Lily, Petunia, and Harry. However, the Dursleys are abusive to Harry, including acts of emotional and physical abuse and neglect. The abuse is intentional; it's not as if the Dursleys are simply incompetent or incapable of caring for others, because they over-lavish affection on their own son, Dudley, while giving Harry a single toothpick for a Christmas present.

---

1 *Harry Potter and the Half-Blood Prince*, p.78

Headmasters, Mentors, and Therapists

Although Dumbledore is protective of Harry at Hogwarts, he still requires that Harry return to the Dursleys to live when school is not in session, despite knowing what Harry endures. This is not because Dumbledore is careless with Harry's well-being, though, but because of the magical protection against the death eaters that Harry has while still living with his biological family. The charm that protects Harry derives from his mother, Lily's, loving sacrifice of her own life to save his, which spares Harry the effects of Voldemort's killing curse. Because his life was saved by his mother's love, Harry remains protected throughout his childhood as long as his mother's blood relatives remain his guardians. Unfortunately, that means Harry must remain in the custody of the Dursleys.

Love, then, becomes the strongest spell in the *Harry Potter* world. It is why Harry is the only known survivor of the killing curse, and it is the basis for the magical charm that continues to protect him.

But this is not a simplistic fairy tale, and we can't simply conclude, "love is powerful and always protective—ta daa!" and think we've arrived at the ultimate lesson in *Harry Potter*. Love, as it turns out, also has the potential to remove our protections from us when it is applied incorrectly. Dumbledore is careful to place Harry into a childhood home where, despite abuse, there will at least be supernatural protections to guard Harry from magical foes. However, he also fails to keep Harry safe in other ways, and his failures also arise because of love.

While Harry is trapped in the Dursley's house during summers, he survives with no contact from his friends, no news about what is happening, and days of endless frustration. Harry has no idea why Dumbledore seems to have stranded him in such an abusive, lonely situation; is Dumbledore just mean? Why doesn't he just explain the reasons to Harry? There is a reason Dumbledore is reluctant to simply clarify why Harry has to remain in the Durleys' home during his childhood. In order to do that, Dumbledore would have had to also reveal the *full* truth about Harry's encounter with Voldemort as an infant, because the very reason Harry is protected by his mother's charm also includes the detail that Voldemort's killing curse caused Voldemort's own soul to fragment, locking part of itself inside of Harry, too. Harry carries not only the protective charm of his mother's love, but also the remnant of Voldemort's curse that took Lily's life and nearly Harry's own as well.

Had Dumbledore explained all of this to Harry from the start, Harry might have been crushed under the implication that he is a Voldemort Horcrux himself. This information is kept from Harry in order to spare Harry that pain. Dumbledore is motivated by love; it is, again, someone's love for Harry that moves them to try to protect Harry. But in this case, Dumbledore's love for Harry actually costs Harry dearly. By trying to shield Harry from the truth, Harry actually suffers more pain: he cannot understand why Dumbledore becomes distant from him (which Dumbledore does to protect both himself and Harry from a link he suspects Harry still has to Voldemort). He cannot understand why Dumbledore returns Harry to the Dursleys each summer (which Dumbledore does to prolong the magical charm that protects Harry). And when Harry finally learns the truth about his internal link to Voldemort, he cannot understand why Dumbledore had hidden this information from him (Dumbledore hid it to spare Harry the pain and shame of feeling inwardly connected to Voldemort for as long as possible).

Professor Snape challenged Dumbledore over the decision to withhold the truth from Harry: "You have kept him alive so that he can die at the right moment?...Now you tell me you have been raising him like a pig for slaughter..."[2] To Snape, this is just cruelty on Dumbledore's part. Why would Dumbledore shield Harry from a truth about himself, just to make Harry feel better by not knowing it for so long? To Dumbledore, though, this is loving: he has shielded Harry from a truth about himself, just to make Harry feel better by now knowing it for so long.

Dumbledore's flaw is that he is not always able to face painful truths. He cannot face his own grief about the death of his sister, Ariana, when they were younger. In fact, he claims that his "Mirror of Erised" vision is a pair of comfortable socks, when really it is his family, alive and reunited.[3] He is unable to fully accept the reality of his grief, and to deal with it to become healed and thus is unable to reconcile with his still-living brother, Aberforth. When it comes to Harry, he is also unwilling to reveal the painful truth about Harry's life, and the fact that Harry must sacrifice himself in order to destroy the Dark Lord's power once and for all. Dumbledore seems to have convinced himself that withholding that information is for Harry's own good, but it later becomes apparent that Dumbledore has done this for his own peace, not Harry's, and admits as much. Harry is kept miserable because of Dumbledore's reluctance to be fully honest with him, while Dumbledore defends his reluctance as a way to keep Harry from being miserable.

Any of us can completely understand the moral bind that Dumbledore is in. On one hand, keeping the truth from Harry keeps Harry trapped in a confused, frustrated frame of mind for years. It is because of his love for Harry that Dumbledore shields him from those truths, yet doing so misleads Harry:

---

2 *Harry Potter and the Deathly Hallows*, p.687
3 This fact is not stated in the books, but was later revealed by J.K. Rowling.

"Do you see, Harry? Do you see the flaw in my brilliant plan now? I had fallen into the trap I had foreseen, that I had told myself I could avoid, that I must avoid…I cared about you too much…I cared more for your happiness than your knowing the truth, more for your peace of mind than my plan, more for your life than the lives that might be lost if the plan failed. In other words, I acted exactly as Voldemort expects we fools who love to act."[4]

Dumbledore admits that it was his desire to spare Harry from greater pain than he had already suffered by shielding Harry from full knowledge. However, that move causes Harry to feel betrayed by his own mentor, abandoned by his friends, and alone in his struggle because he had not really been helped to face his own reality.

On the other hand, withholding the truth from Harry is an act of kindness, because it allows Harry to grow, develop his strengths, and form the friendships that eventually help Harry to become the kind of selfless person who would be able to make the sacrifice that is required of him:

"Eleven, I told myself, was much too young to know. I had never intended to tell you when you were eleven. The knowledge would be too much at such a young age…I should have recognized that I was too happy to think that I did not have to do it on that particular day…you were too young, much too young."[5]

Love, then, motivates Dumbledore to act in ways that both protect and hurt Harry—"hurt" here meaning that Harry is frustrated by Dumbledore's actions, not that those actions are abusive or cruel. Here we see the contradiction in love's power: loving someone does not always mean shielding them from things they need to deal with, but it does mean protecting them from what they are not yet able to face. That feels manipulative to Harry (and even to readers sometimes), but is the difficult boundary of Dumbledore's therapeutic help. Harry became resentful toward Dumbledore because he was not aware of the difficult tension between protecting and exposing Harry that Dumbledore was wrestling with.

---

4 *Harry Potter and the Deathly Hallows,* film adaptation
5 *Harry Potter and the Order of the Phoenix,* p.838

Many heroes experience an intense disillusionment toward their mentors/ counselors/ministers at some point in their journey. Some feel abandoned when the mentor compels the hero to step forward on their own (like Harry Potter becoming furious with Dumbledore in *The Deathly Hallows*), and others feel disillusioned when the human fallibility of their mentor becomes apparent, toppling the mentor from the position of idealized caretaker the hero had once maintained.

Pardon the non-*Harry Potter* references here, but the original *Karate Kid* film is a fantastic example. Daniel Larusso has found a mentor in Mr. Miyagi, but Miyagi's training techniques are not typical and even begin to seem exploitative to Daniel. Daniel eventually explodes in outrage at feeling taken advantage of and hurt by his mentor, accusing him of failing to teach him anything. Daniel suspects that Mr. Miyagi just wants to use him for common chores, and doesn't truly value or respect him. Cursing and screaming at Mr. Miyagi, Daniel claims that he hasn't learned anything at all, that he is no better off than if he had never met him, that Mr. Miyagi is only in it for himself. In truth, Mr. Miyagi has developed a deep affection and respect for Daniel, and has been using unusual techniques to help Daniel learn advanced skills without even realizing it. Had Daniel broken away from his mentor at that point, he would never have realized what Miyagi's methods have made possible. Blind to this, Daniel is ready to discard his relationship with Mr. Miyagi and continue training from replacement mentors who, while more mainstream and business-like, have no affection for Daniel personally. Only when Daniel realizes that he has misjudged his older mentor can he begin to see that Mr. Miyagi has actually cherished him. No professional instructor would have ever used Miyagi's methods, but through them Daniel truly becomes a more whole person, not merely a trained fighter.

Conversely, Anakin Skywalker becomes convinced his once-loved mentor, Obi Wan, has become a disgrace, and betrays Obi Wan. He attacks Obi Wan, even as Obi Wan protests his affection and heartbreak toward his young apprentice—"You were my brother! I loved you!"—but it is too late; Anakin renounces the path of the hero out of bitter scorn for the mentor he had once trusted and defended. Anakin becomes corrupted by hate, yet remains convinced he has attacked Obi Wan for righteous reasons; Obi Wan, he believes, has misused and harmed him, and he never realizes that Obi Wan's guidance was always earnest.

In real life, many heroes abandon their journeys of healing and opt for self-destructive journeys instead; some even convince themselves for years they are "trying to cope" when instead they are actually cycling through the same self-victimizing patterns. Often this happens when someone cannot yet fully understand the contradiction of protective love, which is that not all love is meant to shield you from pain. The notion that a caretaker ought to always protect you from your own inner pain is not true, but it is so often believed that many victims of abuse discard their own allies from a sense of outrage when those allies don't perform that way. One glance at how many internet articles have been written to accuse Dumbledore of being a manipulator rather than a mentor makes the point, too. People mistake "mentor" for "angel of protection," and become offended when the mentor does not fill that role. Sometimes love means protecting you from what you are able to endure, but sometimes it means refusing to give you easy shelter from that which must be faced.

Dumbledore's Lessons for Therapy

We live in a culture that celebrates "rugged individualism," and sees cooperation, compromise, and work toward the "greater good" as forms of weakness. A consequence of this mindset is that people who struggle with depression may feel pressured to tough it out, go it alone, and refuse help. Even in therapy groups, I have seen clients try to outrank each other with competing stories of personal pain, with the goal of winning status in the group by having the most authentic trauma, resulting in a "pecking order" of ruggedness.

This type of "prove your toughness" approach to healing actually causes even more separation from others, which in turn causes depression to worsen. In some cases, the family members of clients of mine intentionally tried to sabotage the therapeutic relationship between the client and me, usually because the family member was responsible for some aspect of the abuse that my client had suffered. Their goal was to prevent the client from actually improving, in order to protect the abuser's power and secrets. As a result, the clients sometimes were prevented from healing, and became even more depressed because they had begun to believe that "I'm so damaged, even therapy doesn't work." They would be left with no support, only internalized myths about toughness being the only way to cope.

Fortunately, Dumbledore's relationship with Harry Potter gives us a clearer, healthier understanding of what inner strength actually means. As a therapist reading *Harry Potter*, I recognized the same internal conflicts toward my clients that Dumbledore felt toward Harry: the difficult boundary between protecting them from what they cannot yet endure, and exposing them to painful things they need to face. Both of these options arise from a sense of affectionate respect toward my clients, *even when* they might resent my affection for them as a trick. This is Dumbledore's contradiction: for him, love means occasionally sparing someone from pain, and sometimes helping them to face things that are painful.

This loving paradox is not even slightly similar to the abuser's tactic of hurting you and then saying, "this is for your own good; you'll thank me later; I'm only trying to teach you a lesson." Rather, this is a way of helping a person feel *less* shame, not more; *less* trauma, not more; and become *more* whole and healthy, not less. A therapist asking you to become open about what you've survived in order to help heal from it is not like the person who inflicted the wound in the first place. Dumbledore guiding Harry toward truths that Harry must face is not like Voldemort or the Dursleys, who caused those things. A therapist pushing you toward difficult realizations is not the same thing as "you don't care about me, because you're making me face things that are painful!"

Harry comes to the breaking point after the death of Sirius Black, and finally vents his rage toward Dumbledore. When Dumbledore assures Harry that he knows how Harry feels, Harry explodes, "YOU DON'T KNOW HOW I FEEL!" and hurls things in anger across the room. Harry is convinced that nobody, least of all Dumbledore, could possibly empathize with his pain and rage. "I don't want to talk about how I feel!" he roars. What Harry is feeling is how you have probably felt, too, about your own loss and trauma. When people try to assure you that they support and understand you, it can make you bristle with resentment rather than feeling soothed. Many times, clients of mine became furious at me for merely showing them kindness and support, convinced that nobody could ever really understand them. In their minds, being so alien and alone meant that anyone claiming to feel empathy was lying; the helper—in this case, me—must surely have a sinister motive. Did I just want their money? Was I simply intrigued by the horrible stories I could lure out of them? Was I just another man wanting to exploit them? Was I a stone-cold hollow man, claiming to understand them to impress them? When the time comes for you to truly connect with someone who is ready to hear your truths, it won't feel like a breakthrough at first. Your shame and anger will fight against the bond, trying to detach you and scorch shut the open, vulnerable part of you that needs to connect to someone.

Dumbledore knows this, and assures Harry that "the fact that you can feel pain like this is your greatest strength…suffering like this proves you are still a man! This pain is part of being human…" The fact that *you* are hurt by your past is a sign that you are able to heal, too. Grief is the right emotion to feel about your abuse, because it shows that there is part of you that still values yourself as a person, and you feel hurt that an innocent person was harmed. If you did not still think of yourself as worthy on some level, you would have no emotional objection to someone else's infliction of harm against you. As Dumbledore told Harry, "You care so much you feel as though you will bleed to death with the pain of it."

Harry responds with more fury, because his emotions are in control of his thoughts. To him, someone that *feels* true must *be* true, even if the evidence is to the contrary. He howls at Dumbledore that he doesn't care, yet the very fact that he howls it while smashing things suggests that Dumbledore is right, Harry cares beyond measure. That is why Dumbledore does not move a muscle to stop Harry from acting this way. In my past work as a therapist, I remember clients who would shriek at me, throw notebooks from across the room at me, and even curse me out when their traumatic feelings and memories finally broke through. Unless they were harming themselves, it was important to calmly and, yes, lovingly allow them to explode that way. The worst thing to do in that moment would be to shut yourself down and cram a cork back into the bottle, forcing your feelings to compress back inside. What needs to happen is for those emotions to be fully expressed, so they can be extinguished. Dumbledore understands this, and refuses to allow Harry to leave the office until the catharsis is complete. That is why, if you are in therapy, it is important that you express your full range of emotions with and toward your therapist, not just the polite, rational ones. Even rage and hate toward your therapist are important, because they are often the emotions that give you the energy to pull out the cork, allowing all the other buried stuff to finally come free.

Therapists constantly face difficult choices in terms of what to help clients deal with, and what is still too difficult. A good therapist is able to help set a pace that allows you to build up your strength so you do not become overwhelmed. When someone would start therapy with me and immediately begin telling me details of their rape, for example, I knew it would burn them out too quickly, and would redirect them into other, smaller, more here-and-now crises first. The time would come to deal with the worst stuff, to open the boxes and let the Boggarts out, to hunt the Horcruxes. Until then, though, we needed to strengthen our relationship and the client's coping abilities. For that reason, processing the worst trauma is usually done near the end of therapy, not at the beginning. Having a regard for their well-being meant shielding them from what they could not yet handle, while preparing them to face things that would hurt them.

On their journey toward the final enemy, heroes usually endure a rite of passage that changes them into a stronger person. This passage is not their final achievement; it is what enables them to face their darkest foe. For Harry, it comes when he is told the complete truth about his link to Voldemort, and what must happen to break it. For Luke Skywalker, it's when he has his vision on Dagobah in which he is warned about his own vulnerability to the dark side of the Force, symbolized by seeing his own face inside Darth Vader's helmet. For many victims of abuse, the rite of passage comes at the moment they can finally identify themselves as survivors: "I am a rape survivor" or "I am a child abuse survivor" or "I can finally say that what happened to me was sexual abuse". In therapy, this often happens after you have learned how to connect your anxiety, flashbacks, self-harm, substance abuse, or depression to the trauma you endured, no matter how many years ago.

Many people get to this point and become afraid to continue, just like Harry felt afraid. It's easy to give up your journey, your "Horcrux hunting", and jump to easy answers that let you turn back from your final work:

"Put it in a box and forget about it."
"Give all those painful memories to Jesus!"
"Just claim victory over your past!"
"The Bible tells us to let our minds dwell on good things. So why even think about anything negative?"
"You need to forgive and forget."
"That's all in the past; just move on from it."
"Pour another beer; light another joint; cut another cut."

One of the most difficult things I faced as a therapist was seeing a client struggle, and being tempted to save them from the stress. So many times, I wanted to make it all better for them with pep-talks, positive thinking rhetoric, or giving them permission to move on without really talking about what was upsetting them: "We can come back to that," or "I think we talked about that previously, so let's move forward" or the worst cop-out of all: "And how does that make you feel?" I could send them home feeling better and they'd be thrilled with me as a therapist, even though I would not have helped them one bit in actually overcoming their PTSD.

Clients of mine would resent me for not rescuing them, too. "Why is Matt making me go through this? Is he punishing me?", and "I thought you were supposed to be *nice!* You're not doing anything to make me feel better about all this stuff!" Learning to feel your feelings all the way through is such a difficult lesson, but it's one every trauma survivor has to achieve. The urge to make painful thoughts disappear back into a state of comfort is actually a symptom of post-traumatic stress, but until those painful thoughts are fully extinguished, they will remain under the surface. Sending a Boggart back into a dark corner doesn't mean it's gone.

In my work with rape victims, clients who were nearly finished with therapy would finally be ready to hand-write and read their entire narratives out loud to the group. These narratives would include every detail they could remember, nothing left out, including descriptions of what all of their senses experienced. This was their way of breaking open their final Horcrux. Writing their stories often caused all of their worst symptoms to flood back to them again, making them question why they were even proceeding. Some clients would spend days writing their stories, and during that time they would lose sleep and be unable to eat. Occasionally, they would skip sessions or even drop out entirely, going back to a lifetime of carrying the Horcrux with them.

Many clients would arrive with stories to read, but their stories were so disconnected from emotions that there was little effect from reading them. They were written more like police reports ("And then he… and then I…"), without any emotional language at all. They could read them calmly. It was tempting for me to just let them get away with that, too, because I knew that redoing it properly would bring up difficult emotions. *That's the point, in fact.* The "Dumbledore" in me, though, wanted to keep them shielded from that pain.

Clients have often said they fear writing their stories because it makes it real. It's black-and-white fact. They plead with me, "can't I just skip this?" or "can't I just say it instead of writing it?" The "realness" of the writing is, however, exactly why it should be written. By writing your story, you are not making anything real that wasn't already real. What happened, happened. You can't recover from something that you refuse to face or pretend was something it wasn't.

When it came time to read their stories aloud in therapy, I would first instruct the other group members about what to expect, and how to react. They were not to all rush over to them and hug them, say things to make everything better afterward, pass tissues to them, or interrupt the complete eruption of emotion at all. In fact, when someone was finished reading their story, I would often let several long moments of absolute silence pass, because sometimes the grief would finally begin to come out during those moments. The urge to make all of the discomfort go away with hugs and inspirational feedback is totally natural, but it would end the moment of pure healing that the client needed to finish.

One of the ways I helped clients build their strength was with the phrase, "I'm going to help you by not helping you with this." Therapists see warning signs when a client tells them, "you're the only one who can help me!" because that's a sign of a client who wants a Patronus, not a therapist. They want a protector who will drive their pain away for them. They see more healing strength in the therapist than they see within themselves. When clients would over-praise me for how helpful I'd been, I would deflect it back and remind them that this is *their* work to do. My basic rule of therapy was simple: I will work my butt off for you, but I will not work harder than you. A client who expects their therapist to protect them and make all the bad feelings become good feelings isn't looking for a Dumbledore-like mentor, they are looking for someone to play Vernon or Petunia Dursley to their Dudley. This is not love, and it's certainly not therapy.

The paradox of protective love, then, is very much at work in therapy. You will resent your therapist for pressing you onward toward honestly, fully facing your pain. Your therapist may even seem cruel at times for not saving you from those truths. But in the therapist's mind, they are usually being very cautious with how much they expose you to, and what they still shield you from. Both of these are acts of compassion and support. To heal, you must be guided toward facing your traumas, while still being kept safe from the parts of it that you're still not ready for. Protective love, then, can allow you to endure painful feelings on the way to healing, while at the same time supporting you as you heal from that pain.

CHAPTER FIVE

Boggarts and Trauma

Anything you refuse to face because of fear, you are allowing to remain hidden somewhere in your mind. But each time you let those memories and feelings surface, face them, write them down, and tell them to someone, you are gradually taking strength from them, little by little. It may not be as instant and gratifying as shouting "Riddikulus!" at your Boggart, but it's the same idea, just over more time.

A Boggart represents a wizard's worst fear given physical shape. Boggarts are "non-beings" that have no known basic form, because the form they take is determined entirely by the mind of the person looking at them. For example, Molly Weasley saw a Boggart in the form of her family, including Harry (whom she loves as a son), all dead. Harry sees a Boggart as a Dementor. Even Muggles can see Boggarts, although they do not realize that it is a magical creature, and instead become convinced that the Boggart is something from their imagination or subconscious. Each Boggart appears differently to each person who sees it, which is why we should never minimize our own pain or anyone else's; there's no such thing as a traumatic pain or fear that is more or less "real" or deserving of care than another's. Any person's Boggart is their own personal worst fear, and for them it brings up the same intensity of dread that yours brings up for you.

Boggarts And Trauma

At Hogwarts, students are taught to face their Boggarts in a safe way, in order to master their fear and to learn a Boggart-banishing spell that instantly transforms the Boggart into something whimsical and harmless. Nothing about trauma is whimsical and harmless, but the analogy is still a good one because facing our fears in safe ways helps us conjure up the inner strength to overcome them. In therapy terms, we call those fears "stuck points" or "triggers," and they are the things we most need to face in order to heal. Too often, I have seen victims of trauma use the word "triggered!" as a sort of faux protective charm, as if uttering it can push challenging thoughts and experiences back into the "Boggart box" and make everything safe again. Not only does trauma not work that way, but repeatedly using "triggered!" as a protective charm to avoid the trigger can actually diminish your strength by becoming a habitual form of hiding from your Boggarts. We can't look for something like a "Riddukulus" spell in real life, but we can still draw on the concept of facing our Boggarts in safe ways until we have overcome them.

In real life, a trigger is a "brain hijack" caused by your brain matching incoming information (stimuli) to past experiences that it associates with danger. For example, certain sounds or scents may be associated with your abuse, and when you encounter those stimuli, your brain kicks into "fight or flight" mode because it recognizes signs of danger again. The danger might not even be real (heck, reading a book or watching a movie can be triggering, even though there's no actual danger), but your brain hijacks you anyway. In the center of your brain, a small, primitive part called the *amygdala* is responsible for these reactions. Your amygdala scans all incoming sensory information for anything it identifies as a threat. Any scent, sound, sight, or physical feeling can be interpreted by the amygdala as an indication of danger, and when it detects a threat it triggers your brain into crisis mode. This routine can be very useful when the danger is real, but the amygdala often gets it wrong, too, because it is not a part of the brain that can think or reason. It simply detects a sensation that it identifies as danger, and hijacks you into "fight or flight" modes. People whose amygdalas have been programmed by trauma to over-identify sensory input as "danger" become easily triggered into panic, rage, and anxiety. They tend to see the world as unsafe, people as devious, and love as risky.

A trigger, then, is your brain recognizing a Boggart; even though you're not actually in danger, you recognize something you fear, and you react to it as if the danger is real and all-powerful. Triggers are not mere reminders; simply being unpleasantly reminded of an uncomfortable experience is not a trigger. Rather, triggers are overwhelming physical responses that prevent you from functioning normally. The word "triggered" has become over-used to describe any uncomfortable reminder, though, and should be applied correctly. Harry Potter *thinking* about Dementors may make him uncomfortable, but actually encountering a Boggart of a Dementor is a true trigger. In your case, remembering your abuse may make you uncomfortable, but being reminded of those things is not the same as being triggered. A true trigger causes your brain to veer into an uncontrollable "fight or flight" crisis mode, and is a serious interruption of your normal brain processes.

To cope with triggers, a trauma survivor must learn how to interrupt this "Boggart hijack" by learning to prevent emotions from capturing all of the brain's decision-making processes. This can happen by therapeutically and repeatedly processing your trauma in excruciating detail until your brain no longer mistakes minor reminders in everyday life as indications that another trauma is imminent. This is not easy at first, because our brain is conditioned to accept something as an absolute truth if it merely feels true. Consider your abuse as an example: you may be convinced, despite all evidence to the contrary, that you are a worthless, degraded, filthy person—simply because you feel that way. "Emotional reasoning" is a pattern of thinking in which we assume that our emotions are the only evidence we need to verify a belief. If I feel ugly, that's all the proof I need that I am ugly. If I feel stupid, it is undeniable that I am stupid. Even Molly Weasley, a tough-as-nails wizard who defeats Bellatrix Lestrange in battle, is overcome by her Boggart; being susceptible to fear is not a weakness. It is a natural reality.

In order to reprogram your amygdala, you have to expose it to the very triggers that cause it to think you are re-experiencing danger. Sounds awful, doesn't it? But what happens is that your amygdala encounters those sensations, although without you actually experiencing any harm. You *feel* like you are going through it all again—at first—but you aren't actually being re-abused. Gradually, the amygdala changes its response to those trigger sensations, because new data replaces old data. Instead of hearing the word "rape" and being triggered into a defensive crisis by an amygdala that fears your past experience, it "learns" that this trigger is not associated with actually being presently raped at this moment. Therefore, it can change your brain's response to the trigger. All of the scents, sounds, and feelings that you have associated with being abused have been interpreted by your amygdala as new risks of repeated abuse every time, which is why hearing your abuser's name or smelling something that reminds you of being abused might send you into a panic. But when you talk about your traumas, you bring those same feelings back to your amygdala in safe ways that re-program it to change its reactions. Instead of, "Oh no! I'm feeling emotions that I associate with my abuse—PANIC!" your amygdala can begin to respond, "I recognize these sensations, but they don't correspond to me being hurt because I've felt them during times when I've been safe too. No need to panic." The best way to do this is by writing and speaking about your abuse in a safe, therapeutic setting, because it confronts your amygdala with all the repressed feelings it brings up until it "learns" not to take over your brain with panic every time. It changes your neurological reactions to traumas from "Oh my God! FREAK OUT!" to "These memories suck, but I'm not in danger. Remain calm and in control."

Triggers feel like hell, but they're not dangerous. A trigger occurs when your subconscious mind is trying to resolve some conflicted or painful detail about your trauma. It can happen when the mind is sufficiently at ease that the subconscious can inject the troubling memory into your conscious without the defensive walls of numbness, dissociation, or intoxication holding them back. This is why people who suffer flashbacks often abuse substances: the mind can't retrieve these memories when it is incapacitated. But unless the conflicted memory is acknowledged, fully expressed in your mind, and resolved, it will continue to percolate as a flashback/amygdala hijack that you can't always control. Or to put it another way, until you have faced your Boggart so often that the Boggart no longer terrifies you, it will continue to manifest. The longer you postpone resolution of these memories in these ways, the more difficult it will be to manage them when you can't resist them anymore. As Dumbledore said, "Numbing the pain for a while will make it worse when you finally feel it."[1]

The *good* part of having a trigger is that it indicates you are finally ready to resolve these traumatic memories. Although they feel frightening, they also suggest an unusual form of mental strength, as long as you don't sacrifice that very strength in destructive efforts to suppress the memories! It's like having the "check engine" light come on in your car: it doesn't tell you what's wrong under the hood, only that something needs your time, attention, and correction. Having a Boggart means you know what worst fear you most need to face. "But won't that just make my Boggart change into the next thing I'm afraid of?" Yes—and that "next thing" will be something that *wasn't* your original worst fear. It's something you feared less. And the Boggart after that will be something you fear even less that the second one. And so on, until your Boggarts no longer have their original power over you.

The most potent trigger is a self-shaming thought about your abuse. This is why flashbacks usually present you with the most painful,

---

1 *Harry Potter and the Goblet of Fire*, p.695

explicit, or humiliating moments of your traumas; those moments tend to be the instances when you had the least power, which triggers the self-blaming talk "that's the part I should have prevented!" or "that's the part that makes me the dirtiest!" (And consequently, "that's the part I have to keep secret from others, so they don't also blame me or know how awful I am!") Flashbacks are Boggarts.

Overcoming Boggarts/triggers requires you to do the exact opposite of what your "comfort instincts" tell you to do: rather than avoiding these memories (with whatever tricks you use to numb them), you have to directly examine them. In every detail. Even the yucky ones. *Especially the yucky ones.*

Boggarts are not real danger, but they are real fears. Having triggers is a confirmation that your pain is real, that your experiences are real. A flashback can be used as proof to yourself that you are hurt(ing), and that the pain does matter, which is important to realize when you doubt your own traumas ("maybe I'm crazy; maybe I'm wrong about what happened; maybe I wasn't raped, I just misunderstood; maybe my pain isn't as bad as other people's; maybe I don't even deserve all this fuss"). Consider reframing flashbacks as proof that what you know is true: the abuse is not a lie you made up, not a false accusation, not an attention-seeking tale, not an excuse. Flashbacks don't prove you are crazy, they prove you aren't. Boggarts don't imitate things you aren't afraid of, they imitate fears that are genuine. There's a reason those fears are genuine. Having a Boggart, then, does not mean you are a coward. It means that your experiences are genuinely true, and you are responding to them. The Boggart, or trigger, is a way to figure out which details of your memories are the ones that most need to be defeated. Triggers are useful in that way, because they point you from step to step through your healing by identifying the next huge thing that you need to face.

Professor Lupin helps his students to do this by showing them a Boggart so each of them has a chance to face it and practice the banishing spell. In this analogy, Lupin is being a therapist! He makes sure he is there to guide them and keep the situation safe, so they are not overwhelmed. He knows that Boggarts do not have the same power as the fear they are portraying (for example, the Boggart of a banshee would not actually have the power to slaughter the students with its scream, and facing memories of abuse is not actually being abused again). It's a controlled environment, and he can let the students reveal their fears, face them, and begin building up their strengths against them. If a student does become overwhelmed, he can intervene and return the situation to normal, even taking extra time to help talk them through it.

Battling Your Boggarts

1. Know your emotions. Work on increasing your self-awareness, the ability to recognize a feeling as it happens. Learn as much vocabulary about emotions as possible, so that you aren't limited to narrow descriptions of how you feel. Instead of just saying "I feel bad/horrible/ashamed" (or worse yet, "I dunno"), learn more complex words that better describe the nuances of your feelings: Fear, Anger, Ambivalence, Disgust, Anticipation, Shock, Conflicted, Disappointment, Envy, Intimidation, Discovery, Loss, Grief, Courage, Cautious, and so on. By expanding the language of your emotions, you will be more capable of expressing your own responses to triggers, rather than having to sort your emotions into simplistic "Good/ Bad," which is hardly ever the accurate choice. The more detail you are able to use to express yourself, the more capable you become in your battle.

2. Regulate your emotions. Improve your ability to handle feelings and to recover quickly from upsets and distress. Your therapist will assist in this area more than I can do from a book. But the tools for doing this seemingly-impossible task are to use self-talk to challenge your emotions, and to begin compelling you to question whether something really is true simply because it feels true. In my work with clients, I called this the "hate it but do it anyway" strength. If you cut your emotions off by distracting yourself or numbing them, they never get to be fully expressed, so they crawl back inside you to surface again another time. Instead, learn to let the feelings roll all the way in, then all the way out, like the tide. That will let them begin to recede. I've seen clients grow from not even being able to say the word "rape," for example, to doing public speaking and educational workshops about sexual abuse because they were able to let their triggers fully manifest and then recede until they were no longer triggers.

3. Motivate yourself. Learn to delay your desire for instant relief when distress sets in. Many trauma victims are so upset by triggers that they will begin a search for some method of quickly suppressing the anxiety, such as alcohol, marijuana, self-injury, or even sex. One of the most difficult things you will learn in therapy is to "sit with the feelings," to let them surge and withdraw like a flood, and re-learn the skill of remaining fully aware and controlled during a painful sensation. One way that I have helped clients do this is to instruct them to sit alone in their home or in nature, with no TV or audio, and just listen. Attentively listen to the silence. Familiarize yourself with every tiny sound. Spend three minutes meditating in this way before opening your journal and writing. The purpose is to re-experience silence (and even aloneness) as

a safe time, a feeling that precedes healing, and a personal time. Another thing I do is to prohibit group members from interfering when someone is experiencing a trigger/Boggart during a therapy session. It appears cruel to my patients at first, but I do not allow members to touch, move closer to, hug, swarm around, or even interrupt someone who is struggling with an aspect of his abuse that brings a flood of grief. The reason is that interference will prevent him from fully processing the anguish. He must fully pass through his emotional state, so that emotions no longer become enemies. If everyone else rushes in to cast their "Boggart banishing" spell *for* him, he never learns how to do it himself.

4. Cultivate empathy. Try to recognize, identify, and feel what others are feeling. Find a person whose approach to healing impresses you, and begin to model them in similar situations. I can tell when a change from "victim" to "survivor" is happening by the way someone responds to other victims' experiences. During the stage of being a victim, it is common for patients of mine to hear other people's stories and respond in these (and other similar) ways:

- "Oh, that's like my story" or "That reminds me of me" or "I'm the same way!" (other people's stories are used to return attention to one's self)
- Criticism of other victims. Blaming them. Talking tough about how you would never put yourself in the same situation.
- "Why do we always have to talk about abuse in group? Can't we talk about something else?!"
- "I'm over that. I've dealt with it, and I barely even think about it anymore. I've moved on with my life, so can we work on otherstuff, please?"
- "I've been through all that stuff too. Look, here's what you need to do…"

But when a person transforms from a victim into a survivor, words like "rape" or "abuse" and the stories of other victims no longer have so much power to knock you off balance. You are able to hear the words, listen to the stories, and respond in a way that honors the other people who tell them. Gradually, you evolve from thinking that other people's narratives have value (or danger) only to the extent that they remind you of yourself, into a new way of thinking where other people's stories become opportunities to relate, to support, to nurture, to encourage, and to uplift. This is not a form of codependence where you feel you must take on and heal every other victim's burdens, but a sense of personal power and calm that allows you to share together in the struggles and successes without always personalizing them. It's a change from "it's all about me" to "it's all about us."

5. Manage relationships. Managing relationships means nurturing the important ones, and avoiding the toxic ones. In the *Harry Potter* books, Draco meets Harry for the first time and immediately tries to recruit Harry into his own cadre of friends. It is Draco's intention that Harry abandon his "loser" friends, and become part of Draco's own elite, powerful group. Harry, however, senses that Draco is dangerous. He sticks with the friends who are kind and clever: "I think I can tell who the wrong sort are for myself, thanks,"[2] he says to Draco.

Never squander a precious friendship or alliance. Do not let a single conflict become the permanent end of a valuable companionship. Develop yourself as a helper who will be able to assist other survivors in the future. It may seem that relationship skills have little to do with triggers and "Boggart hijacks," but they are very much intertwined. The more relationship skills you possess, the fewer threats you will perceive in everyday interactions. And as you become more assertive, you will be better-defended in daily life.

When Harry, Hermione, and Ron do have occasional feuds, they don't last long. They never sacrifice their entire relationships over squabbles. In *The Deathly Hallows,* we learn that once when Ron had become upset with Harry and Hermione and left them to go out on his own, he had actually regretted his choice immediately and tried to return back to them right away because he knew how much their friendships truly meant to him. Buddhist spiritual teacher Thich Naht Hanh once said, "Only your compassion and your loving kindness are invincible, and without limit." The poet Kahlil Gibran echoed that thought when he wrote, "Tenderness and kindness are not signs of weakness and despair, but manifestations of strength and resolution." They could have been summarizing the single most important lesson of the *Harry Potter* series.

---

2 *Harry Potter and the Sorcerer's Stone,* p.109

CHAPTER SIX

Dementors

"They don't need walls and water to keep the prisoners in, not when they're trapped inside their own heads, incapable of a single cheerful thought. Most go mad within weeks."[1]

-Remus Lupin

Dementors are creatures that suck the happiness out of people, leaving them emotionally hollow and despairing. Victims of a Dementor feel powerless to resist, feeling drained of all hope as if they could never feel pleasure again.

In the world of the Harry Potter books, Dementors are most closely associated with Azkaban, the concealed prison island in the North Sea where prisoners are kept powerless by an infestation of Dementors, which continually prey upon them like parasites. Azkaban was originally built as a fortress by the mad dark wizard Ekrizdis, as a way to lure sailors to torture and doom. When the wizarding world decided to use the fortress as a prison rather than as a trap for unwary Muggles, Dementors were allowed to remain as a way to weaken prisoners to the point of helplessness. The Dementors became so abundant and strong, though, that even when Minister of Magic Eldritch Diggory suggested finding another less-cruel way to control the prison population, the wizarding world refused out of sheer fear that the unfed Dementors would depart Azkaban and invade the mainland in search of new prey. And so, the parasitic symbiosis between wizards and Dementors was allowed to continue.

---

1 *Harry Potter and the Prizoner of Azkaban*, p.188

Dementors

Dementors, however, are untrustworthy because they are not loyal, but instead ally with whomever can provide them with the most people as an energy source. They don't differentiate among victims (in fact, they have empty eye sockets and can only sense happiness as a food source that attracts them), and they lack distinctive features, appearing as shrouded, floating wraiths. We can infer from descriptions of Dementors that they lack personalities, and instead function more like emotional leeches, drawn to happiness the way another parasite might be drawn to an animal's warmth.

The symbolism of Dementors is not subtle; they are clear representations of depression personified. Rowling herself, in fact, described Dementors as symbolic of her own battles with depression, stating that she had experienced depression as an "absence of being able to envisage that you will ever be cheerful again. The absence of hope. That very deadened feeling, which is so very different from feeling sad."[2] Those who have also endured depression recognize this vivid, terrifying description.

Clinical depression is a real, studied, fairly well understood physical condition that causes emotional, cognitive, and physical symptoms. Depression is *not* simply a passing emotional state, mood swing, lack of positive thinking, or mental weakness. People who have suffered depression compare it to a form of physical pain, exhaustion, inability to make decisions, and hopelessness. One person described it to me, "it's like my brain has begun to decay, with all the healthy parts going silent and only the dying core of it still there."

Science agrees with that description.

Brain scan technology has helped us see the actual differences between a depressed and a non-depressed brain, and the results are astonishing. The depressed brain has far less energy activity than a non-depressed brain, and long-term depression can even cause physical changes in the brain's structure, including the eventual dying off of neurons ("hippocampal atrophy").[3] Long-term depression can cause permanent changes, the way long-term exposure to a Dementor can cause a person to become permanently drained of energy and hope.

This is why well-meaning advice like "get over it" and "focus on positive thinking" and "go out and *do* something!" simply aren't helpful, any more than they would be effective in healing diabetes.[4] Depression is a

---

2 *The Times*, June 30, 2000, with quote archived at http://www.accio-quote.org/articles/2000/0600-times-treneman.html
3 http://psycheducation.org/depression-is-not-a-moral-weakness/chapter-6-what-happens-inside-peoples-brains-when-theyre-depressed/
4 While it's true that physical activity can have a mood-improving effect, it tends to be temporary rather than depression-curing.

physical condition, not an attitude problem. It can arise from many causes, including situational stressors, trauma, genetic predisposition, other medical illnesses, and even some allergies. Likewise, Dementors do not breed, but rather arise under certain conditions, like mold in a damp, dark place. Likewise, Dementors cannot be destroyed, according to Rowling herself, but people can drive them away and protect themselves from them.

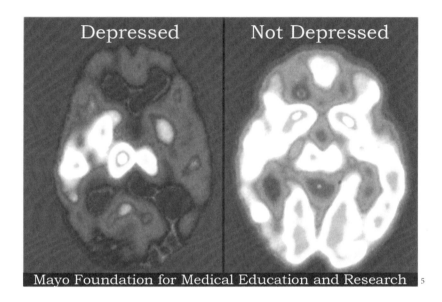

These are good descriptions of depression itself. Depression does not emerge in a person because of some weakness within them, and Dementors are sightless, and choose their victims the way a mosquito or tick chooses a person. That is to say, it is not the "fault" of their victim that they are being attacked, because Dementors simply swarm to what they sense as an available source of energy. The exception to this is that they can be ordered against a specific target, such as when Umbridge sends them against Harry.

Dementors do, however, have a preference for victims who have not only abundant happiness on which to feed, but strong experiences with turmoil and struggle as well, which is why they preferentially attack Harry during a Qiuidditch tournament. Like clinical depression, Dementors find that those with trauma in their past are often less defended against their attacks, as Lupin explains to Harry. This is not a fault of their victims,

5 http://www.mayoclinic.org/tests-procedures/pet-scan/multimedia/-pet-scan-of-the-brain-for-depression/img-20007400; graphically enhanced for print clarify

Dementors

any more than depression is a fault in the depressed person. But it does show us that experiences with trauma can make us more susceptible to the effects, and survivors of traumas such as childhood sexual abuse, domestic violence, rape, and emotional abuse do manifest higher rates of depression later in life.[6] Harry Potter shows us that being "targeted" by depression because of our life experiences is not a sign that we are weak; Harry is also targeted by Dementors because his own traumas do make him vulnerable:

> [Harry] hesitated, and then the question he had to ask burst from him before he could stop himself. "Why? Why do they affect me like that? Am I just –?"
> "It has nothing to do with weakness," said Professor Lupin sharply, as though he had read Harry's mind. "The Dementors affect you worse than the others because there are horrors in your past that the others don't have."[7]

But "vulnerability" is not the same as "weakness"; Harry (like you) may be more vulnerable because of his past, but he's not weak. In fact, Harry becomes so skilled at learning how to defeat Dementors that he becomes a role model for others who want to learn from him. Going through tough experiences doesn't make you weak, and can even make you more able to pass your survival skills on to others who look up to you.

During depression, our tendency is to withdraw inside our own senses. One of my clients described it "as if my emotions got smaller, like I was sucking my own feelings deep inside me so they wouldn't be damaged again." This is a good description of what is happening! We are trying to blunt our own emotional sensitivity to protect our amygdala from having to imprint new data, essentially tattooing our minds with new images of pain. The further we have to withdraw our emotions, the more numb and distant we feel, eventually resulting in a dissociative state in which we become living "blank slates," awake but distant, unresponsive, empty of emotion. Dissociating, or "blanking out," is a classic after-effect of trauma.

6 "Emotional support and adult depression in survivors of childhood sexual abuse." Child Abuse & Neglect, Volume 38, Issue 8, Pages 1331-1340
Katherine L. Musliner, Jonathan B. Singer;
"The Long-term Health Outcomes of Childhood Abuse: An Overview and a Call to Action." Kristen W Springer, Jennifer Sheridan, Daphne Kuo, Molly Carnes
J Gen Intern Med. 2003 Oct; 18(10): 864–870;
"The Mental Health Impact of Rape" Dean G. Kilpatrick, Ph.D. National Violence Against Women Prevention Research Center Medical University of South Carolina
https://mainweb-v.musc.edu/vawprevention/research/mentalimpact.shtml
7 *Harry Potter and the Prisoner of Azkaban*, p.187

One woman described it as being like "there was a talking head on top of this prop called a body."[8]

Other people withdraw their emotions not to dissociate, but to become fierce in response to danger. This is the "shields up, claws out!" approach. Armed and upset, ready to explode, we react to others by becoming tough and angry. I once saw a man in therapy who kept my group in an intimidated state, snarling from his chair whenever he felt confronted. He had lost his job after making a face-to-face death threat against his boss, and his wife had threatened to leave him because he had lacked warmth and empathy for years. His response to conflict was to become a warrior, and he told me that he regarded the world as "no different than the jungles of Vietnam" and that he perceived "enemies all around" whom he had to defeat. He did not see the world as a place where trust or vulnerability with others could ever be safe.

His was not the healthy anger that we need to feel. Anger is not a forbidden emotion, and expressing it does not make us like an abuser. If anything, righteous anger is healthy because it represents our desire to restore an unfair situation to justice. It is a refusal to accept a circumstance that needs transformation into *shalom*, the Hebraic word that describes peace, completeness, and fairness.[9] But his anger was explosive and hurtful, and it came from a place of distrust and disconnection from others. His anger was not toward things that are wrong, but toward people who he wanted to repel in order to stay isolated. He thought it would make him safe—it only made him lonely.

Do you suffer from depression? Then you have something in common with Harry Potter and J.K. Rowling.

Are you willing to struggle against it, not give up, to fight back, and learn how to overcome it? Then you have something in common with Harry Potter and J.K. Rowling.

Fighting Against the Dementors

In my work with wounded people, I have seen that trauma causes an injury even worse than depression alone. The experience of being neglected, abused, molested, or raped causes such a sense of betrayal

---

8 Meyer, Rick. *Through the Fire: Spiritual Restoration for Adult Victims of Childhood Sexual Abuse*, p63.

9 "Shalom" comes from the words *Shelem* and *Shulam,* meaning that all restitution and debts have been resolved. Thus, "Shalom" indicates a restoration of equality and righteousness.

that you may even feel banished into loneliness.[10] You may have come to see yourself as a misfit, alone in the world, cursed to a life that is never understood or accepted by others. Even in a crowd, you may still feel inwardly alone, as if nobody near you could ever possibly understand what you feel. As one woman said to me once, "being raped was the loneliest experience of my entire life." If you relate to those feelings, chances are, you read the parts of the Harry Potter books where Harry is banished into the dark, cobwebbed crawl space beneath the Dursley's stairs and forbidden to speak, or even belong, and you felt more emotional connection to that suffering than most other readers ever could. That sense of being alone, unknowable, and disconnected from the rest of life is perhaps the worst misery a human can experience, and it's why solitary confinement is considered a form of torture. The emotion of loneliness is your Azkaban.

And it can get even worse. If you've been abused, you may have also come to think of love as a resource that is very rare, a treasure in limited supply. Something there's not enough of to go around. I'm not talking about romantic love, I'm talking about unselfish regard for another's well-being in a way that brings joy to both the giver and receiver of it. To a victim, love is rare, and when it is given to someone else, the total amount of it you have left to give becomes smaller.

That's why you might sometimes even live in fear that love will vanish. If you're not sure if this actually describes you, here's one way to tell: if you've ever felt that it's safer and smarter to keep your feelings to yourself so nobody else can hurt you, even though it's a very lonely form of protection, you are who I'm describing.

Now contrast this to Harry's parents, and in particular his mother. Lily Potter was so overwhelmingly full of love, so open with it, that rather than becoming a weakness, it became something strong enough to actually protect Harry from the strongest, deadliest forbidden curse of all. Lily shows us that sharing love doesn't diminish us. And she does this, even to the point that she is willing to die rather than withhold her love from another who needs her, and that sacrifice gives Harry his magical protection.

In real life, this doesn't happen. Being loved, or loving others, does not charm us with a magical protection from harm. But the Harry Potter books do still give us important lessons in what love means in human relationships, and how it relates to our struggles against our Dementors.

A few years ago, I went through a severe depression. But over time, I realized something. Each surge of despair would almost drown me, and

---

10 Gaudin, J. M. , Polansky, N. A. , Kilpatrick, A. C. , Shilton, P. (1993). Loneliness, depression, stress, and social supports in neglectful families. *American Journal of Orthopsychiatry, 63,* 597–605.

then it would obsess my mind with churning, bleak thoughts. But gradually, they would soften. I would settle. My mind would relax, and I would find myself able to accept the truth of what was happening. Eventually I recognized my own pattern of emotions: feeling drowned in emotions, becoming stunned and shell-shocked, feeling hopeless, enduring thoughts that wouldn't stop, and slowly depression would lose its boa constrictor grip on my body and mind. As more and more bad news mounted, I was able to understand them as pangs of despair, which were not permanent. Previously when depression had ravaged me, I had felt defeated, but my thinking evolved to a realization that those wounds were not fatal, that they would slowly heal, and that I would get through it. Depression was the worst thing I had ever felt, but it was not going to win. Even when I finally broke down in tears after the worst panic attack in my life, I told my wife that I was hurting so badly "not because I want my life to end, but because I don't—I want my life to come back again. I want to keep going. I want to be happy again, and I'm not." Yet.

I did not find comfort in inspirational slogans, or reciting bland affirmations, or in temporary pleasures. What saved me was becoming able to listen to my emotions rather than dodging them, allowing them to express whatever information they carried, examining that information ("why am I feeling sick to my stomach, but I am unable to become angry at the situation that is harming our family? What is it about me that transforms anger into a physical symptom so I can't express it in words?"), and to know that my emotions were not wrong—they were simply data.

As this insight dawned on me, I realized that feeling victimized was normal and inevitable, not some failure of strength or faith. All wounded people pass through victimization, where we feel weak, beaten, embarrassed, taken advantage of, with no apparent way out. I also realized that as long as I refused to build a nest inside my victimization, I could outgrow it and become a survivor. To do this, I would have to allow myself to fully feel the pain of the experience I was in, nurture my connections with others rather than isolating, and begin to plan for what my life would be like after my trauma. I learned that I had to be honest about my feelings, such as telling my wife at times, "I can feel my depression coming on again, but I don't want you to worry because I'm aware of it and I'm already planning how I will cope with it," as opposed to dishonesty about my feelings ("I'm fine! Nothing's wrong!") I was not very optimistic, but I was very hopeful—and they are not the same thing.

In the books, Dementors cannot be destroyed, but they can be repelled, and the damage they cause can be eased. After a Dementor's attack in *Prisoner of Azkaban*, Harry is left feeling so cold and unable to move that he feels he is drowning in sadness. The despair he feels is so strong that even those around him can feel it (something that is also true of depression), and Professor Lupin has to expel the Dementor with a spell. After doing so, Lupin provides chocolate to the children, advising them to eat it as a sort of medicine, and Harry feels a warmth begin to spread to his feet and fingers. Later we learn from Madam Pomfrey that administering chocolate is apparently the usual protocol to treating Dementor traumas.

The use of chocolate as a medicine is a cute storytelling device, and it has deeper symbolism. The lesson is that depression cannot simply be cured by wishing it away or being tough; sometimes it requires a medicine that strengthens us. In real life, that medication can often be found in antidepressants.

Years ago, science tended to fumble with medical treatments for depression, and all sorts of barely-helpful methods of treatment were tried and abandoned. Medications that did work also tended to have awful side effects which could sometimes be so miserable in themselves that patients simply abandoned treatment.

Medical treatment for depression has improved vastly, and while not yet perfect, the treatments really are quite remarkable. I cringe when I still see ignorant internet memes that claim that antidepressant medications are worthless because "science doesn't even know how they work," or "antidepressants are just fake moods in a bottle," or "the belief in 'chemical imbalances' is not true." None of those statements, in fact, is true. Medical science actually knows quite exactly how antidepressants work. Antidepressants are not mind-altering drugs that cause fake moods, and taking them is not a form of creating a phony personality to hide the real you. What they do, very simply, is to help your brain's natural transmitters carry nerve signals across the gaps between the tips of nerve cells so that those signals can complete your normal thoughts at normal speeds. Therefore, antidepressants don't drug the real you, they actually set the real you free. They allow your genuine thoughts to finally flow freely through your brain, rather than becoming stuck by nerve gaps they can't cross. "Stuck" brain activity is what makes the depressed brain feel slower, and why your thoughts become obsessive cycles of worry, like wheels spinning in mud. Once those signals become un-stuck, your brain can slowly whirr back to life, lighting up the long-underused parts again. Antidepressants simply help you produce enough of those natural transmitters to help carry your thought signals across those nerve ending gaps.

The cool thing is, none of this is guesswork. Today we can actually see this happening inside the brain using real-time scans. Images of depressed brains that are treated with antidepressants are remarkable;

the fullness of the brain "lights up" again after being under-energized by depression. And here's the coolest thing of all: accepted medical research now shows that not only can antidepressants help revive a depressed brain, but they can also help protect brain cells from further damage by depression, and even begin to repair and re-grow atrophied brain cells! For years, this was thought to be impossible—once those cells die, they're dead—but antidepressants are now so well understood that we can see this happen. In real life, *right now*.

I don't mean to imply that every antidepressant method is perfect. In fact, it can still take trial-and-error to find the specific form of medication that works best for each person. There are also still some side effects from them that people dislike. My point is that the science is improving, they are an incredibly effective and safe method of treatment, and it's important to understand that depression is a physical brain condition, and that's why medications can be effective in treating it.

Imagine if Harry's method for coping with Dementor attacks had been to simply say, "leave me alone, it's none of your business, I'm fine," and just play tough. Or worse, imagine if that hadn't been his method at all, and that he actually *wanted* help, but had nobody around to provide it. This is exactly what happened to J.K. Rowling herself; when she sought medical care for her depression, a stand-in physician failed to truly understand her needs, and discharged her. It was later when a subsequent doctor recognized the urgency of her depression that she was provided with treatment that worked.[11] Not only did Rowling battle her depression through counseling, but also by speaking out publicly about it. This not only helped her personally, but helped others struggling with depression to find a role model who could explain that depression is a treatable medical condition, not a weakness.

Depressed people often need help getting help. Fortunately for Harry, Professor Lupin is there with exactly the right medication at the right time. Again and again, other professors and Madam Pomfrey are able to also help Harry by providing him with the medicine he needs, and Harry trusts them. He cooperates with their treatments, and he finds that they work. Don't skip over the whole "chocolate" part of the story as just a cute detail; Rowling is telling us something about what it can take to repair ourselves after the Dementors have attacked.

As Harry's magical powers grow, he also learns about a spell which is the only known way to actually defeat Dementors. While there is no known method for destroying them, there is one advanced charm that can repel even an entire horde of Dementors at once. As Lupin explains

11 http://www.howibeatdepression.com/how-jk-rowling-beat-depression/

Dementors

to Harry in *Prisoner of Azkaban*, "The Patronus is a kind of positive force, a projection of the very things that the Dementor feeds upon--hope, happiness, the desire to survive..."[12] Only instead of providing Dementors with an abundance of the very emotional energies they gorge on, it repels them. It works as if the happiness the Dementors crave to feed upon emerges from the human in a totally different quantity, changing the dynamic from one in which the Dementors have control over the happiness, to happiness having power over the Dementors. To conjure it, a wizard focuses on one moment of purest happiness from their entire lives while uttering the charmed words, *Expecto Patronum!*, which expels a magical symbol that embodies the source of the wizard's own happiness.

Once a wizard identifies their personal "truest moment" of happiness, that moment powers their protective charm each time the charm is used, unless a newer moment of even more happiness replaces it. Furthermore, the power to conjure a Patronus charm can be lost, too, if a trauma overwhelms a wizard's previous happiness; for example, J.K. Rowling once revealed that George Weasley lost his ability to cast a Patronus charm after his beloved twin brother Fred died during the Battle of Hogwarts. Harry has to try several happy memories before he is truly able to cast a Patronus. He tries using his first memory of riding a broomstick, which almost succeeds in producing his Patronus, but flashbacks of his parents' deaths intrude, and his charm fails. Even as you struggle to maintain your recovery from abuse, there may be times when flickers of memories or sensations interrupt, causing you to falter. Remember, these are not defeats, only obstacles. They do not mean you are weak or incapable of facing your own Dementors, they only mean that Dementors fight back, and you'll still need practice.

Next, Harry tries a memory of a Qiuidditch victory. Even though this, too, is a happy memory, it is also insufficient to overpower a Dementor during his lessons with Lupin, and traumatic childhood memories flood him again.

Finally, Harry uses his memory of leaving the Dursley's home (where he was abused) to attend Hogwarts for the first time (where he finds his true friendships), and that memory works. Although Harry does not cast a full Patronus, the power of the silvery-white glow that rushes from his wand is the strongest yet, and it is clear that he's identified the true source of his Patronus.

What we learn here offers much wisdom about combatting depression. Depression is a serious, even deadly, medical condition that cannot be treated with weak or powerless methods. We have to read the story of Harry's Patronus lessons with Professor Lupin very carefully to get

12 *Harry Potter and the Prisoner of Azkaban*, p.237

the correct point; this is *not* a story that teaches us that thinking positively is a cure for depression. In fact, the story goes out of its way to show that positive thinking is not a successful form of defense against depression. Focusing on mere feel-good memories gives Harry enough power to produce a very slight, mild wisp of silver magic, but nothing capable of actually defeating a Dementor. Harry tries repeatedly to use "positive thinking," and the memories of trauma just overwhelm them each time.

But wait, isn't it just a case of Harry needing to find the right happy memory? Doesn't the story just mean that if your positive thinking efforts don't work at first, just keep trying until you luck into the right positive thoughts that finally make your Dementors go away? No, that's not what the story is teaching at all, although it could look like that if we don't read carefully. Harry's memory of leaving the Dursley's to come to Hogwarts works, but not because it's just a better brand of happy memory that makes Dementors go away. Rather, it's the symbolic importance of that memory that teaches us what really works.

When Harry leaves the Dursley's home and comes to Hogwarts, he doesn't just gain a new sense of personal pleasure about his life that adds enough sugar to his positive thinking to win the battle against depression. This memory represents meaningful, life-altering changes that Harry makes in his real life. By leaving the Dursley's house, Harry becomes physically free of his abusers, which is a crucial life change to someone healing from trauma. Trauma cannot be extinguished if you are still experiencing the same kinds of harm that cause trauma in the first place. In my work with rape victims, for example, I've noticed that rape trauma just doesn't really heal while someone is still in a relationship with an abuser who causes them to still be devalued, ashamed, and at risk. But Harry is able to finally see a light at the end of the tunnel of his abusive childhood, and even though he does still have to return to the Dursley's to live sometimes, he does have one important resource that makes all the difference: he has, for the first time in his life, a support network.

Harry can't always get out of his toxic environment, but that doesn't mean he is powerless to still heal from his abuse. In real life, abuse victims are also not always able to be free of their abusers. For example, in my work with domestic violence survivors, I heard so many stories about how they were unable to find true support because people who were ignorant about domestic violence would judge and scold them: "why don't you just leave? Just walk away! Nobody's forcing you to be abused, so you must like it! Are victims just stupid? If it was *me*, I would…" Meanwhile, victims who were financially stranded with their abusers, too young to live freely, threatened with worse harm if they left, coerced into staying by threats made against their pets or children, and being programmed for years to think they are unlovable, worthless failures, find that they cannot simply walk away from abuse and be free.

Harry Potter shows us that being trapped in an abusive situation does not make you a failure as a person. It does not happen because you are weak. In his case, he simply does not have a way to be free of his abusers. Harry also shows us that even though we cannot fully heal from trauma while still being traumatized, we are not forever "stuck" as trauma victims, either, and he does make progress toward healing. If you have ever been trapped in an abusive situation and were unsure how to cope because you couldn't escape it, it doesn't mean you're weak. It means you're very much like Harry Potter, and you have the same potential to recover and heal that he does.

What makes the difference to Harry is that he is able to find a true support network. For the first time in his life, he forms real friendships. Ron and Hermione understand Harry's life, and they never judge or mock him for it. Instead, they both become eager to show Harry all of the wonders of the world he's never seen, and to help him develop his intelligence, his humor, and his skills. When Harry is overwhelmed by images of his traumas, they support him gently. In short, Harry has found people he can be honest with about his pain, fear, and self-consciousness.

At workshops and during counseling sessions, I've often been asked, "how do I know when I've changed from being a victim to becoming a survivor?" My answer is that we become true survivors when we reach a point where we are no longer ashamed that we were ever victims. We become able to speak our truths honestly and to the right people at the appropriate times. For you, that may mean that you no longer feel defined by rape, or child abuse, or emotional abuse, but you are not ashamed that it is part of your story, because you have truly, genuinely learned that these experiences do not degrade your worth as a person. They do not make you unlovable, or ugly, or damaged goods. They do not define or limit your goodness; they define and limit the goodness of those who inflicted hurt upon you. The fact that the Dursleys, or Professor Umbridge, despise and abuse Harry does not make Harry less precious as a person. Readers are able to direct our scorn against those abusers for what they have done to our Harry; we don't see Harry as a pathetic person for having been abused by them. Once you can apply this same clear-headed point of view to yourself and your abusers, you begin to shed some of that shame, too. If you can see Harry's abusers as villains while still seeing Harry as a good person, the same is true of the villains who were abusive in *your* life.

Harry is not able to instantly see these truths. Neither can most abuse victims at first. Like other victims of trauma, Harry needs others to help guide his thinking until he can gradually correct some of his misunderstandings. Many victims of abuse have come to believe that violence is normal in families, and that most men and most women have similar roles to the roles they saw in their own lives. I've found that abuse victims also tend to over-criticize themselves, even while showing such compassion to others who have been hurt. In group therapy, for example, I saw case after case where someone would punish themselves for any mistake—"I'm so stupid! Why did I...? It's all my fault!"—while showing forgiveness and understanding to others in the group who had similar traumas. This kind of Dobby-like self-punishment is so common in abuse survivors that it may even be the most difficult wound of all to heal from, because it silences victims from sharing their truths with other people out of fear of being rejected the way they reject themselves.

In order to heal from those wounds, the victim must take the courageous step of finally revealing their truths to another person, who I call the "compassionate hearer." This is partly to help the victim finally find their voice and speak bravely about what they have been through, but partly to help extinguish the sheer terror they have that "if anyone else knew all the details of what happened to me, they would reject me!" Opening up to someone and having kindness returned to them rather than scolding and rejection is an important step toward healing, and it's why healing *cannot* take place alone. Healing *cannot* take place just by reading a book, writing a private journal, or thinking positive thoughts. It comes from healthy connection to others *in combination* with internal work and growth. Harry is careful to choose friends who aren't constantly embroiled in drama, crisis, chaos, or craziness. Enemies certainly cause all of those things in their lives, but Harry's friends are functional people. They're not maladjusted losers. They don't make his life worse. Harry has chosen friends who challenge him to develop his intellect, his humor, his abilities, and his internal life. To put it bluntly, *do not choose Slytherins as your friends.*

Friendships, then, become healing medicine to Harry. Harry is not a stoic, tough, Wolverine-like warrior who needs nobody and rides into his tough-guy sunset at the end of his war. His strength actually comes from *not* being like that; he is made stronger by being emotionally vulnerable and open with his loved ones, finding those he can truly trust, and seeing love and connection to others as his primary strengths. This is why his Patronus was not just a form of "positive thinking" and "happy thoughts." Harry's Patronus is generated by his experience of finding a world beyond his abuse, in which he can find healthy relationships with those who will love him rather than rejecting him. Every aspect of his Patronus, from the form it takes (a stag, representing his loving father) to the memory that produces it, relates to Harry's connectedness to others as his real strength. For Harry, the Patronus is a charm that comes from within, but it is only possible because of strengths he has that *don't* just come from within, they come from his loving companionships with others.

Can a Patronus show us lessons about defeating real-life Dementors? Yes, as long as we understand the lesson correctly. As long as we don't minimize a Patronus into a cheap sort of "happy thoughts" remedy, and truly see the depth of Harry's Patronus as a lesson about finding strength through connection to others, yes. The very words "Expecto Patronum" translate as "I await my protector" (or even "I call upon, or expect, my protector"). The protection you need comes partly from within yourself, such as in making wise choices of friends and behaviors, not causing harm to yourself, enriching your curious mind with smart activities, and nurturing your sense of goodness. But your protection also comes from outside of yourself as well, such as supportive friends, role models, and teachers. In overcoming depression, we have to learn the same insights that Harry has learned: work with experts who know more than you about how to treat it, find others who understand your experiences, use medication responsibly, and value the moments that give your life meaning and hope.

CHAPTER SEVEN

Horcruxes and Trauma

Over many years, countless people sat with me in my counseling office, ready to finally tell me the big, dark secret they've been keeping that they're certain will finally repel all of my care for them. Leg bouncing nervously, fingers fidgeting, eyes down, they begin to really open to me about what's hurt them most in their lives. Despite all the therapy they'd received, sometimes for years, they had never actually put into words the one thing they believe is their worst truth. In a moment that they think will finally horrify me to the point of rejecting them, they begin to speak…

The secret is different for everyone, but it's also somehow the same. The trauma itself varies—"I was raped," "my father molested me for years, and sometimes I even liked the attention," "my mother hated me all of my life, and let people do horrible things to me"—but in each case, they feel so ashamed that they are convinced their entire soul is ugly because of it. Each and every one has become exhausted from pretending to be fine, which they've done for years because they are convinced that people only care about them because nobody knows their real true secret. The common belief of a survivor of trauma is this: "if I had been worthy, nobody would have treated me as hurtfully as they did. Their harm to me caused me to become damaged. And to this day I still suffer, which proves I am still unworthy and damaged." The strongest effect of shame is the belief that you have some trait or truth that, if known by other people, would have you unworthy of connection. It is the idea that others would not want to relate to you if they were aware of some flaw that you keep hidden, because you believe that flaw makes you unbearably bad or repulsive. I have never yet met a single survivor of abuse who did not have feelings of shame.

People who have been victims also expect me to respond to their shame in certain ways. They think I'm going to pester them with questions that subtly blame them: "Did you report it? Why did you let it go on? Why didn't you tell someone?" or that I'm going to become defensive to them about my own qualities as a man: "Well, you know *not all men* are bad" and "That's an irrational belief we'll need to work on" and "Okay, but you can trust me" and "That could block your therapy, you know." All of these are common responses, that all miss the point.

The great lie of abuse is that it causes a permanent emotional wound, a scar that can never heal, a stain that can't be removed. Sometimes for years, the victim of abuse may feel empty, valueless, unlovable, and frightened. It can feel like a contradictory entrapment: you may wish desperately that someone would accept and know you, and yet you fear that someone might truly know you now, and then at other times it also feels like everyone can tell you've been abused by merely looking at you. "I'm afraid nobody will ever know me, and I'm afraid anybody might ever know me."

In the beginning of coping and recovery, you may find yourself using very stark, dreadful words when you describe yourself:

- Scarred for life
- Worthless
- Damaged
- Filthy
- Unknowable

You may notice yourself using extreme and permanent-sounding terms to describe yourself, your pain, and your life, such as "always, never, forever, nobody, everybody, nothing," etc.

Many trauma victims repeat the same ineffective patterns of coping, such as turning to alcohol or marijuana to numb their emotions, taking up smoking; injuring themselves; and using sex as a form of self-harm. During your "victim" phase, you may become more and more frustrated with yourself because nothing you try seems to work for longer than a moment. You exhaust yourself in a scavenger hunt for new ways to feel, or new ways *not* to feel; new ways to struggle with your abuse, and new ways to avoid struggling with your abuse. You criticize yourself for how long the process is taking because you say to yourself (and other people say to you), "Aren't you over this yet? It's time to let it go!"

You're not sure how to try different, so you just keep trying the same things *harder*.

You may be feeling guilty and depressed. You may have trouble eating and sleeping. You may feel empty and grey inside, confused even about who you are. You may find yourself becoming angry with people who do not correctly guess how to respond to your needs, and wind up driving others away (and perhaps even feeling even more victimized by the loneliness that results—"See? Nobody understands me! Nobody sticks by me!").

These should not be the feelings you carry for the rest of your life, but for right now, at this point, these are the normal and reasonable emotions that trauma will stir. Don't deny your emotions because you have guilt or pressures telling you not to feel them. People who are unable to genuinely accept what they feel during this process have much more difficulty getting through it.

Emotions are forms of communication within you and they have some important things to say. If you shove them away, ignore them, suppress them, blur them with alcohol, or find other ways to counterfeit how you truly feel, your emotions will not be able to finish their task of expressing data to you, which will cause those emotions to persist in more confusing forms. Allowing our emotions to be heard and understood will not result in being "drowned" in a tidal wave. In fact, the opposite happens: they are able to be expressed, then finally withdraw and fade into vapor.

However, this is not an easy process. After people have taken the step to finally reveal their "deep, dark secret" traumas to their therapists or helpers, they tend to become even more disgusted with themselves. The feeling of relief doesn't come at first; in fact, they usually feel worse, not better. All of their shame floods up because now somebody else knows what happened to them, and all of the ways to cope with it that they're now ashamed of. Someone knows about the molestation, the abuse, the years of being humiliated—and they also know about the substance abuse, the cutting, the dangerous sexual behavior, that they've been doing for years. Revealing these things doesn't make the feelings of disgrace immediately lift; at first it makes them *stronger*.

While helping people talk about those feelings in therapy, I've learned some amazing things about why revealing "trauma secrets" (or "secret traumas") can actually make you feel worse at first, not better. When I first started doing this work, I would have guessed that someone finally revealing their secrets to me in therapy, and not being rejected by me for it, would give them a sense of relief, but that's actually wrong. It turns out that what usually happens instead is that they now not only feel ashamed of what they've told me, but they also still feel like the horrible things their abusers did to them *are still part of them.* They feel like these aren't just secrets they remember and need to talk about, but that their abusers, their rapists, their molesters, have left part of their contamination symbolically inside them, where they continue to corrupt them to this day. As one woman put it to me, "I know my rape was a long time ago, but I haven't been able to get over it because I feel like he's still inside me. Not physically, I don't mean that, I mean it's like what he did to me bonded me to him in some way, so that all his ugliness, all his hate, all his badness, is now part of *me*, too, and I'm rotting from it." Or as a young man put it to me, "I've cut myself all over, but it's not because I'm crazy. It's because I feel like [my abuser] is still part of me, and I keep trying to let it out so I can be free." Or to say it another way, "I feel like my abuse isn't something from my past. I feel like it's something that still spoils me from within, like it's become mixed into everything that makes me, me."

The idea that your abuser is still affecting you from within yourself is both true and not true. There's a lot of work to do with this idea: "Of course it is happening inside your head…But why on earth should it mean that it is not real?"[1] Your pain is real because your trauma is real. Being wounded by it is not an over-reaction, and spending years working to heal it is not time wasted.

Throughout his young life, Harry feels a connection to Voldemort that he can't seem to close. He sees Voldemort in dreams, flashbacks, and visions, and even Harry's own emotions are sometimes changed as if Voldemort is still living and acting from within. Even the Sorting Hat can sense the presence of Slytherin-like traits within Harry. Harry can't understand why he still feels corrupted inside by Voldemort, because he hates Voldemort and rejects everything he represents. He wants nothing more than to be free of feeling Voldemort in his own emotions. Hermione begs Harry to block out those flashbacks, and Harry swears he's trying but just can't. Dumbledore even assigns Harry to private lessons with Professor Snape to learn how to protect himself from his sensations of Voldemort in his mind.

Harry, then, is the abuse victim who still feels like his abuser's effects are not in the past, but still part of him. It is not until many years of this have passed that Dumbledore finally reveals the reason Harry feels this way: he'd become a Horcrux for Voldemort during Voldemort's first attack against Harry.

---

1 *Harry Potter and the Deathly Hallows,* p.723

A Horcrux is an object into which a dark Wizard deposits part of his own soul, which he splinters off from himself through an act of extreme evil; in the books, it's a murder. For our symbolism, it's inflicting an act of abuse on a victim. The act of extreme evil against another person is enough to damage the abuser's soul, which the dark Wizard would rip off from himself and encase inside an object. That fragment of his soul retains the personality of the original dark Wizard, and can continue to manifest his mannerisms. Voldemort was the first dark Wizard to have created multiple Horcruxes, and perhaps also the first to have created Horcruxes out of living things rather than just objects.

Harry is the Horcrux that Voldemort never meant to make. When Voldemort murdered Harry's parents, Voldemort's soul was broken, and a remnant of it encased itself into the nearest living thing, the infant Harry. Harry, then, carries a portion of Voldemort within himself for years without understanding why he still feels an internal connection to someone he despises. All he knows is that he can't seem to free himself from constant flashbacks and nightmares about his abuser, and even though he tries to reject everything about Voldemort and be a good person, he somehow still seems corrupted inside by what Voldemort had done to him years ago. Harry, then, is identical to the abuse victims who have told me in therapy that they still feel internally ruined by their abusers.

In order to defeat Voldemort, Harry must locate and destroy six Horcruxes—or so he thinks. Dumbledore only names six of them to Harry, even though he knows there are seven. He knows that if he reveals the truth to Harry about Harry himself also being a Horcrux, it would overwhelm him. Harry would collapse under the significance of such a thing. It's important for Harry to achieve victories over Voldemort in order to develop his own inner strength, so that when the time comes for Harry to face the final horrible truth, he'll be able to understand what he must do.

In therapy, I found that victims who tried to take on all the aspects of their own traumas too quickly were also overwhelmed. They would become flooded, have a surge of nightmares, and sometimes even drop out of therapy. If you are working with a therapist for your traumas, it is important that you know that beginning to address your abuse may actually make you feel worse at first, not better. You are starting to purge all of the stuff you've been terrified or ashamed of, and it's like vomiting out a poison. At first, trauma therapy feels awful. Flashbacks can become worse, you may have headaches or stomach issues, you become exhausted and angry, and you might find yourself even feeling defeated. When Harry, Hermione, and Ron are carrying an undestroyed Horcrux with them, it makes them increasingly miserable and argumentative. Each of them can sense the harmful effects of the Horcrux from the one who is carrying it. Likewise, carrying unresolved trauma will affect your relationships, including with yourself. When they finally open the Horcrux to destroy it, what bursts out is a manifestation of their fears, resentments, and anger. Inwardly, you may even tell yourself that therapy was a mistake because it's not working; you're not feeling better, you're feeling more awful than ever! All the trauma stuff starts coming up, and it feels like it will drown you. This is all normal, and a good therapist will be aware of it and help you understand that feeling worse is a common part of trauma work.

The way I would help the process along is to put off the heavy trauma work until much later in therapy. In fact, having someone write and read their memories of being abused or raped would be one of the last things we'd choose to do, not one of the first. Taking it on too soon would collapse you, until you've built up strengths and coping skills. Dumbledore knew this too, and made sure Harry accomplished other tasks that would each help prepare him for handling the "final truth," the worst thing, the "Voldemort within." As he explained, "Harry must not know, not until the last moment, not until it is necessary, otherwise how could he have the strength to do what must be done?"[2]

Each Horcrux that Harry finds must be destroyed, which means damaging the containing object beyond repair. In each case, there are certain ways to do this, and mere brute strength will not work. For example, basilisk venom can destroy one, as can the Sword of Gryffindor. But merely striking at the Horcrux and bashing it around won't do it. Again, we have a good symbol for coping with trauma. Brute force won't work for that, either. Years of forcing yourself to be fine don't actually make the symptoms of trauma go away. In my work, I frequently saw adults who had been abused as children, and they were convinced that since the abuse was so long ago it was a non-issue. They thought they only needed therapy for current anxiety, job stress, substance abuse, etc. In fact, they thought it was silly of me to put any focus at all on childhood abuse! But in reality, trauma remains under the surface, keeping its power, like a Horcrux. When the time comes for it to emerge, it can't be stopped. Defeating the Horcrux of abuse means using specialized tools and techniques that help open the Horcrux so the trauma inside can be faced and overcome. When you begin to open up and speak honestly, and grieve, and scream, and really, really let this stuff out in therapy, you are killing a Horcrux.

But wait, if killing a Horcrux means destroying its container, doesn't that mean I'm telling you to do something that will damage *you*? Not quite. In this case, what you are breaking apart is not *you*, you are

2 *Harry Potter and the Deathly Hallows*, p.685

breaking apart the many shells inside of you that have kept you from setting your trauma free. Those shells have kept you from functioning in healthy ways, and from understanding your traumas. You are breaking open the layers of denial, alcohol use, cutting, sex, self-hate, and despair that you have carried for so long. Those are the things that have contained your trauma inside of you like a Horcrux. *You* are not a Horcrux; *you* are not infested with abuse, contaminated, or spoiled. You are the being that can go free when the Horcrux you have carried is finally destroyed.

I cannot overstate how important that distinction is. Comparing the effects of trauma to a Horcrux does not mean that you really do carry your abuser's or rapist's contamination inside of you. That is *not* what the Harry Potter story teaches, and it's not true in real life either. In *Harry Potter*, Harry does indeed carry part of Voldemort's soul inside of him, but this is symbolic for us, not a literal concept that means you are inwardly contaminated. Harry, despite being a Horcrux, is able to function morally, make his own choices, defy Voldemort, love and support others, and make people proud of his choices. As Dumbledore told him, "It is our choices, Harry, that show what we truly are, far more than our abilities." If he'd been a therapist, Dumbledore could have said, "It is our choices that show us who we truly are, far more than our traumas." That's probably the most important insight in this entire analogy: being affected by the actions of your abuser does not ruin you. You do not lose your worth, your goodness, and your choices because you still feel unhealed trauma inside.

The Trauma Horcrux

Trauma is any safety-threatening event that is sudden, unexpected, or not within your normal experiences, exceeds your ability to cope, and disrupts your healthy mental and physical functioning. After a trauma, you may have access to whole memories of the incident, or parts of those memories may be suppressed. Fragmented memories are common and normal responses to trauma, and it is also common for memories to change over time. Post Traumatic Stress Disorder (PTSD) is diagnosed from these symptoms:

- Recurring and intrusive recollections of the event. This can include memories, flashbacks, nightmares, etc.
- Inner distress when you are exposed to cues that relate to the initial trauma. For example, talking about rape causes you to feel nausea, gagging reflexes, or anxiety. Triggers for these

reactions can include sights, smells, certain music, anniversaries of trauma, scenes in movies or TV shows, dental and OB/GYN exams, being grabbed, sexual intercourse, etc.

- Physical symptoms of stress when you encounter triggers related to the trauma: pounding heart, adrenaline, shakiness, or tunnel vision.

- Efforts to avoid anything associated with the trauma. For example, avoiding certain places, skipping or dropping out of therapy, using self-injury or drugs to suppress feelings, and being unable to talk about the trauma.

- Heightened fear of danger, and increased arousal of the senses for the purpose of remaining on "high alert." You may experience irritability, anger outbursts, difficulty concentrating and remembering, exaggerated startle/flinch responses, and sleep difficulties. Have you noticed that since the trauma, you become more alert and uncomfortable when someone walks behind you? Or that you suddenly stiffen up when you are hugged, even by someone you love? Or that footsteps now cause waves of fear? These are "startle responses."

- Changes in emotion: numbness, loss of pleasure, and depression.

- Symptoms last for more than a month, and interfere with your daily life.

In addition to these, victims of abuse tend to also feel guilty about anything they did to try to survive or minimize the abuse itself. For example, complying with what an abuser told you to do is a normal way to try to prevent the attack from being even worse, but afterwards many victims feel they deserve guilt for "going along with it." I've worked with rape victims, for example, who remained still and quiet during the rape, or went to a place they were told to go with their attacker, or catered to their family abuser's whims, in an effort to reduce the violence. Research shows that *most* rape victims become quiet and still during the attack, but because this doesn't match the fighting, clawing, resisting depictions of rape victims in movies or in self-defense classes, the victims feel ashamed afterward: "Why did I just freeze? Why didn't I do more?"

The damage of betrayal trauma is far-reaching. It affects us physically, emotionally, and spiritually. It even affects the people close to us. But many wounded people have difficulty even identifying how trauma has affected them because there may be gaps in memory and a resistance to acknowledging the pain of trauma. "Because silence has shrouded our lives, we probably have not talked about what lies beneath the surface that we carefully maintain," writes Mari West Zimmerman. "Many of us don't realize that not everyone has difficulties with dissociation, lack of feelings, depression, lack of trust, fear of intimacy, inability to set boundaries, and countless other problems. Even when we do acknowledge that we have problems, we tend to minimize them and we fail to realize or admit that these may be the effects of abuse."[3]

Harry shows symptoms of trauma that you might relate to, as well. After he witnesses Cedric Diggory's death, he has disturbing dreams in which he re-experiences the event; this phenomenon is actually one of the symptoms of post-traumatic stress. If you have nightmares or flashbacks to your own traumas, you are not weak, you have this in common with Harry Potter. Harry's traumas also begin to affect his relationships:

> And what were Ron and Hermione busy with? Why wasn't he, Harry, busy? Hadn't he proved himself capable of handling much `more than them? Had they all forgotten what he had done? Hadn't it been he who had entered that graveyard and watched Cedric being murdered, and been tied to that tombstone and nearly killed?
>
> *Don't think about that*, Harry told himself sternly for the hundredth time that summer. It was bad enough that he kept revisiting the graveyard in his nightmares, without dwelling on it in his waking moments too.[4]

Harry is displaying many of the common symptoms of trauma, such as recurring and intrusive memories of the event ("It was bad enough that he kept revisiting the graveyard in his nightmares"), and trying to suppress his thoughts and memories of the trauma to avoid stress ("Don't think about that, Harry told himself sternly for the hundredth time…"). As in real life, Harry's traumas even begin to affect his relationships with other people; his resentment toward Ron and Hermione is not something they deserve, but Harry's grief causes him to lash out at them. If you find yourself becoming bitter or closed-off from loves ones and allies, remember this passage from the book and question whether your relationships are actually being affected by your trauma. Since abuse causes people to feel abandoned and disconnected from others, the flickers of pain you still experience even years afterward can re-create that same sense of being alone, which can cause you to have inaccurate beliefs about whether others really have forsaken you:

---

3 Zimmerman, Mari West. *Take and Make Holy*, p26.
4 *Harry Potter and the Order of the Phoenix*, p.8

So it went on for three whole days. Harry was alternately filled with restless energy that made him unable to settle to anything, during which time he paced his bedroom, furious at the whole lot of them for leaving him to stew in this mess; and with a lethargy so complete that he could lie on his bed for an hour at a time, staring dazedly into space, aching with dread...[5]

Harry responds to his feelings of loneliness and resentment by becoming *more* volatile, rather than working through his feelings. Like many abuse victims, Harry becomes prickly with emotions, ready to explode, eager to fight. His feelings of being unfairly victimized (he's right) combined with feeling misunderstood, abandoned, and owed special consideration from others because of it (he's wrong) produce an attitude of entitlement and hostility:

Harry watched the dark figures crossing the grass and wondered who they had been beating up tonight. *Look round,* Harry found himself thinking as he watched them. *Come on... look round...I'm sitting here all alone...come and have a go...*
If Dudley's friends saw him sitting here, they would be sure to make a beeline for him, and what would Dudley do then? He wouldn't want to lose face in front of the gang, but he'd be terrified of provoking Harry...it would be really fun to watch Dudley's dilemma, to taunt him, watch him, with him powerless to respond...and if any of the others tried hitting Harry, he was ready — he had his wand. Let them try...he'd love to vent some of his frustration on the boys who had once made his life hell.[6]

His impulse to lash out, to take revenge, is boiling. Harry is wallowing in self-pity here, and it fills him with rage. He's convinced that his abuse entitles him to special treatment, such as constant service from friends who must be available on demand, and urges to retaliate. At this point, Harry is dangerously close to adopting the same abusive mindset that has hurt him in the first place: he should be allowed to hurt others when he thinks they have it coming. People who let him down or don't tend to his needs deserve punishment for it. Ironically, I have seen many victims

5 *Harry Potter and the Order of the Phoenix,* p.44
6 *Harry Potter and the Order of the Phoenix,* p.11

of abuse adopt this *exact* mindset—"I have a special status that entitles me to be served by others"—without realizing that this is a controlling attitude that their abusers had as well.

This bitter, hostile kid isn't the Harry we love. But it's honest storytelling, because this is the kind of resentment and hostility we feel while there is still unhealed trauma inside. If anything, we relate to Harry even more, because we recognize those feelings. If Harry had been perfectly virtuous and never slipped up, and never had moments of struggle because of his traumas, we couldn't identify with him. So often, victims of trauma mistake being fierce with being strong, as if their anger is its own evidence that they are "no longer a victim". They have come to believe that being mighty with outrage also makes them strong and healed: "I am not a victim!" they howl, and to prove it they display anger like porcupine quills toward others. Sadly, this is not evidence of being healed, but evidence of being *un*healed. In fact, it's like an inner Horcrux using anger as a form of protection from truly being destroyed by repelling allies, mentors, therapists, and loved ones from being able to really connect with the gentle, vulnerable part of you that most needs love and care.

In addition to his outward anger, Harry becomes inwardly angry at himself for still thinking about Cedric's death and other painful memories. He tries to suppress his own thoughts in order to squash his depression. But at the same time, suppressing his thoughts also causes him to be incapable of dealing with them accurately. After trauma, you may also find that remembering key details becomes impossible. It's common for abuse victims' memories to become distorted, such as remembering things out of sequence, forgetting major details, and recalling lost memories later. Many people who don't understand trauma see this happening, and think it's evidence that a victim is lying, but that's not actually the case. During trauma, the conscious brain can even simply stop forming memories until the trauma has passed.

Even years later, victims often cope with trauma by dissociating from it. Dissociation is a temporary flatness of mood and thought in order to separate from stress. A dissociating person may seem to "go blank" for a period of time so that the memory of a trauma can be kept distant, as if a blanket had been draped over it. The end result is a sort of temporary "Obliviate" spell, a feeling of emptiness and emotional vacancy, floating passively in an imaginary world. It is as if the person sends their conscious mind outside of their own bodies so that the sensations within their bodies are not felt. The younger you are when trauma occurs, the more likely you are to use dissociation.

Horcruxes And Trauma

Survivors of trauma often create a mental "wall" between their conscious thoughts and the memories of the trauma. But this isn't a solid wall; it leaks. Triggers such as sounds, smells, touches, and images that remind you of the trauma drill little holes into that wall, allowing suppressed memories to burst through into conscious thought. Dissociation is an attempt to patch the cracks in the wall again. You may have noticed that memories and triggers that cause you to dissociate are highly emotional, and usually nonverbal; that is, they are not logical thoughts that are easily managed. They feel powerful and unchallengeable, which convinces many trauma survivors "I just can't deal with this." Even Harry experiences this sometimes: "Harry's whole body went numb" and "His mouth was dry now" and "Harry's brain seemed to have jammed" and "inside his head, all was icy and numb."

Dissociation is a short-term suppression of emotional pain, but it also prolongs the total duration of trauma by postponing the re-emergence of those painful feelings. It's not a form of erasing emotions; it's a form of compressing them into a mental box. Imagine stuffing more and more laundry into a drawer until it's full; it takes more pressure, more effort to keep the drawer shut, and each time you have to stuff more into it, the risk of the contents overflowing increases. Dissociation is shutting a drawer on compressed contents within it; when it finally erupts, it explodes.

Dissociation isn't entirely good or bad; it's a normal thing that most people do to escape anything from boredom to distress. Dissociation doesn't mean you are "crazy"; on the contrary, for many people it has been a part of their emotional survival. That doesn't mean it's a good choice for a permanent coping skill because it only postpones dealing with memories, it doesn't eradicate them, like hiding a Horcrux in a cave and forgetting about it. In time, those memories will continue to intrude more and more until they are processed.

One of the worst wounds caused by abuse is the sense of betrayal. When the abuser is a caretaker, such as a parent, a spouse/partner, or a teacher, the relationship has been so broken that you may find yourself obsessing over discovering the reason for it. A father is not supposed to molest a daughter, and a boyfriend is not supposed to rape a girlfriend, so why did they cross that line? Why did they violate the relationship in that way? So often, victims cannot come up with a reason why someone else would damage a relationship with such severe abuse, so they look inward for the cause: *I* must have done something wrong; *I'm* bad; *I* should have fixed whatever problem caused this. You begin to see yourself as a Horcrux in the sense that you feel flawed and ruined inside, even though you're not. Horcruxes are formed when someone else damages their own soul and forces someone or something else to carry the effect of it afterward; they are not caused by someone or something being bad and *attracting* evil. When Harry becomes a Horcrux, it is Voldemort whose soul is damaged and broken apart; Harry's soul is still whole and clean inside of him. Harry does indeed bear damage that has to heal, but he is not broken. His soul remains pure. Yes, you have been damaged by abuse. That is not the same as saying that you are contaminated or that your soul is dirty because of it. Like Harry, you still carry a pure soul. It is your abuser whose soul was broken by what he did, and your wounds are not your soul. Harry's scar is not his soul. It is your abuser whose humanity has been broken apart. They, not you, are dehumanized by the abuse.

Trauma, then, means that you do indeed have damage that needs to be healed. There are emotions, like shame and inferiority, which need to be purged out of you once you have become open enough to release them from inside. You are a Horcrux in the sense that trauma has embedded those feelings inside of you, and that makes you sometimes feel like you are as inwardly ruined as your abuser. You are *not* a Horcrux in the sense that you actually carry evil inside of you because of your abuse. Harry does literally carry part of Voldemort's soul inside of him, but that's a plot point, not something that actually describes you. What does apply to you is the realization that Harry, like you, is able to set himself free of it by facing it, and that Harry's actual soul is not corrupted because of what Voldemort has done to him.

What if I Become Like My Abuser?

Because evil is real, we need to begin to think about abusers not as psychopathic lunatics, but as people who made deliberate choices to inflict harm on others for the purpose of taking power and control. Thinking in these terms can free you from self-blaming thoughts because it relocates the cause of the evil to the abuser, where it belongs. It is *their* traits that brought evil to you, not *yours.* Furthermore, understanding abusiveness as a chosen set of values and beliefs, rather than an illness, places the abuser into a position of accountability. People who think of evil as an illness are more likely to believe the myth that being abused turns victims into abusers (an idea that drains the hope from any victim of abuse!), whereas those who see abuse as a response to beliefs and values know that being abusive is a *choice,* and that victims of abuse are not destined to become abusers too. Abuse is on purpose, not an accident that abusers can't help.

Horcruxes And Trauma

In the film adaptation of *Harry Potter and the Order of the* Phoenix, while talking alone with Sirius Black, Harry confessed his own fear that because he had experienced evil, he would become evil himself. Sirius points to the tapestry on the wall, which has the Black ancestry embroidered into it. Over Sirius' name, the tapestry is burned. "My mother did that after I ran away. Charming woman. I was sixteen…" Sirius' voice trails off, and tears come to his eyes. When Harry is confessing his own fear of becoming like Voldemort, why would Sirius answer with a family history lesson? What has that got to do with anything Harry's talking about? The lesson Sirius is teaching is that our pasts do not always determine who we will become; we choose our values for ourselves. Growing up with hate does not have to make you hateful. In fact, Sirius was rejected by his family for not becoming hateful, as they were.

Harry then confesses that he has doubts about being able to choose not to become evil. He reveals that despite his desire to be completely unlike Voldemort, he still has glimpses of the world as Voldemort sees it. To Harry, this is a terrifying warning that perhaps he, too, is destined to also become evil:

> This connection…what if the reason for it is that I am becoming more like him? I just feel so angry! All the time! What if, after everything that I've been through, something's gone wrong inside me? What if I'm becoming bad?

Sirius steps closer to Harry, looks Harry in the eye, and solemnly says to him,

> I want you to listen to me very carefully, Harry. You're not a bad person. You're a very good person who bad things have happened to. You understand? Besides, the world isn't split into good people and death-eaters. We've all got both light and dark inside us. What matters is the path we choose to act on. That's who we really are.[7]

As an abused child, Harry learned that people who feel anger will inevitably hurt the ones they are angry at. Anger, in his experience, takes something from other people. It diminishes them. When someone is angry, they are rejecting the person they are angry at, regarding them as worthless. Abusive anger works that way, and he's afraid it means that his own anger is a sign that he is also becoming abusive. He does not realize

---

7 *Harry Potter and the Order of the Phoenix* film adaptation

that anger can also be righteous, because it opposes situations and actions that we know are not right. What matters is the path we choose to act on. That's who we really are.

I once saw a 19-year-old young man, Andrew, in an inpatient therapy program because he was self-destructively angry. Andrew had been molested as a little boy, and an ignorant therapist had told him that his molestation meant he was likely to become a sex offender as well. Because the therapist was a trained expert—an authority with a license—Andrew assumed that her comment was true, and was disgusted with himself. Andrew could not cope with the prediction that he would become a sexual abuser someday, and began to hate himself. Even more destructively, subsequent therapists supported this prognosis!

This is the result of ignorance in mental health work. The urban legend that abused victims grow up to become abusers is *mostly false*, especially in the case of sexual abuse,[8] but it has been repeated so often that even clinicians repeat it as gospel truth. Andrew refused to approach his newborn brother for years, would not change his diapers, would not wrestle and tumble with him like a big brother should, would not snuggle, hug, or hold hands with his little brother, or go for walks with him, or show him any affection. Andrew withheld his love out of fear that people would see it and mistake it for abusive grooming. Consequently, Andrew lost eight years of big brotherhood.

When I explained that his previous therapists were wrong, and that his own values determined how he would live, Andrew was enraged, sad, and relieved. He had spent years despising his own mirror, believing that at any moment a switch would flip and he would become a molester—the thing he hated most. So he became a violent, self-destructive drug user to manage his self-hatred. He had been psychologically vandalized by people who did not understand the role of choice in the person you become. To them, he was simply a pure Horcrux of his abuser, and rather than being able to overcome it, it would overcome him. Hearing for the first time that he had a choice to be free of that meant so much to him. He had to overcome

---

8 There is a correlation between being abused and becoming abusive to others, but even the most significant study conclusions still find that the overall rate is low. While some victims do go on to continue the cycle of abuse they themselves experienced, it is not "all" or even "most"; it is still a minority of victims overall. Clearly it is true that people learn what they are taught, but the role of personal choice seems to be critically important as to whether someone will practice the abuse they have learned by being abused, or whether they will become more protective toward others as a result of being abused. For example, one in five women will experience a rape or attempted rape during her lifetime, yet we do not see one in five women becoming sexually abusive.
See: http://bjp.rcpsych.org/content/bjprcpsych/179/6/482.full.pdf
And: https://www.havoca.org/sexually-abused-kids-become-abusers/

the heartbreak of years of time missed being a loving big brother, but he was also free to choose for himself to be the kind of man he knew he could be.

You will slip up. You will lash out, become angry, and find yourself doing things you will later be ashamed of. Those moments do not make you like your abuser. When you do feel that anger and that hate rising in you, remind yourself that the emotions are simply part of you, but your choices will determine whether they are expressed abusively or not (there are people I hate, but I would never lash out at them or hurt them, because that is not the kind of man I want to be). Being angry is not abusive. Here, however, are some traits of abusers to help you know what to avoid in your own life. Abusers tend to:

- Choose victims who have less power than they do;
- Blame the person they hurt for what they've done ("it's your fault; you made me do that; I wouldn't have done it if you hadn't…; you deserved it")
- Treat women and men as if they are not equal;
- Use tricks to get out of trouble with their victims, ranging from romantic gift-giving and promise-making to outright threats and guilt trips;
- Try to make their victims feel crazy;
- Try to make their victims feel like they caused and deserved what happened;
- Isolate their victims from supportive family and friends;
- Control how their victims look, dress, spend money, and spend time,
- Deny their victims any privacy, by sneakily monitoring their emails, phones, purses, and whereabouts;
- Feel entitled to sex, and treat sex as a way to manage relationship problems;
- Expect total agreement and loyalty, and punish or reject those who don't give it to them;
- Treat the humiliation of others like a joke

Those are the traits to watch out for, not anger. In fact, there are times when the healing process itself will provoke your anger. Therapists are even skeptical of the progress someone is making if they never seem to become angry at all. Being angry, like Harry is, does not make you like your abuser. Being abusive would make you like your abuser. My friend Beth wrote of her own experiences:

By claiming "abuse begets abuse" we delude ourselves into believing that evil is something that can be quarantined to a certain group, like a contagion. Society can never be healed as long as we quarantine evil because we each play a role, however small, in making the world better or worse. I suppose the biggest impact on me of my childhood and my rape is that it made me yearn for a better world: not by waiting until I die and move onto the next, but by trying to understand and change the world for those who live in it. I haven't yet found my way of doing this, but seeking it out is something I need to do in my very bones.

In human behavior, every action represents a person's attempt to meet an internal need. Scratching an itch, moving hair out of our eyes, getting high, reading fantasy novels—they are all ways to meet a perceived need, either to feel something or to stop feeling something. The same is true of those who commit abuse; they are also behaving in ways that fulfill something they think they need. Once we understand that actions are attempts to satisfy needs, it becomes easier to interpret the real motives and beliefs that underlie abusiveness.

Many abusers, for example, complain that "nobody understands *me!*", insisting that they are the real victims of other peoples' failures to consider their needs. But in reality, abusers intentionally make sure they are not understood; they *depend* on people being confused. Abusers impose contradictory rules on their victims such as, "you should always be interested in my needs" versus "quit getting into my business", and "I can't live without you" versus "you're so terrible that you deserve what I do to you, and you should be grateful to have me." The motive is to keep the victims confused and in despair so that the blame will be turned inward ("why can't I figure out how to respond the right way so this will stop happening?"), and to keep outside observers from truly recognizing what is happening ("How can you say you're being abused? It seems to me that you just want pity when *you're* the one who can't make this work"). The last thing an abuser wants is to be truly understood, to have their needs really exposed, and to have their actions genuinely examined. Being unpredictable, cunning, and inconsistent is a way for an abuser to fulfill their need to remain in control.

Some clients of mine were too troubled by the word "abuse" to be able to fully commit to therapy, because the word is so loaded with stigma and pain. They thought that being abused meant they had succumbed to some inner flaw of theirs that "let" another person mistreat them, an idea that stems from the lousy, false meme that "nobody can mistreat you against your will" (*of course* they can; that's ridiculous and victim-blaming!). Furthermore, misunderstanding abuse as a form of "anger problem" or "sexual perversion" or even "mistake" has harmful connotations to the survivor, because it turns anger, sexuality, and imperfection into taboos and flaws. The fear that being angry, enjoying sex, or making mistakes makes you like your abuser can lock you into an anxiety-causing routine of stoic, emotionless avoidance of outrage, pleasure, or spontaneity. Or worse yet, it can make you feel awful about yourself for having those impulses, as if they are sick.

Instead, consider abuse as an intentional form of strategy, not a random explosion caused by someone else's failure of self-control. Abusers cunningly and methodically use whatever forms of coercion will meet their own need for control and power. Voldemort, for example, forced his followers to comply with his whims, he punished dissent, he was cruel when he felt disappointed, he constantly questioned the loyalty of his followers to make them over-prove their dedication to him at their own expense, and he offered scarce rewards to manipulate his followers into over-valuing his approval. Likewise, abusers strategically maintain power and control by making their victims (who can be partners or children) feel less important, blaming you when they feel displeased, making you constantly prove your devotion to their needs, and sometimes using gifts, approval, gestures of affection, or small acts of mercy to manipulate you into over-valuing them. Abusiveness is strategic, not random. For example, provoking you into hysterics in front of witnesses while they seem calm is meant to cause others to judge you, disbelieve you, distance themselves from you, and see your abuser as more stable in contrast. When Harry tries to convince others at Hogwarts that Voldemort is back, Voldemort cleverly remains reclusive. The result is that Harry, despite being right, becomes an outcast, mocked for being delusional and attention-seeking.

Once you understand that abuse is strategic, you will come to understand their tactics more clearly. Your abuser's actions will be less confusing (especially when you keep in mind that confusing you *is* one of their tactics), and will be able to gradually release some of the shame that comes from years of wondering, "what did I do wrong? Why couldn't I fix it? Why is everything my fault?" You will also see the difference between being abusive, and being a normal person who has normal senses of anger, annoyance, sexuality, and imperfection. It is such a relief to realize that having those feelings is *not* what makes someone become an abuser; rather, using anger, cruelty, sexuality, and arrogance to take power over others is. Harry had so many parallels to Voldemort—nearly being sorted into Slytherin, being a Parselmouth, feeling angry and alone, desperately wanting to prove he is not weak, and even answering professors' questions similarly ("is there anything you wish to tell me?" "No sir...nothing")— and yet be nothing like him. Why didn't Harry become an abuser? Because despite having all those feelings, he *chose* not to see himself as entitled to special pity or glory, or use them as tools for gaining control over others. Harry, like you, carried the impact of abuse inside himself, but was able (again, like you) to become different from his abusers.

At the end of *Harry Potter and the Deathly Hallows*, Harry does something that symbolizes this very choice between becoming like your abusers or rejecting their mindset. He rejects the Elder Wand, a choice even Dumbledore was not able to make. "I'm putting it back where it came from. It can stay there." His last magical act with the Elder Wand is to use it to repair his own true wand, the wand he has had since childhood. Harry has chosen to reject might. He has intentionally refused the option of being more powerful than others, of having supreme control over people. Instead, he repairs his own original wand, representing his choice to simply be the person he truly is. He heals himself, restores the parts of him that need restoring, and refuses to accept the privilege of dominance. Nineteen years later, Harry's son Albus Severus Potter confesses his fear that he might be sorted into Slytherin. He worries that he is not good enough and that he'll be seen as bad. Harry assures him that the kind of person young Albus Severus will become is determined more by his own choices than by any other trait, a lesson Harry has learned for himself, too.

Healing from Horcruxes

But we don't live in Harry Potter world, and we have no basilisk venom or Swords of Gryffindor to free us, so how are we supposed to destroy our own internal Horcruxes?

To begin, you must first identify what would be different about yourself if you were to become healed of trauma. Knowing that will give you a goal to strive toward. The contrast between your healed self and your traumatized self reveals the set of symptoms that most need attention. What is the difference between a victim and a survivor? A victim is not less than a survivor; this is not about moving from having less worth to more worth, and "victim" is not a bad word or a put-down. They are simply different states of being, defined by different sets of reactions to pain. As a therapist, I would ask each person to write what he or she thought the difference would be between being a victim or a survivor. Here is what one woman wrote to me:

Victim: Says it's her own fault.
Survivor: Says "hell no, it's not my fault! He chose to rape me. He made the decision." She puts the blame where it belongs.

Victim: Says, "I'm dirty."
Survivor: Says, "What happened to me was dirty. He was dirty."

Victim: Says, "I'm unlovable."
Survivor: Says, "My rapist tried to convince me I'm unlovable, but I'm worthy of love. I'm full of love. I'm love. He can't take love away from me."

Victim: Keeps the secret.
Survivor: Breaks the silence, be it talking with a therapist, trusted friend, writing about the rape and reading it aloud, or attending a support group.

Victim: Self-injures, in the form of cutting, bingeing, purging, drugs, alcohol, or sex.
Survivor: Confronts her rape with great courage, instead of numbing the memories that haunt her by injuring herself over and over. She realizes that the rapist still has the power if she chooses to destroy herself. A survivor chooses against these behaviors.

Victim: Says, "I'm powerless."
Survivor: Takes her power back, by talking about the rape. Writing about it.
Encouraging other survivors. Attending support groups. She begins to speak out about this crime.

If you truly want to do the work to transform into a survivor, one of the fundamental first steps is to forgive yourself for how long you have already struggled, and to preemptively forgive yourself for however long the process will take. This isn't like getting over a cold, and well-meaning people may heap pressure on you to "hurry up and get over it." Abuse is a life-changing experience, and it is perfectly acceptable for you to work at your own pace. Try not to be rough on yourself for the time it's taken to arrive at today.

If you wish to successfully transform into a survivor, you must take care of yourself. You cannot succeed at this work if you are skipping therapy sessions, avoiding homework, using drugs (including alcohol) during the process, or ignoring medical self-care. If you are not willing to form a personal covenant to manage your physical, emotional, and even spiritual health during this process, this transformation will be more painful than healing. Every week in therapy, I saw people begin this process who had not committed to taking care of themselves, and then became overwhelmed. Those who do commit to self-care tend to do very well.

This doesn't mean you are failing if you have slip-ups. From time to time, every abuse victim I've counseled has lapsed and relapsed in some form: a night of binge drinking, an episode of cutting, a regretted sexual experience with an unloved person. They are hurtful things to go through, but I can understand them. If you slip up, make a pledge that you will immediately divulge the incident to your therapist, rather than hiding it. You can use these lapses to learn more about recovery by identifying the triggers and stressors that might have preceded them, and tracking down the inner thoughts ("self-talk") that promote relapses. There is a Buddhist teaching that no experience is a failure if it promotes new learning. That's very similar to Dumbledore's teaching that we are defined by our choices, not by our abilities.

The goal of each day is progress, not perfection. I've had clients who are reluctant to even do journaling because they are afraid their writing will be imperfect or that they "won't say it right." Other clients of mine have hidden the fact that on weekends they got drunk or had compulsive sex with someone they didn't even care about. They are afraid I will judge them (because they are already judging themselves). The progress in therapy halts, and I can sense something has happened, but until they divulge what happened we cannot cope with the issue. Remember, if you do slip up or relapse, it does not mean that every sign of prior progress is suddenly erased. It does not mean that you start again at "square one," with no strengths and no victories. You still get to keep and draw on all your previous successes, and relapses do not suck them away from you like a tidal wave. If you slip up, acknowledge it and explore what triggered it. Remember how many tries it took Harry, Ron, and Hermione to figure out how to destroy their Horcruxes? Remember the horrible struggles they each had to go through just to even find them sometimes? Recovering from trauma means you have to develop your "hate it, but do it anyway" courage.

Horcruxes fight back against their own destruction. They can sense threats, and lash out against those who threaten them, such as when the locket shows Ron a vision that taunts his fears to the point that Ron is paralyzed with dread. As you face your traumas, this can happen to you at certain points in your healing. You will begin to open up about your traumas, which means naming them ("I was raped"), identifying their effects on you ("I have trauma from child abuse"), and confiding what happened to you to a therapist or mentor. Each step is progress toward destroying your trauma Horcrux, and as you get closer and closer, the work gets harder. Harry even felt like he was worthless sometimes:

> He felt dirty, contaminated, as though he were carrying some deadly germ, unworthy to sit on the Underground train back from the hospital with innocent, clean people whose minds and bodies were free of the taint of Voldemort...[9]

That is exactly how many abuse victims feel at times, because the memories and stories of the abuse are still locked up deep inside. Harry even considered running away in order to protect other people from his own contamination: "The feeling of being unclean intensified..." What he really needed to do, though, was to open up and talk to others about what he was feeling, but he was too afraid of being rejected.

In therapy, people who were finally ready to share their stories with me would hand write them, and then read them aloud. Sometimes they would read stoically, with little emotion. Nothing had budged. I would ask them to start over, and this time read their own words as if they were reading something written by a child—not in a child's voice, but to imagine they had found a child's journal and they were reading what had happened to that little boy or girl. Whatever it took, the important thing was to really open and release all the stored up emotions. When it finally "clicked," a tremendous rush of sad, angry energy would finally come. It was like the locket had opened, and the horror hidden inside was bursting out.

After reading their stories, people would usually have troubled nights with nightmares, panic attacks, and nausea. Sometimes they would even skip the next therapy session. All of their shame was fighting back, trying to crawl back inside them and close up the walls again. The shame wanted to stay inside them, and hated being exposed and forced out. When you have come face-to-face with every detail of your trauma, every trigger you've ever avoided is now laid bare. Ultimately, pulling them out of hiding and revealing them is a very healing thing to do, and it begins the process of ridding yourself of those shameful thoughts. It's like cleansing your house of a mold infestation. But the positive results aren't immediate. Before the benefits show up, what impacts your emotions first are those

---

9 *Harry Potter and the Order of the Phoenix*, p.492

fearful beliefs and self-talk about the shameful, embarrassing truths you have revealed. "I have exposed myself, and that exposure is going to cost me dearly. It is going to change what people think about me now!" So the first reaction you have to deep therapy isn't always positive relief, a lifted weight, and freedom—it's terror and disgrace. It takes time, and then the healing comes, both emotionally and physically.[10] Horcruxes fight back, so don't give up before they're destroyed.

The important thing to remember is that battles are painful until they are won, and being overwhelmed when you talk about your traumas is normal. You might feel like you've made a mistake, that you shouldn't have said anything, that you should have left it all in the past, but remind yourself that Harry had to face Dementors over and over, and destroy all of the Horcruxes to become free, and every battle was painful. What Harry didn't do, though, was to retreat, hide from his tasks, or turn off his emotions and friendships. Once the battles are finished, we begin to heal our wounds for real, and then, like Harry, the time comes when our scars no longer cause us pain.

Becoming Stronger Than Your Abuser

My friend Bill grew up being beaten by his father day after day. His father also molested Bill's sisters, beat his wife, and terrified the entire family. Bill described his father as "pure, solid muscle, a badass." The trauma Bill endured had caused him to have nightmares, flashbacks, and waves of depression to the point of contemplating suicide on several occasions. Bill couldn't even feel comfortable in the presence of his friends' kindhearted families, because he was so on-edge with fear that adult men could snap at any moment and attack him.

Bill's trauma lasted for years, even into adulthood. After he moved out of the house, he avoided going back home and had very little contact with his father for years until he got a call that his father was dying in a hospital. Bill reluctantly went to see him one last time; this was Bill's version of Harry walking back into the forest to confront Voldemort one last time.

---

10 Pennebaker, J. W., et al. "Disclosure of traumas and immune function: health implications for psychotherapy." 1988 J Consult Clin Psychol 56;2:239-45. "Healthy undergraduates who wrote about traumatic experiences had significantly increased physical symptoms and negative moods immediately after writing, but at six weeks were happier and had had less health center visits than a control group. Students who wrote about something they had never disclosed before also had significantly enhanced immune response."

Horcruxes And Trauma

In the hospital room, Bill finally said everything he needed to his father. With tears running down his cheeks he confronted him over years of abuse, and was able to finally put his pain into words. This was no gentle final moment of mercy or father-son reunion; Bill finally released all his hate and anger at his dad over what his dad had done to the whole family. "I hate you! I *hate* you! Look what you did to all of us!" When he was finished, he suddenly saw his father differently than he ever had before. Suddenly, the solid-muscle badass seemed like such a frail, weak, tiny man in a deathbed. His father had no more power, and was just a pathetic shell of an old man at the end of his life.

When Harry finally confronts Voldemort, Voldemort wields all of his power to hurl a killing curse at Harry. What neither of them had realized, though, is that this curse would not ultimately destroy Harry, but the portion of Voldemort that was "Horcruxed" inside of Harry. Both of them are struck by the single spell. Harry and Voldemort each find themselves in an afterlife, but the difference between them has become remarkable. Harry, now purged of Voldemort's presence within him, is whole and pure—at last, healed. Voldemort, however, is now banished into a tiny, frail embryotic body, where he lacks any power. Voldemort's soul has been so damaged by his evil abusiveness that there is nothing left of him to purify. Harry, at last, realizes that just because he carried the effects of Voldemort's evil inside of himself, it is not actually part of his own soul. He, Harry, is innocent and pure, and he is able to heal from his traumas. Like my friend Bill, purging himself of his anguish helps him finally see that he is a more complete, stronger, and more righteous man than his abuser had been. In contrast, the man he had seen as such a powerful threat turned out to be a broken, disfigured being whose own soul was shattered by what he'd done to others.

I'm not being literal in the sense that you have to actually confront your abuser at some point. Sometimes, that can be helpful, but in many cases that's not wise, because abusers almost never offer the kind of closure that victims seek when confronted. They don't tend to show remorse, or apologize, or even admit fault. In my example, Bill was able to transform how he saw his abuser, but the significance of it is symbolic, not literal. In your case, becoming stronger than your abuser means cleansing yourself of the effects they have had on your life, and intentionally becoming a different person than them.

One friend of mine shared his story with me about his own experiences growing up with abuse. Chris' childhood family had been terribly unhealthy, including habitual meth use, violence, child exploitation, and repeated imprisonments that left Chris homeless as a minor. The abuse he endured from his mother in particular later manifested as habitual self-harm. As a teen, he was in and out of psychiatric hospitals, and even saw me as a therapist for a while. Now an adult, he told me how he had been able to heal from his traumas.

"Yes, I absolutely felt like my abusers had become part of me," he said. "I totally relate to that feeling. For me, I was terrified that I carried something of them inside of me, and that at some point it could awaken in me and turn me into something like them. It was like having my own personal Voldemort in me, waiting to take over." (Yes, he actually invoked the image of an "inner Voldemort" to explain his feelings.) I asked him how he was able to heal, and he said, "I had to first acknowledge what I had going on inside of me. I had to face the fact that they were my family. I've been told I even look like my mother. Plus, she cuts herself all the time, and then I'd started doing it when I was a teenager, so I had to be aware that her effects on me were real."

Chris showed me his arms, lined with multiple tiny white scars from where he'd cut himself. "This is what I did for a long time." He thought for a moment and said, "to heal from it all, I had to really understand what they were like, and then make choices to be completely different. They [Chris' abusers] were not smart or educated, so I chose to read and learn science and develop myself that way. They don't care about anyone else's needs, so I chose to become kind to people. All they're about is harm, so I had to choose to be different. Even dressing and grooming myself in a dignified way is how I can help separate myself from them."

"It's like Dumbledore said, that our choices make us who we are, then," I replied.

"That's exactly it. I had to face that I have the same DNA as them, and make sure to not let any aspects of their personalities become part of my own personality." He also had to learn as much as he could about why his abusers were like that, so that he could understand their motivations and intentionally choose to reject similar ways of thinking. It was his own "Defense Against the Dark Arts" study, learning about something so that he can become strong enough to resist it. He had to accept what was in his past so he could learn from it and overcome it.

Chris said that people still notice his scars sometimes, and he'd made a decision to not hide them. "I chose to be open about them, because I don't cut anymore, but I'm not ashamed of what I went through. Other people who are going through things see them, and they recognize what they mean. So I make myself a safe person for their sake, and it helps me be able to talk to them as someone who's been through it too. Instead of being a victim, I've been able to become a supporter of other victims, because they know, hey, I've been there, and I came out of it."

What Chris has done is to face the Horcrux that had been put into his mind as a child by his abusers, and then make choices that defy and destroy that Horcrux. Instead of becoming an invulnerable tough guy to hide his pain, Chris became thoughtful and gentle, his entire life becoming an antidote to abusiveness he'd seen in the world. He saw his family embracing a life of meth, violence, and cheap thrills, so Chris became as different as possible from them. He devours science books, has taught himself advanced mathematics, explores art museums, and creates complex worlds for role-playing games. He has intentionally become as opposite as possible from the lives and mindsets of those who hurt him.

Harry's final act of becoming separate from Voldemort is an act of self-cleansing. He purges Voldemort from his life, becoming everything opposite of Voldemort that he can become. By becoming as different from your abusers as you can, you defy them. If your abusers were selfish, angry, hateful, and tough, you can defy their effects by becoming compassionate, gentle, thoughtful, and accepting. If you were raped, you can defy your rapist by developing healthy relationships, respecting the equality of men and women, supporting other survivors (both male and female!), and demonstrating that being raped does not make you feeble. It takes no strength to mimic your abusers in your own life. Using others for your personal sense of control and power is easy and lazy. But by becoming morally better, uplifting others, taking care of yourself, and treating yourself with respect, you become stronger than them. You also show that it's a lie that people can't help being abusive, because you live an example of someone who was put through trauma but *chose* to develop other values instead.

CHAPTER EIGHT

Mental Health and Creative Maladjustment

So many adults who write novels for young readers try to cram in such drama and moral lecturing that their characters become almost constipated with integrity and seriousness. Their acts of rebellion are grandiose uprisings, and really, who can relate to that? One of my favorite attributes of the *Harry Potter* series is J.K. Rowling's obvious delight in sheer weirdness. Her characters don't succeed in their quests because they are always predictable, obedient conformists. They are quirky, funny, bewildered, curious, prank-playing personalities. For example, imagine a scenario where an all-too-serious, romantically bland 100-year-old teenage vampire tries to flirt with Luna Lovegood! It's such a bizarre set-up, it's nearly impossible to even imagine. Rowling is able to give us deeper parables about wisdom, courage, and integrity from a bunch of weirdo characters, than most other books can do with all the cramped seriousness they can shove into our faces.

For Rowling, good and evil are not constructs of obedience to rules. In fact, rules, in Rowling's works, can often be hindrances to goodness, so she gives us plots where morality manifests not as obedience, but as actions which uplift the greater good and reduce the amounts of cruelty and abuse in the world. When abusers sometimes *make* the rules, Rowling's more creative approach to rebellion gives us a totally radical, more interesting, and more useful concept of what it means to be a healthy, functional person.

Mental Health and Creative Maladjustment

In the *Harry Potter* series, some acts of nonconformity are simply harmlessly odd: Luna wears radishes for earrings, and Dumbledore gives a comically-nonsensical "speech" consisting of nothing more than words that are fun to say, to introduce himself to Harry's first year. Some acts of non-conformity have greater weight: students band together as Dumbledore's Army to train in secret for battle against dark Wizards, even though they risk actual torture by Umbridge if they are caught. One consistent theme through all of it is that those who have the official power to make rules and policies are not always those who represent actual moral goodness. It's not that the rule-makers are necessarily evil, but they're often so convinced that "rules" and "righteousness" are the same thing that they cannot see past them.

Unquestioning obedience to authority is *not* how I define good mental health. Rather, *good mental health is the ability to accept reality as it actually i*s. Reality, however, includes the fact that unhealthy and abusive forces do exist in life, and they ought to be eliminated. I'm not saying that overcoming abusive systems means you have to become part of some Katniss Everdeen uprising against all the forces in the world. What I am saying, though, is that a bit of healthy nonconformity actually does help chip away at the Umbridge-like systems that keep people locked into personal traumas.

One of the wounds caused by abuse is the belief that you aren't allowed to "step out of line", for fear of being targeted again. In my years of work with both victims and perpetrators of abuse, one thing I found in every single instance of abuse was that abusers would blame their victims for what had happened to them. "You made me do this!" or "you provoked me!" or "I told you what I would do!" Victims learn from this to become small, diminished in importance, and self-blaming. Or to put it another way, they learn the lessons abusers pass on to them about abuse: it's their own fault. Harry lived in dread that anything he might do could accidentally provoke the Dursleys into fits of abusiveness, so he remained as quiet and still as possible, locked away from sight, desperately hoping nothing he did would attract attention to himself.

I once had a client who would answer every question I asked her with a question-asking tone of voice right back. If I asked her what a successful journal assignment meant to her, she would reply, "um, that I'm strong?" If I asked her what she had learned from a reading assignment, she would answer, "that it's not my fault I was raped?" This was a woman who could not make declarations because she had to seek my approval of her thoughts before she would own them herself. I learned from her pattern of approval-seeking that she was terrified that if she made a mistake or said the wrong thing, she would be punished in some way. As a result, her triggers were constantly flaring and she spent most of her day suffering through anxiety and panic attacks, needing alcohol each night to calm herself. Her progress in treatment screeched to a halt because her alcohol use (and self-harm) prevented her from developing inner coping skills, and thus she was never confident of her own beliefs. She's not all that different from Harry Potter when we first meet him.

J.K. Rowling is able to recognize this form of oppression, and gives us creative ways to act out against it. While other novels set up a conflict between the hero and some massive villainous power, such as a warlike district that devastates entire communities through forced combat, or conflict between "I love him, but he doesn't love me"/"She has no idea how much I love her, but *gasp!* It's forbidden, and it could annoy the werewolves, because reasons!", Rowling is able to identify much more nuanced and realistic forms of evil that many of us actually face every day. Being squeezed and compressed by your abusers info a life that has little freedom is something millions of trauma victims truly understand, even if they haven't had to shoot arrows at a dictator to win a rebellion.

In case you are wondering by now, yes, I am seriously making the point that being just a little bit weird, rebellious, and non-conformist can actually be both self-healing and abuse-resisting. If abuse forces people to stay "inside the lines" drawn for them by their abuser(s), healing will mean that you begin to grow outside of those limits. Every time you develop part of your spirit in a way that goes beyond what your trauma let you experience before, you are fighting back against that trauma. By *not* being the kind of person your abuser wanted to force you to be, you are resisting abuse.

This kind of "healthy nonconformity" takes guts because it will confound and threaten many people who cannot perceive the good in such a thing, and will only see it as attention-seeking. The Dolores Umbridges in your life will certainly condemn you for it, and try to nail up new rules that rein you back under control. If, like Luna Lovegood, you defy the rules of "being cool" and do your own weird thing, you will be mocked for it, just as she was mocked for it. But if you come from a background of suffering, then you will also begin to realize that being well-adjusted to a dysfunctional system is a dysfunctional state of being! To be maladjusted is a healthy state when it means we live at odds with unjust treatment of others. To put it in *Harry Potter* terms, making Dolores Umbridge happy is not a way to become morally healthy; Harry becomes stronger and more moral when he defies Umbridge and the Ministry of Magic. Fitting in with them, like Percy Weasley does, does not put you on the right moral side.

Mental Health and Creative Maladjustment

There are times that being condemned by a system that is itself unhealthy is a good thing, and you ought not to follow its rules. Refusing to buy into a culture that degrades you is a form of healthy rebellion.

Healthy mischief, sanity-producing oddness, and creative maladjustment are all parts of a life fully lived. One of greatest examples of good mental health in popular culture is the character Dumbledore, the wise and brilliant headmaster of Hogwarts. Everyone, including his foes, knows that Dumbledore is powerfully skilled, one of the greatest Wizards in history, but nobody seems to know what to make of his eccentric personality. Dumbledore is frequently described as having a "twinkle" of mischief in his blue eyes, making self-deprecating jokes, talking to students with respect, and saying things that can only be described as "completely nuts." But he's not crazy; he may even be the most mentally healthy person in the series, capable of being completely self-aware without being the slightest bit self-conscious. Rather than being a stuffy, stale headmaster, Dumbledore can be playful. You can just as easily imagine him shuffling down a Hogwarts hallway in funny mismatched socks, as battling Voldemort.

None of Dumbledore's expressions is insincere and Dumbledore is never out of control, yet he is perfectly willing to become a clown as well as a mentor. He acknowledges his character defects, his ego is in check, and he never lets his tabloid critics demolish his compassion, even though they condemn his unorthodox conduct and squawk for his removal. In fact, he is one of the most sincere, authentic people in the story. When Dumbledore takes Harry into his care as a guide and trainer, his affection and respect for Harry are clearly genuine, yet scandal-mongers take great delight in their insinuations that there is something exploitative, unhealthy, even wicked, in Dumbledore's bond with Harry as an apprentice. Even Harry himself begins to doubt Dumbledore's character and intentions, angrily chastising him for all the mistakes that Dumbledore has made in their friendship. Yet Dumbledore does not respond with force or retributive anger; he continues to do what he feels is right, regards Harry as a wayward but beloved apprentice, and persists in his efforts to overcome evil with intelligence, love, humor, and patient wisdom. Dumbledore allows his life to be taken, which appears to be a victory for the forces of evil, but is eventually revealed as a careful decision of his to promote the well-being of his loved ones which they cannot understand until much later.

Is Dumbledore an example of perfect mental health, then? No, he has weak spots like we all do. Dumbledore is never really able to "accept reality as it actually is" with regard to his sister, Ariana, or his brother, Aberforth. In his youth, Albus and Gellert Grindelwald had become very close friends, and Albus crossed the line into experimentation with dark magic and "might makes right" beliefs. But their friendship fell apart, and a duel between the two of them and Aberforth Dumbledore resulted in the death of Ariana, who had tried to intervene. Until the end of his life, Albus is never sure who actually cast the curse that killed Ariana, but he is forever devastated by even the fear that it may have been his own spell.

Ariana's death is one of Dumbledore's worst traumas, and he never deals with it. It remains a tragic secret of which he never speaks. The grief of this loss tears apart Albus from his brother Aberforth in a rift that never heals. Albus Dumbledore's Boggart, the lifeless body of his sister, represents the trauma that wounds him most through his entire life, and yet he never faces it, heals from it, and banishes that Boggart from his heart. Dumbledore exhibits superb mental health in so many aspects of his life that he reminds us that even role models can have flaws and weaknesses. I'm quite glad that J.K. Rowling left that weakness in Dumbledore's character rather than making him perfect, because a perfect character is unrelatable to us. We can't aspire to be perfect. But a character who is otherwise emotionally healthy, playful, kind, and brilliant but who still has weaknesses like we do….that is someone we can relate to. Dumbledore's imperfectness makes him a more honest role model for us. I've seen abuse survivors spend years and years of their lives, well into their old age, still frantically chasing down every Boggart in their traumas, desperately terrified that they have not yet healed every wound, solved every problem, and undone every speck of trauma. That sort of impossible standard of healing would cause you to become more miserable, not more whole. It's good to always continue your progress, but Dumbledore reminds us that we can be good, mentally-healthy people even while we still have weaknesses.

I wish Albus Dumbledore had worked to repair his relationship with Aberforth; if I were Albus' therapist, I would have advised him that caring for here-and-now relationships is so crucially important. Perhaps even just doing that might have released Albus from his Boggart of Ariana's death, since her death symbolized not one, but many lost relationships. Albus undoes so much of the harm he had caused as a young, power-hungry, reckless Wizard: he honestly acknowledges the part of himself that craves power, and passes lessons on to Harry in hopes that Harry will do a better job of resisting; he rejects the lure of dark magic; he strives with all his might to guide Tom Riddle into better paths; he withdraws from Harry when he fears that his relationship with Harry could be exploited by Voldemort (a decision Harry resents, but later comes to understand was an act of wisdom); he works behind the scenes to protect Harry, Hermione, and Ron's attempts to press on against the Death Eaters. In so many ways, Albus Dumbledore displays genius and boundless energy in his efforts to right wrongs, protect others, and model good morals. At the end of his life, reconciling with Aberforth remains an undone task. No, Dumbledore is not perfect. But he exhibits creative maladjustment with positive results, rather than remaining passive, even though he is still flawed.

Another aspect of J.K. Rowling's writing that I think is really important is her description of the friendships that develop throughout the books. Amid the intricate plot lines, we also see Harry, Ron, Hermione being normal teens: they play jokes, compete, become fascinated with dating, screw up on those dates, have arguments, make up, and just act like normal kids. Those details in her storytelling tend to be overlooked as just "fun stuff" that decorates the real plot, but in fact I think revealing the characters to be full of genuine humor, anxiety, self-doubt, happiness, and so many other feelings show us much about what it takes to be healthy. The essential task of defeating Voldemort is obviously the main plot of the series, but along the way the three friends manage to also develop the skills that will keep them emotionally healthy through the parts of their lives that continue on. If they were focused only on one task, their relationships would dissolve after their success, because there would have been no underlying qualities shared among them to preserve their friendships. Instead, we see that defeating Voldemort is only part of what keeps them together in a set of friendships that become life-long.

When twenty-five women gathered in north Oklahoma for a spiritual wilderness retreat for trauma survivors I had organized, they were tense and nervous. What if they didn't like one another? What if they were judged and excluded? What if they weren't at the same "level" of healing as the other women they admired? What if I frightened them, being a large male? But as they began to relax during the first few hours, something remarkable happened. They began to tease each other, hug, joke, and venture out alone for walks. They became able to openly identify themselves as survivors, without shame or judgment.

The second night of the retreat, I could tell by the giggles, whispers, and glances that the women were up to mischief and that I was clearly not meant to be aware of it. After midnight, the women cleared the tables and chairs out of the dining hall, gathered brooms, set up cardboard boxes at both ends of the room, and played a midnight game of "broom hockey." They tumbled over one another, laughing, accusing each other of cheating, cheering, challenging one another to tournaments, and losing track of the score altogether.

Then they got the idea to cram into a van and sneak out at 2 a.m., invading the local small-town 24-hour Wal-Mart, where they refused to leave the night crew alone until they had each agreed to smile and pose for silly photographs with the group. They pushed each other up and down aisles in shopping carts, singing and shouting, not particularly caring whether they would be asked to leave. Giddy with silliness and stocked up on art supplies, they returned to the campground where they spent the rest of the night decorating humorous signs to be worn around the necks of each person for the final day of the retreat. Each woman was awarded a sign to wear for the entire final day, and each sign bore a humorous slogan that made humor of the wearer's habits and traits. I received one that read, "I don't speak for my wife, do I honey?" decorated with glitter and kid's stickers.

To a person without imagination, this whole story might be nothing more than the nonsense of grownups who hadn't acted their ages. But if you can see something more in what had happened, if you can see it with your heart, then you see an experience of healing from evil by a group of women who, as children, *never* got to act their ages. I realized that these women had never been able to be little girls at a slumber party, for their childhood dreams were kicked awake by nightmares. They had also found a brilliant way to resist the negative labels—the "signs"—they had borne for years as victims of rape, by creating new *actual* signs with positive descriptions on them. By spontaneously becoming a "slumber party" with laughter, games, mischief, jokes, and staying up all night, they had seized back a remnant of joy from what they had lost. The very act of experiencing delight is a way of fighting evil.

One of my all-time favorite characters in the series is Luna Lovegood, the odd misfit girl who wears necklaces made of butterbeer cork, reads magazines upside-down, and is teased with the name "Loony Lovegood" by the other students. Luna is conspicuously strange, and she knows it, but her strangeness is not an intentional performance to get attention. It's just genuinely who she is. Her strangeness has an innocence to it. She wears weird clothes because they delight her, not because she's trying to make a statement or be the subject of conversation. Even her gentle sweetness isn't enough, at first, to overcome other students' derision of her. Harry, Ron and Hermione, while not joining in with the more spiteful insults against her, tend to avoid her at first. Luna's smart and gentle and accepting of others, but she's just so different from the others that she's avoided.

I've always had a special place in my heart for heart-of-gold misfits, artists, and outcasts. I like that J.K. Rowling tells the truth about being a bit weird: creatively maladjusted people are not typically met with pure acceptance. They're usually given a hard time for it. But what's amazing about Luna is that even though she knows she is being mocked, she seems

Mental Health and Creative Maladjustment

immune from shame. She is grateful for her friendships with people like Ginny, who sticks up for her when other kids call her "Loony" in class (a name that Ginny herself once called Luna). When her shoes are taken and hidden by other students (as a mean prank, not as a friendly tease), she simply stops wearing shoes to prevent the problem. But in Luna's case, this is not a form of her giving in to bullying, but simply her adapting to a situation and moving on without changing who she is inside. I like to think that Luna knows what her own true worth is, and that she is just abiding until the time will come that she knows others will see it, too. That simple inner confidence in her own value is her immunity to shame. Luna never collapses from the bullying and rejection she endures, she just remains her true self, happier in her own choices and personality than in any craved fantasy of being accepted by bullies.

When you have been mistreated, degraded, or rejected by others who are unkind, it's easy to make the mistake of trying to figure out what you should change about yourself so that you will finally be accepted by them, and your abuse will stop. Many abuse victims spend years trying to cope with their abusers by telling themselves, "If I could just figure out what I need to do differently, what I can change about myself, then maybe I'll be the kind of person who they won't abuse anymore"! One of the effects of this kind of thinking is that abuse victims often try to become more of the kind of person they think their abusers will value, which results in the abuser actually becoming more powerful. For example, Draco Malfoy wants to win status for his family, yet his father is repeatedly humiliated by Voldemort. Rather than resisting Voldemort over it, Draco strives to become *more* of the kind of person Voldemort would value. Honestly, I don't fault this one bit. If *you* did the same thing, don't feel "picked on" by me pointing this out as a Draco Malfoy tactic. In real life, learning to comply with an abuser's expectations is a rational, logical form of survival, not weakness. Many of the abused women I've worked with felt ashamed for how long they had tried to please their abusers, sometimes even siding with them, because it was the only way they could try to be safe. I get that. When you're powerless in an abusive situation, trying to reduce the harm done to you by complying with the abuser is absolutely normal.

Luna is not a model for how to handle abuse, but she is a model for how to develop your personality on your own terms during your healing. Rather than spending energy obsessing over "why am I not accepted?" she simply decides what kinds of things she loves, and she makes them part of her life. Even though she takes her outsider status in stride, she doesn't back down when her ideas are challenged. She's able to accept that others don't always accept her ("I think they think I'm a bit odd, you know"), but when she sees others being treated badly too, she intervenes. Whether it's sticking up for her father's tabloid newspaper, or defending her belief in the existence of possibly-imaginary creatures, Luna knows she's been devalued by others, but she doesn't devalue herself. Even Hermione disparages Luna at one point, scolding Harry for befriending the likes of her:

> "Oh, for heaven's sake, Harry, you can do better than her," said Hermione. "Ginny's told me all about her, apparently she'll only believe in things as long as there's no proof at all. Well, I wouldn't expect anything else from someone whose father runs *The Quibbler*."[1]

Hermione, although clearly brilliant, is not open enough to accept Luna at first. Luna's father, Xenophilius, confronts Hermione about this: "Luna has told me all about you, young lady. You are, I gather, not unintelligent, but painfully limited, narrow, close-minded." Harry, though, is beginning to see Luna with a fresh set of eyes, because she is one of the only people who believes him about the return of Voldemort. To him, simply being believed matters more than whether a potential friend is popular. As Harry becomes more accepting of Luna, he realizes she has had qualities all along that he'd missed, and his appreciation of her grows. This is not to say that your value as a person depends on other people noticing and approving of it; Luna's value was inherent all along, regardless whether anyone else ever accepted it. It's not that Luna suddenly feels (or becomes) worthwhile because someone finally accepts her; that would mean that our value as people can only come from others, and not from within. In fact, much of Luna's worth is revealed in the moments when she is *not* accepted by others. It's her outsider status that allows her to become a truly honest, independent, unique person.

If those qualities were there all along, why does it take Harry so long to notice them? Of all the encounters he's had with Luna, why is it that Luna simply believing Harry's claims about Voldemort suddenly changes all of Harry's attitudes toward her?

In my work with rape victims in therapy, I learned that it was more important to listen without judgment, than to give advice or explanations. As I listened, one amazing thing became clear to me. Of all the fears that victims have in the moments after being raped, the first fear in nearly every case was "*Oh my God, nobody is going to believe me!*" The fear of not being believed is so immediate and so strong that it keeps most victims from reporting their abuse for a long time. And I totally get it. It makes complete

---

1 *Harry Potter and the Order of the Phoenix*, p.262

sense to me. As I've seen how poorly abuse victims are treated—being insulted online, being blamed, lectured, guilt-tripped, accused of lying, accused of wanting attention, being blamed, and being blamed—I can completely understand the valid reasons people have for making the choice not to report.

It's a choice that protects people from being subjected to even more pain, but the side effect is that it causes the victim to become even lonelier. For years, there's a fear that you have one big secret that would destroy you if anyone else ever knew it. Or worse, you would be rejected if you did reveal it, only to find that nobody believes you. When the worst moments of your life become the very thing people use against you, it's like when Harry Potter starts telling people that Voldemort is back. Rather than being supported and protected, Harry is despised, treated like a liar, and even punished for it.

One of the ways I teach people how to support loved ones who have been traumatized is to simply believe them. No lectures, no "Why didn't you? Couldn't you have? Shouldn't you have? Are you sure?" interrogations, just support and patience. If trauma causes a profound sense of loneliness and separation from others, one of the ways we heal from trauma is to find others who support us, so that we can reconnect again. Simply telling a victim of trauma "I believe you" is one of the most healing things we can do.

Believing Harry when almost nobody else does is Luna's gift to him. Luna stands by Harry, supporting him when he's isolated, dueling beside him at the Ministry of Magic, and nearly dying during the Battle of Hogwarts. Luna doesn't even realize how valuable her support is to Harry; at one point she even confesses, "People expect you to have cooler friends than us." Harry responds, "You are cool. None of them were at the Ministry. They didn't fight with me." To Harry, being supported and accepted and believed matters more than whether cool people think he's cool, too. At one point, Luna even asks Harry if the "DA" club ("Dumbledore's Army") can continue, but Harry points out that there's no real reason for it anymore, because Umbridge is gone. Luna says, "I enjoyed the meetings…It was like having friends." The sad sweetness of this moment is that, of course, it was not *like* having friends, they *were* friends. Luna had become so accustomed to being rejected that she didn't even realize how accepted she had become. Weird kids everywhere were moved while reading this simple moment, knowing exactly how this feels.

Harry, who used to be slightly embarrassed to be seen in Luna's company, becomes protective of her, too, sticking up for her to others and inviting her to be his guest to dinner. During the Battle of Hogwarts, Harry specifically names Luna as one of his closest friends who he wants to see one last time before he sacrifices himself. It is Luna who senses that Harry needs time to himself during the victory celebration, and creates the distraction that allows him to slip away. She is sensitive to his needs in ways that others can't be. By rejecting "normal" ways of life and being a bit weird, she has been able to open herself to wider ranges of emotions, intuitions, and wisdom than most others. Even the name of her father, Xenophilius, carries a clue about her upbringing: a "xenophile" is someone who embraces novel, foreign, and different experiences.

As a survivor, your healing will be enhanced if you reject narrow, mainstream, conventional views about what's cool, because those views are created by groups of other people, and the definition of what's trendy isn't relevant to what you personally need in your development. Like Hermione says, "Excuse me, I don't like people just because they're handsome!"[2] Instead, shape your life around what truly makes you happy and healthy, the way Luna does. Throughout Rowling's books, it's always the "outsider" characters—the uncool misfits—who turn out to be the heroes, and it's because being outsiders opens them to insights and feelings that "mainstream cool" characters can't access. The Weasley family is dreadfully unpopular in the wizarding world; they're not wealthy, they're not prideful, they refuse to discriminate against others, and they're not shy about speaking out against abusers. Neville is an uncool student, but nobody realizes that his family has been traumatized by death eaters, and that he is coping with his grief every day. He's teased for being a sensitive, clumsy kid, but it turns out that Neville has genius gifts in potions, and bravely fights the death eaters on several occasions.

Rowling's storytelling teaches us that connection to others on the basis of shared values of kindness, intelligence, and wisdom do more to heal us than fitting-in with a mainstream, popular crowd. Being something of an outcast is, in the *Harry Potter* parable, a strength, not a weakness, even though it comes with a burden of being misunderstood and rejected by the mainstream. But for those who have endured abuse, this can be a hopeful message, too. Feeling somehow different from the "normal" people around you doesn't mean you should change to become more like others. It means you should embrace what truly brings happiness to you, and find allies who respect those same traits about you. After all, Harry himself learns that "family" is not always about literal blood relationship, but can also be about finding acceptance among others who truly welcome you— *all* of you. Who is Harry's true family then, the Dursleys, or the Weasleys? Who lets Harry fully become the good man he is meant to be, rather

---

2 *Harry Potter and the Goblet of Fire*, p.236

than forcing him to remain quiet and meaningless? Who lets Harry make mistakes, and forgives him, rather than forcing him to live in terror? Who lets Harry form his own personality, rather than forcing him to live within very narrow cages of rules?

When Harry, Ron and Hermione visit the Lovegood home, they see Luna's bedroom for the first time. She's not there, because unbeknownst to them, she has been captured by death eaters. But what they see fills them with such understanding of why creative maladjustment matters. They see her ceiling painted with five murals that depicts each of them, Neville, and Ginny, connected by painted golden chains that spell out the word "FRIENDS." Over and over, "FRIENDS." This simple gesture is so heartbreakingly beautiful, so honest, so sincere, that Harry overflows with affection for Luna.

CHAPTER NINE

Dobby and Self-Harm

Part of the recovery process is to finally make connections between your trauma itself and your current feelings that affect your behaviors and relationships now. The connection may seem self-evident at first, but until you really examine it, write about it, and learn to successfully challenge it, the belief that you are worthless or damaged will continue to drive a constellation of other symptoms such as anxiety, panic attacks, substance abuse, self-injury, and sexual dysfunction. Alice Sebold, in her book *Lucky*, describes her recovery as the struggle after her struggle, meaning that "I was about to begin my real fight, a fight of words and lies and the brain."

In your recovery, it is important to change the language of trauma that you might use. I have found that abuse victims can be very cruel to themselves and recycle awful self-criticisms in their own minds. For example, "I'm scarred for life." A person in recovery will reconsider what "scarred" truly means: a scar is a healed place, a marker and reminder of what was formerly a wound but is now a protected and useful (and even useable) growth. While we cannot lose our memories of the wound that caused the scar, we carry the evidence of our healing as the scar. Examine the self-talk you use:

- Do you continually degrade yourself, criticize yourself, and expect rejection?
- Have you begun to believe that because of your abuse, you no longer have anything worthy inside to contribute to another person's life?
- Does it feel like you have "hurt me" printed right on your forehead?
- Do you find yourself accepting all of peoples' criticisms, but none of their praise?
- Do you continually produce art or writing obsessed with images of defeat, injury, or despair?
- Do you start conflicts with people, or have a "chip on your shoulder," and then criticize others for failing you when the clash starts?
- Do you behave in ways that you think will cause people to reject you because you believe "they'll reject me anyway, so let's get it over with"?
- Do you tell yourself that nobody can love you now?
- Do you warn people who love you that you are no good, and suggest that they abandon you?
- Do you deliberately provoke people who love you in an effort to drive them away to "save" them from you?
- Do you find yourself asking permission to speak, apologizing for seeking help, or feeling undeserving of time?
- Do you make comments like, "you would be better off without me" or "I'm sorry to be such a burden on you" to people who try to support you?

One way in which your trauma will affect you is by planting this type of "I'm a victim and nothing more!" thinking. This is the self-rejection and self-hatred that rape and abuse victims experience: "I'm damaged goods," or "nobody will want to marry someone like me" or "I can't take the pain anymore. God has even forgotten me." While you have no control over the victimization you endured, you can learn how to overcome this part, which is good news because it is this level of harm that is most damaging and potentially fatal (through suicide, eating disorders, self-injury and addiction). Remember, Remus Lupin went through all of these same feelings, too: "'And I've told you a million times,' said Lupin, refusing to meet her eyes, staring at the floor, 'that I am too old for you, too poor...too dangerous...'"[1] He, too, had to overcome his own "I'm no good, nobody would want someone as ruined as me" beliefs.

1 *Harry Potter and the Half-Blood Prince*, p.624

Dobby and Self-Harm

You should define recovery. But here are some things to look for: you can begin to think and talk about your trauma without feeling shame or fear, and you should be well-informed enough to confront and challenge ignorant comments by others. Nightmares and flashbacks should subside. You should be able to experience conflict or sadness without using self-destructive coping measures. You should be able to accept your innocence in this crime, and not just intellectually—you should feel innocent again. You should be inspired to assist other people who are struggling with this issue. These are good "shoulds", not scolding "shoulds", in that they return control and decision-making to you in your healing.

Meanwhile, you are probably facing a lot of negative "shoulds", as well: "I should have stopped the abuse or rape"; "I should be over this by now"; "I should have been stronger." All of these self-accusing thoughts can cause you to feel ashamed and deserving of punishment, especially if your abusers used shame *as* a punishment, such as intentionally humiliating you, actually telling you that you are no good, ugly, unlovable, etc., and putting you down for any attribute they saw as weak. While guilt is actually a good thing (it represents remorse for something you actually did wrong, and for which you can atone), shame is purely unhealthy (it represents the feeling that *you* are bad). Shame, then, leads to self-punishing thoughts and acts that are not deserved.

Many abuse victims punish themselves by depriving themselves of pleasure, or even intentionally harming themselves. Like Dobby, they may feel that anything they do that disappoints someone "superior" to them, or anything they do that makes them feel pleasure or importance they don't feel they deserve, warrants self-punishment. Dobby punishes himself any time he feels he has disappointed his masters or Harry, but he also harms himself any time he finds himself feeling too proud, because he feels he is too lowly to deserve any pride. As a result, Dobby is trapped in a cycle of self-punishment, because he cycles between feeling ashamed of himself, then feeling too good about himself, then feeling ashamed again because he doesn't think he is worthy of feeling good.

As we come to know Dobby, we see that he has several quirks in his thinking that make it hard for him to break out of his cycle of shame and self-harm. First, he thinks of himself as having low worth. This belief causes him to approach relationships with others as their inferior, not as their equal. In fact, being treated with any respect is shocking to him ("Dobby has never been asked to sit down by a wizard — like an equal —").

Second, Dobby is terrified of ever disappointing anyone who he feels dependent on, such as his masters, the Malfoys. Despite resenting them, he feels he has to please them. Even having negative thoughts about them causes him to punish himself, bashing his head on furniture. Dobby is trapped in a contradiction in which he simultaneously dislikes the Malfoys, yet regards them as his superiors and sees himself as inferior. To resolve this contradiction, Dobby transfers his resentment of them to *himself*, seeing himself as the one who is flawed for thinking ill of them. They are, after all, his providers, even though they are cruel to him. The worse they are to him, the worse he feels inwardly. Consequently, he over-values approval from those who abuse him, and faults himself for having any bitter thoughts toward the very abusers he over-values. In psychological terms, this is called "splitting": the tendency to hold contradictory love-and-hate thoughts about someone else. A person "splits" their feelings about someone when they both resent and idealize them, but they cannot combine these views into a realistic, cohesive whole, so instead they view others in all-or-nothing terms.[2] Sirius Black, on the other hand, teaches us a more sophisticated way to see the people in our lives: "The world isn't split into good people and Death Eaters. We've all got both light and dark inside us. What matters is the part we choose to act on. That's who we really are."[3]

Splitting makes it hard for Dobby to realize that good people like Harry can have flaws, and he idealizes Harry Potter to unrealistic degrees. Normally, we are able to accept that people can be good and loving and worthy, and yet sometimes disappoint us. We don't completely discard their worth when they fail. Dobby, however, splits his view of the Malfoys ("They are bad, but if I think they are bad, *I* am committing a sin for which I should be punished, because they are my masters and must not be thought of as bad!"), and his view of Harry ("Harry is supremely good! Nobody must ever think badly of Harry or they deserve to be punished!"). Since neither of these are actually accurate ways of thinking, Dobby simply punishes himself for the flaws in his beliefs rather than correcting the beliefs.

People who resort to splitting tend to use very stern, inflexible words when they describe others: always, perfect, never, impossible, evil, best, worst, and so on. Because of this, such people often have stormy, chaotic relationships in which they alternately feel elated (when their caretaker/superior/other acts as expected) or outraged (when their caretaker/superior/other disappoints or hurts them in some way). As a result, their self-image also suffers, flipping back and forth between "I am good" and "I am evil". We see Dobby do this constantly, spinning between intense happiness and intense despair.

---

2 https://www.verywell.com/what-is-splitting-425210
3 *Harry Potter and the Order of the Phoenix,* film adaptation

Third, Dobby is often paranoid about how others are behaving, and uses manipulation to manage his stress. Probably because of his tenure in the Malfoy home, he has become accustomed to people behaving in dishonest, unreliable ways—much like someone who has grown up with abuse. He is constantly afraid that people will abandon him in some form, such as his dread that Harry will be killed at school. As a result, he sabotages Harry's life in ways that hurt Harry, all for Dobby's own agenda of keeping Harry from leaving him. Dobby intercepts Harry's letters from his friends in order to cause Harry to think his friends have forsaken him and choose not to return to Hogwarts. When Harry discovers this, he is furious with Dobby, but Dobby feels justified and rebuffs Harry's anger ("Dobby is used to death threats, sir. Dobby gets them five times a day at home."[4]). Dobby then incapacitates Harry's access to the Hogwarts Express to physically prevent Harry from leaving for school.

In Dobby's mind, these are all things he has to do to protect his idealized Harry Potter, but to everyone else it makes Dobby seem chaotic, reckless, and intensely difficult to deal with. Dobby is behaving in ways that frustrate other people and risk his relationships with them, but he believes he is doing what is necessary to keep them from separating from them ("Harry Potter mustn't be angry with Dobby. Dobby did it for the best —"). The very things he is doing to manipulate others into remaining with him are the things that drive those same people away. When Harry becomes angry with him, Dobby responds by becoming even *more* difficult, wreaking havoc in the Dursley home to intentionally cause Harry trouble.

Even though Dobby causes others to lose patience with his behavior, he also feels ashamed, and takes it out on himself. He simultaneously repels others with the drama he causes, and then feels rejected when those he repels lose patience with him. His most common reaction to these stresses is to harm himself, such as burning his hands, hitting himself, and throwing himself against furniture and walls.

Self-harm is the practice of inflicting harm on one's own body to effect a change in inner emotions. To someone who is not a self-injurer, it may seem baffling that anyone would deliberately cause himself pain or inflict self-injury. Even to many self-injurers, this may also be a point of shame: "What would make me do something like this? Am I sick? Am I a freak?" But to a self-injurer, the compulsion to cut or scratch (or otherwise harm) yourself can feel so overwhelming it becomes almost a need, not a desire or habit. If you are a self-injurer, you may not even be aware of the inner motivations that drive these behaviors. Some people have recognized the connection between their self-injury and trauma, but others may have

---

4 *Harry Potter and the Chamber of Secrets*, p.177

mistaken them as separate issues. I suggest that the link between the two is very strong.

People who self-harm say that they typically have one of two reasons for the behavior: to feel more, or to feel less. By inflicting an injury on the body, they divert emotional energy away from anxiety, depression, or frustration, and the replacement sensation—either pain or numb dissociation—becomes a sensation they can control. For a person whose inner pain is the result of abuse or trauma in which they had no control, this can become a clever, but addictive, way to find temporary relief.

In my work with self-injurers, I have observed several thoughts and beliefs that precede the act of self-harm. These include:

- I can trick my brain into becoming numb so that I don't feel distress
- I am shameful and dirty, and I deserve punishment
- This is the only form of pain in my life I can control by myself
- These injuries are the only ones I can successfully nurture and heal
- This is the only way I can express inner feelings with an outward action
- This is proof that what I feel is genuine

But one thing that isn't part of those thoughts is "I need to end my life." Self-harm is not a form of suicidal behavior, because it is usually done to make life feel more manageable, not to make life stop. It is done to manage whirlwinds of thoughts and feelings, rather than to fulfill the all-or-none goal of suicide. Like Dobby, people who self-harm are trying to purge themselves of shame, using pain to complete an act of punishment they feel they deserve, as well as to release endorphins that cause a temporary soothing feeling that keeps stress at bay.

Many people who have been through abuse, especially childhood and sexual abuse, have developed rituals of self-harm that can last for years. Although not usually done as openly, publicly, and flamboyantly as Dobby's self-harm, people who self-harm after trauma do tend to share the belief with him that they are responsible for their own badness, and that they have to submit to self-punishment in order to express that blame.[5] They are often caught between "I don't belong/I don't matter" thoughts, and tend to be very self-critical. They fear public judgment, and will often "mind read" others, convinced that people are silently judging and reject-

5 Nelissen, R.M., & Zeelenberg, M. (2009). When guilt evokes self-punishment: evidence for the existence of a Dobby Effect. *Emotion, 9 1*, 118-22.

ing them. I have found that people who self-harm will simultaneously feel that everyone knows thoroughly what their faults and flaws are, including their rape or abuse, and yet nobody can ever truly know them. She feels shunned but analyzed, ignored but investigated, all at once. One woman even told me that her cuts were a way to satisfy other people in her own mind: "It was my way of saying, 'see? I know I'm as bad as you know I am, so I'll do this to show you that I'm not blind to it. This is my way of telling you that I agree with what I think you're thinking about me!'"

As we follow Dobby through the years, we find that he, too, has exhibited these same traits, but he is able to grow beyond them. Rather than continuing to hurt himself, Dobby learns to change the *thoughts* that cause him to feel like self-harming. He becomes a free elf, and changes his routines: he takes up the hobby of making socks, gets a job at Hogwarts, works on his own terms, becomes more confident, and forms new friendships. He no longer lives in isolation, and research shows that ending isolation and forming relationships is a key part of overcoming self-harm.[6]

Ultimately, Dobby's success in overcoming his self-harm is achieved by both inward and outer growth. Not only does Dobby develop his life in healthy ways, but his friendships also help him overcome his habits. His friends know of his urges, and intentionally intervene (in one situation, Ron physically stops Dobby from flinging himself against a table), and they grow to respect him more and more over time. Their friendships with Dobby evolve from one of simply asking him for favors and giving him orders, to becoming respectful. Harry knows how it feels to grow up in an abusive home, he recognizes that Dobby has experienced similar traumas, and they grow a relationship that becomes protective and kind. In fact, their development mirrors one another's when it becomes Dobby's turn to rescue Harry from the Malfoys, just as Harry had once done for him.[7]

Notice that Dobby does not overcome his self-harm through "positive thinking" or merely expressing his inner pain. Changing your behavior is much harder than expressing your pain is. Rather, he refuses to accept his former limitations as the borders of his life as a free elf, and he becomes someone who no longer fits into the confines of his pain. His self-harm does express real anguish, but merely expressing it changes nothing for him; he has to also become *more than his pain*. He has to develop other emotions, such as empathy, friendship, trust, humor, and comfort, so that pain itself is not the supreme description of his life.

6 Skegg, K. (2005). Self-harm. *Lancet, 366,* 1471–1483.
7 LaBouff, L. (2015). The Dobby Effect Part II: Analyzing Dobby. *Psych Central.* https://blogs.psychcentral.com/bipolar-laid-bare/2015/07/the-dobby-effect-analyzing-dobby/

Dobby and Self-Harm

Watching Dobby, we see that self-harm does not end simply because we want it to. Self-harm stops when it no longer works the way it used to, which can happen when you have grown stronger than your pain. You no longer need to force your feelings to change when you have faced those feelings and overcome them. As his behavior changes, Dobby becomes able to manage his relationships with others in ways that do not repel people because of his repeated manipulation, constant need of soothing or pity, and reckless behavior. He becomes someone who is able to accept the goodness of his friends, even though he sees their faults. His all-or-none thinking is gone, and he is able to see others in a more complex way so that his own contentment is not based on whether others are perfect or not.

CHAPTER TEN

Dobby, Winky, and Finding Strength

When we meet Dobby, the Malfoys' house elf, he is terrified to say anything critical about his family, even though they are vicious to him and he knows that they are not as blameless as they seem. Dobby sees himself as a degraded, unlovable creature, and cannot imagine anyone ever treating him with respect or kindness. He is very familiar to readers who have grown up with family abuse. In those families, victims are often warned to keep abuse secret and to maintain a falsely positive public persona. So often, adult and teen victims of family violence, sexual abuse, and emotional abuse told me in therapy what it was like to hear people praise their abusers—"Your parents are just wonderful! Your dad is such a good man! Our church is so blessed to have him!"—while inwardly they knew what was really happening in secret. Many rape victims, too, know the feeling of seeing their perpetrators adored in public.

Over and over, victims learn the lesson to keep their abuse a secret, just like Dobby does at first. Victims of sexual abuse are often harassed online, especially if the abuser has celebrity or high social status, and comments sections under online news about abuse become rotten with victim-blaming, abuser-supporting comments. They learn quickly to keep their mouths shut and not reveal their secrets because of the likelihood of retaliation, and then when they do speak up, they are retaliated against for that, too: "Why'd you wait so long to say anything? If this was true, you would have spoken up before now!" Dobby is no exception; he has been programmed to keep the Malfoy family secrets so that the Malfoys can enjoy public status while committing evil in private.

As soon as Harry invites Dobby to sit down, Dobby bursts into tears: "Dobby has never been asked to sit down by a wizard — like an equal —" It's easy to think of Dobby's tears as signs of gratitude or pride, but they're not. They're tears of shame. For Dobby, kind treatment isn't something he'd ever desired, because he had been raised to believe kindness was something that would never be shown to him. He simply *was* lesser than others. In fact, Dobby's very next action is to begin beating himself, banging his head on furniture, and repeatedly insulting himself for the crime of "speaking ill of his family."

Wounded people know exactly what it's like to be surprised by respect and equality shown to them by others, and to not feel they deserve any of it. When someone shows respect to an abuse-wounded person, the "Dobby" in them feels they don't deserve the positive regard. In fact, they often feel that it is an insult to other more-deserving people to even accept respect for themselves. In the back of their mind, they are nagged by the fear that "if you knew how low I *really* am, you wouldn't respect me!" Since accepting respect they feel they don't deserve makes them feel like a fraud, even feeling for a moment that they matter becomes a reason to later feel they deserve more remorse and punishment: "I don't deserve to be respected! If someone respects me and I don't deserve it, it means I've led them on—lied to them!—and that makes me even *worse!*"

When I worked with rape and abuse victims, I noticed this. If I assured them that I saw them as innocent people who didn't deserve what had happened to them, they didn't feel consoled or encouraged or more comforted by me. They felt the opposite: even more isolated, more resentful, and more misunderstood. In their minds, their abuse or rape was *clearly* their fault, and they were bad, inferior people who didn't deserve kindness. If I offered them kind words or equality, they felt that "here's just one more person who thinks he 'gets it' but clearly doesn't; either that, or he's just flat-out lying to me about me being a 'good person' when I'm obviously not." Or as Harry himself says to Dobby, "Whatever you've heard about my greatness is a load of rubbish!" They either concluded that being abused or raped had made them so pitiful and so disconnected from others that they were impossible to understand, or they felt that people who treated them with any respect were fakers who were manipulating them. It couldn't possibly be that someone might actually see them as valued people. To them, I was "one more guy who clearly just doesn't get it." The question of whether they were ruined, bad people wasn't in doubt—that was the one thing they were sure of—so my encouraging words changed their minds about *me*, not about themselves.

Children who have grown up in abusive homes have also absorbed another "Dobby" lesson, as well: never question the family behaviors, and protect the family reputation. Keep the secrets. Make up excuses for the family misery, if you can't hide it entirely. Questioning the power and control of the primary abuser is Sin #1; telling anyone outside the family what's really going on is Sin #2. Dobby expresses this when he begins punishing himself for almost speaking ill of his family, even though the Malfoy family to which he "belongs" is just awful with abusiveness. In real life, it can take years for an abuse victim to grow from being loyal to the family and its secrets, to eventually becoming independent and healthy. Sometimes, becoming independent and healthy earns you the scorn of the family that had caused your wounds.

Dobby's first meeting with Harry is an incredible parable about how abuse victims cope. Dobby retreats back into his family brainwashing against revealing family secrets, and Harry does the same thing: "Please," Harry whispered frantically, "please be quiet. If the Dursleys hear anything, if they know you're here —" Harry, too, is committed to protecting the integrity of his own abusive family, for the same reasons as Dobby: he fears the consequences, the punishment, that will come to him if he doesn't. While abuse is happening, victims learn that their primary survival skill is secrecy. Denying the abuse is not only a way of protecting the family's secrets, but a way of minimizing the grievous feelings that come with being abused. That can sometimes be another reason why abuse victims reject words of kindness from others—when someone else offers support and encouragement, it also affirms that the abuse itself is real, which bursts the victim's denial.

When Harry's mind wanders even for a moment to Hermione and Ron, it causes him emotional pain. Why? If you've lived through abusive experiences, you know the answer, too: they represent the healthy, confident, abuse-free alternative lives that others have, which you didn't. Hermione and Ron represent support and encouragement, which is like water behind a wall in a desert for someone trapped in an abusive home. They're relationships Harry can't participate in when he's confined in his abusive home. When Harry sees Dobby right in front of him, going through the same things, and even despising himself for being a victim of abuse too, Harry sees not a kindred spirit, but a tragic symbol for what his own life could become if Harry isn't able to become free of the abuse, "looking like a large and very ugly doll." In real life, I have seen abuse victims resent and

Dobby, Winky, and Finding Strength

reject other abuse victims during their earliest stages of healing, because at first those other victims represent mirrors to their own tragedies, rather than kindred spirits.

Harry even begins to repeat some of the same scolds and guilt-trips at Dobby that he probably subconsciously holds against himself: "But why don't you leave? Escape?" This is the question almost every abuse victim is asked by people who simply don't understand what abuse is actually like. This is also the question many victims torment themselves with for years: "Why didn't I…? Couldn't I have…? Shouldn't I have…? I'm so weak and stupid for not…!" In my work with rape victims, I found that perhaps 90% of the trauma was caused by self-blame and shame, and 10% was everything else. Even years later, rape victims continued to attack themselves with these questions. Harry Potter isn't immune to victim-shaming either; he directs it at Dobby, but those are questions he would probably have a hard time answering about his own abuse, too.

Dobby takes his traumatized thinking even further than Harry, by engaging in outright self-harm. Every time he does something that makes him feel ashamed, even when there's clearly no reason he ought to feel such feelings, Dobby leaps to the conclusion that he's just done the most horrible thing possible, and begins physically beating himself. He bashes his head against furniture, slams his hands in doors, claws at himself, and even burns himself.

Jump ahead a few books: what's different? Dobby is entirely changed. He's no longer the self-harming, ashamed, abused, wilting creature he had been when we first met him. By *Order of the Phoenix*, he's self-assured, committed to a cause, sees himself as an important part of a group, no longer feels defined by his abuse by the Malfoys, and he's even brave enough to face the most dangerous enemies in the series. He helps Harry find a place to hide his "Dumbledore's Army" meetings, and proudly wears multicolored clothing as a sign of happiness and freedom. What changed?

Dobby is able to find a small community of other victims, survivors, and allies who treat him well. But it's not just that Dobby's change comes from the influence of those outside of himself; if the answer was as simple as "other people uplifted him and healed him," that would be a terrible answer. That would suggest that you remain a victim until *other* people turn you into someone better. Waiting for others to rearrange your thinking does not work; healing work happens at both levels, inwardly and socially. Dobby is able to heal on both levels.

Inwardly, Dobby learns to express his needs and speak up about what matters to him. He is able to change himself from being a slave to asking Dumbledore directly to be paid for what he does. That may seem like a minor transformation on Dobby's part, but consider the process: he doesn't approach Dumbledore with a sense of being owed anything *because he's been a victim*. He doesn't use his traumas as ways to convince himself or others that his poor, sad story becomes everyone else's debt to him. Rather, he asked for what he is owed on the simple, rational basis that *it is what he is owed, period*. If Dobby had used his abuse and his traumas as leverage in convincing others that being a victim gives him special entitlement to anything, it would not only cause resentment in others ("Dobby's playing the Victim Card again!"), but it would mean that being a victim was the most important resource he actually has! If "I'm a victim, so take care of me" had become Dobby's only way to negotiate his needs, he would never be able to heal. He could never relinquish victimhood, because victimhood would have become his go-to form of pressure others to do for him. He couldn't have healed from something he constantly uses as his tactic for getting his way.

Outwardly, Dobby learns to form meaningful connections with others. He chooses his friends carefully; he doesn't form bonds with bullies, abusers, or lowlifes. He also doesn't exclude possible friends on the basis of their gender, race, or whether they were also abused or not. To Dobby, a person's value as a potential friend is defined entirely by whether that person has a core of compassion, decency, and respect for others. The antidote to abuse trauma is reconnecting with others to form relationships that strengthen your sense of worth[1], which Dobby does.

In so doing, Dobby learns to develop a new personality for himself, which defines him differently than he had been defined by the Malfoys. For example, Dobby begins to proudly wear clothing. Anyone who's familiar with the *Harry Potter* books knows that clothing has a unique symbolic role among house elves; it is taboo for elves to wear anything other than a dirty rag. Being given a single item of clothing by their master is a transaction that awards (or imposes) freedom to the elf. When Dobby is freed after Lucius Malfoy is tricked by Harry Potter into giving Dobby a sock, Dobby not only becomes freed in the literal sense, but he also begins to develop outward representations of that freedom: he collects and wears unique and whimsical articles of clothing.

What's that got to do with abuse victims? How are Dobby's fashion choices parables of healing? To Dobby, wearing clothing at all is a form of symbolic defiance against the system of abusive ownership under which he had been tormented. He is expressing his resistance to that former state of

---

1 "The protective role of friendship on the effects of childhood abuse and depression." Powers A[1], Ressler KJ, Bradley RG. Depression And Anxiety. 2009; 26(1): 46-53.

Dobby, Winky, and Finding Strength

his life. He is identifying himself outwardly as a rogue elf now, embracing his freedom with zest, and very intentionally, openly making a statement that his life is no longer defined by the limitations of his former masters. When Dobby proclaims the words "Dobby is a free elf!" that's not a minor comment he's making. To him, those words epitomize all that it means to become unburdened by a traumatic past. He is stating that the person he is now becoming is different than the victim he had once been. "Dobby is a free elf!" is another way of saying "I am no longer a victim! I have become my own person!"

Contrast Dobby's journey with that of Winky, another house elf who had very similar life experiences. Winky, the elf who served the Crouch family, had also lived in deplorable conditions and experienced mistreatment by her human wizard masters. Winky was freed by Barty Crouch, but not as an act of kindness or favor toward her, but in order to exile her after scapegoating her. Winky had been found holding a wand under suspicious circumstances, and not wanting to be suspected of association with dark magic, Crouch sacked her, essentially piling blame onto Winky in order to maintain a public family reputation. In real-life abusive families, victims are often scapegoated as well, treated as crazy problem-causers who deserve punishment and banishment for their non-compliance with the family's power structures. Many of the victims of childhood abuse I have worked with have very similar stories of being vilified by their own abusers later in life, rejected by a family system that remains stagnant in generational cycles of abuse and dysfunction. For many victims, this feels justifiably unfair: "Why are they calling *me* crazy? I'm the one who grew up with this stuff, yet became a good parent, got educated, and moved on to have a good life!" It may not have occurred to them that being rejected by a toxic family is actually a form of acknowledgement by the family that the scapegoat has rejected those abusive values. Being rejected by sick people isn't an insult, it's a testimony to your goodness in spite of them.

That's an important lesson to learn. It's a lesson Winky *never* learns.

Rather than separating from the Crouch family and its messed-up secrets and schemes, Winky became even more bonded to them. She knew full-well what was going on in the family, and was even required to help keep the family secrets (including her knowledge that Barty Crouch Jr. had been smuggled out of Azkaban by his father, an official in the Ministry of Magic). Winky was even physically harmed by her devotion to the family, when her concealment of Barty Jr.'s fugitive state resulted in her being stunned and flung to the ground by Ministry officials who thought she had aided death eaters.

Despite all this, Winky remained emotionally bound to the family, even after the Crouches disowned and banished her. In fact, their rejection of her caused her to shriek with grief! One of the reasons Winky is not able to heal is that she continues to prioritize the needs of the man who banished her over her own. "My poor Mr. Crouch, what is he doing without Winky?" she weeps. "He is needing me, he is needing my help! I is looking after the Crouches all my life, and my mother is doing it before me, and my grandmother is doing it before her…!"[2] Winky is astonished when she is told that Crouch is actually doing just fine without her. In her mind, the man who cast her out is the one who must surely be suffering, and she feels responsible for *his* plight.

In my work with domestic violence victims, I noticed a very similar pattern, often set up intentionally by abusers after their victims had left the relationship. The abusers would intentionally become pitiful and ill, grief-stricken and morose. I saw cases where abusers would starve themselves, give up their sobriety, live in filthy apartments, and feign physical illness to manipulate their victims. The victims would feel guilty to think of the poor wretch, struggling without them: "He needs me! See how terribly he's doing without my help? He could die at any moment; how can I just let him suffer?"[3] The goal is to lure their victim into a sense of guilt and pity, so that they feel responsible to "save" their own abuser from torment and despair. Winky, like many abuse victims, was taught that her own needs were less worthy than the whims and privileges of someone else, so she doesn't tend to her own health and freedom while obsessing with her former master's circumstance. Because she does not value her own health, growth, and freedom, she is not able to nurture any of those qualities in her life.

Cast out by a family that took her for granted, forced her to keep scandalous secrets, coldly rejected her, allowed her to take blame for crimes, and even caused her to be physically harmed, Winky becomes depressed. She does not see herself as "set free" from a dysfunctional family; she sees herself as tragically banished and despised, even though her rejection comes from her own abusers. She becomes ashamed of herself, believing she has disgraced her family, and begins to drink heavily. She allows her rag covering to become ruined, shuns efforts at friendships, and has very little interest in her work. Winky is the epitome of depression that stems from traumatic bonding between a victim and her abuser.

---

2 *Harry Potter and the Goblet of Fire*, p.381
3 For more examination of this tactic, see Lundy Bancroft's *Why Does He Do That? Inside The Minds Of Angry And Controlling Men*, especially chapter 9, "The Abuser and Breaking Up."

Dobby, Winky, and Finding Strength

Winky and Dobby are contrasts to each other in fascinating ways. Both come from such similar backgrounds, where they experienced abuse, scapegoating, cruelty, and were forced to do the bidding of their abusers. Why do they take such different paths in life after they are each freed from those experiences? Dobby transforms from being an elf who constantly hits himself, burns his hands, and throws himself against furniture, to becoming free and healed; why can Winky never achieve that same growth?

Winky can only see herself as defined by her abuse. For her, even though her abusers mistreated and betrayed her, she can only see them as powerful, and herself as weak and powerless. She sees herself as different from her abusers, but not in the "I'm going to become different from them, and grow to be healthy rather than messed up" way. Rather, she sees herself as different from them in the "they are strong and powerful, and I'm unlike them because I'm weak" way. Unfortunately, many abuse victims in real life adopt this way of thinking, too, and become drawn to icons of power and control, which they misunderstand as being forms of genuine strength. Over and over, I worked with children and teens who had ben abused by their fathers, for example, growing up seeing their fathers brutalize their mothers. But when the family finally fell apart, those children would often be resentful toward their mothers, and crave companionship with their fathers because "they're strong" and "mom was weak"! When we mistake abusive power and control as forms of real strength, we adopt Winky's mindset: "They hurt me, but it's not their fault, it's mine. They're strong, and I'm weak. What's wrong with me, that caused them to reject me? Why am I so useless?" Winky sees herself not as a free elf, but as a rejected elf—"properly ashamed of being freed"—and it hurts her even though the rejection comes from her own abusers.

By refusing to form bonds with healthy, supportive friends and allies, Winky remains isolated in her grief. She becomes the victim who believes that gestures of support and encouragement from others aren't genuine and only demonstrate how naïve her supporters are. She can't accept support because to her, statements that are meant to uplift her only clash with her core belief that she is a weak, defeated victim. She makes sure nobody can reach her with kindness. Her entire life becomes limited by her belief that she is nothing more than a victim who has been rejected by the very abusers who victimized her. Since she identifies abusers as "strong" and victims as "weak", and sees herself as a weak victim, she is constantly in emotional pain. She is no longer abused by the Crouch family, but she still inflicts daily abuse on herself! "I'm no good; I'm alone; I'm weak; I'm nothing; I'm ugly..." Like many unhealed abuse victims, Winky even defends her abusers and insists she deserved the abuse: "Mr. Crouch is a good wizard, miss! Mr. Crouch is right to sack bad Winky!"[4] Oh, how many times I heard the same things from both children and adults who had also been abused! "I deserved it; I made him do that to me by provoking him; I had it coming because I was bad..."

One vital mistake that Winky makes is her belief that she can selectively numb only a specific emotion at a time in order to suppress her shame. It is a mistake many people who have been through also make. Winky cannot handle her feelings of shame and self-loathing, and she resorts to substance abuse in an effort to push those feelings down. But it's not possible to crush only certain feelings while letting the rest of them flourish. When we try to suppress negative feelings with intoxication, sex, self-harm and other tactics, *all* of our feelings become increasingly numbed, too. We might be able to experience brief pleasurable distractions throughout our days, but the full, colorful range of happiness, curiosity, courage, joy, gratitude, connection, vulnerability, and love become blunted. During my worst depression, I would spend hours binge-streaming sitcom reruns because the friendships and humor those characters had became a substitute for the feelings of belonging and hope that were missing in my own life. It gave me pleasure and I could laugh at the jokes and enjoy the episodes, but it was like eating a bowlful artificial sweetener as a meal. I was gazing on fake friendships from the outside, because my depression had gradually isolated me from real connection in my life. Like Winky, all of my emotions, not just the ones I wanted to avoid, were becoming withered.

Dobby and Winky teach us such an important lesson. They teach us that abuse itself does not force us to become a certain type of person. Rather, how we interpret our traumas seems to make the most difference. I am not saying that healing from traumas is a simple matter of thinking positively or merely changing our minds about our lives; in fact, I resent that sort of simplistic feel-good advice. But we do have ways to gradually change how we understand our experiences and what they mean about us now.

For example, Dobby makes a conscious effort to change his habits and thoughts from "abused house elf" to "free house elf," and it doesn't come easily. It takes years, and it happens in little steps. He has to become physically free of his abusers first. Then he has to begin creating a different lifestyle for himself, such as gathering and wearing various socks and knitted hats made by Hermione, which he had never been able to do before. By comparison, I remember taking a walk with a friend who had recently left an abusive marriage, and I was amazed by her comment that "until I'd become free, I couldn't even go out in public and do something as

---

4 *Harry Potter and the Goblet of Fire*, p.380

simple as this. So now for me, just taking a walk is a way of staking as claim on my freedom!" This is what Dobby's clothes-wearing represents for him: "staking a claim on my freedom."

In fact, other house elves are made uncomfortable by Dobby's bold statements that he is free: "The Hogwarts house-elves had now started edging away from Dobby, as though he were carrying something contagious."[5] Indeed, he is carrying something contagious: his individuality. Many abuse victims I have worked with in therapy were rejected by their own abusive families when they, the victims, began to heal and become free. They were scolded as "not knowing their place" or "thinking they're better than us" or "just wanting attention." Some of my clients had to walk away entirely from their original families, because they could not remain attached to an abusive system and still be healthy. But their independence and confidence and wholeness did indeed become contagious, and they often found new support systems. One client of mine decided that the day she was actually born into her abusive family was not something to celebrate, so she changed her celebration day to the anniversary of her graduation from therapy. She had spent months working hours a day in intensive group work to address the abuse—physical, emotional, and sexual—that had lasted from childhood into adulthood. In her mind, completing therapy was when she had actually become free and emerged into this world. To this day, she has no contact with her abusive biological family, but maintains close bonds with fellow survivors with whom she shares a deeper connection. Like Dobby, her freedom is contagious among those who support her, and she knows she owes nothing to those who had formerly abused her. As Dobby even said defiantly, "They isn't my masters anymore...Dobby doesn't care what they think anymore!"[6] Like Dobby, she also found an external, decorative way to announce her individuality: Dobby wore hats and socks, and my friend had the words "Loved Survivor" tattooed upon the very wrist she had once contemplated cutting.

Next, Dobby has to begin to put his experiences into words. "Dobby has no master! Dobby is a *free elf*!" Such a simple two-sentence phrase carries such poignancy to those who know what it means for him. Those two sentences represent Dobby's ability to identify exactly what has changed in his life; he sets himself apart from his past ("Dobby has no master!") and then makes a proud assertion that he is no longer a victim ("Dobby *is* a free elf!"); both statements are made in present tense. In real-life terms this is like being able to state, "I have grown from being a victim into being a survivor!" The word "victim" is not a bad word. It

5 *Harry Potter and the Goblet of Fire*, p.378
6 *Harry Potter and the Goblet of Fire*, p.381

isnot pejorative to use that word. In fact, it is entirely the right word to use to describe yourself in certain times of your life. Identifying yourself as a "victim" does not mean you are labeling yourself as "weak," it means you are clear that what happened to you was wrong, and that you were a victim of it. The term "survivor" is another stage of recovery you enter over time. "Dobby has no master! Dobby is a free elf!" is just as powerful and correct as stating "I have been a victim of abuse, rape, or other trauma. I am a survivor of that trauma, and am now free." It does not happen in an instant of stating it; you become able to state it after taking the time to make it true.

Notice that Dobby's emancipation doesn't result in a sudden and complete healing from his traumas. For example, at one point Dobby speaks ill of the Malfoys again, and "horror-struck by his own daring," instinctively returns to his habit of self-harming, throwing himself at a table. Harry grabs Dobby to prevent him from hurting himself, and as Dobby calms again he thanks Harry. "You just need a bit of practice," Harry replies.[7] Your traumas won't heal all at once, either. It happens in steps, and there are setbacks.

That exchange between Harry and Dobby contains much truth about healing from trauma. There will be times when old feelings will flood back again, and you will probably have instinctive returns to older, less-healthy reactions. Self-harm, substance abuse and addiction, dissociation, rage, and grief can sometimes make "return visits" to you. Like Harry said, being healed takes practice. It's not an all-or-none thing, and it doesn't happen at a point in time and then stay in place, like nailing a "survivor" certificate to a wall. Dobby slips up because his old traumas still flicker back into his mind, and that will happen to you, too. But like Dobby, don't give up on your progress because of setbacks. And like Harry said, keep practicing.

How to be like Dobby:

1. Dobby's development really begins after he is freed from the Malfoys. To begin healing from trauma, you have to first be apart from relationships in which you could be traumatized.

2. Dobby creates his own personality according to what makes him feel happy and fulfilled, and in ways that do not infringe on the rights of others. He does not remain stuck in the personality and role that the Malfoys imposed on him. Begin making choices for yourself about what you enjoy doing,

---

7 *Harry Potter and the Goblet of Fire,* p.381

how you look, where you go, who your friends are, and what beliefs and ideas you will claim as uniquely your own. Dobby's new way of life departs from the traditions and habits he had learned as an abuse victim.

3. Dobby becomes incredibly curious about life. As an abused house elf, he has never experienced a world beyond the misery of serving the Malfoys. As a free elf, Dobby becomes fascinated with the world and observes all of it that he can, choosing carefully which parts he will absorb and which parts he will reject. When you are free from abuse, don't stall. Become insatiably hungry for knowledge and experiences, being careful to only embrace the ones that strengthen and fulfill you. Devour books, learn about other cultures, interact with people who are different from you; your friendships should include people of many races, lifestyles, and belief systems, just like Dobby's.

4. Dobby explores his world. He has a "home base," Hogwarts, but he journeys and sees amazing moments. To be like Dobby, remember that it is more important to spend money on experiences rather than things. See as much of the natural world as you can: stand on mountaintops and in streams. Find strange and wonderful places and really experience them. Don't just take a quick cell phone picture and move on. Stop, be silent and thoughtful, and feel the wonder of the world you're in. It's important to remember how much beauty there is, especially after you've survived ugliness. Make that beauty part of you. Absorb moments and time into your heart the way your body absorbs food.

5. Dobby redefines himself, but he doesn't deny his past. When Dobby states that he has no master and is a free elf, he is acknowledging that there was a time when he did have a master/abuser, and yet he is not that victim anymore. To become healed of your abuse, perhaps the most important step you can ever take is to become unashamed that you were abused. Acknowledging your trauma is not "being stuck in the past" or "not getting over it," it's being honest about what has been part of your journey. Just be sure not to leave your personality stuck in that past. Like Dobby, who is now "a free elf," remember to add the current, free stage of your life to the story you tell about who you are.

6. Form healthy relationships. Dobby is remarkably able to

draw clear boundaries. When people insult his friends, he speaks up and objects. When people are kind, he notices and values their kindness. Dobby chooses his friends based on a very simple but important criteria: Are they kind? That's all. At first, Dobby is obsessively fascinated with Harry Potter because he is dazzled by Harry's reputed power, and Dobby associates power with value. But as he heals from his abuse (which was inflicted by others who also over-valued power) Dobby's friendships come to include men and women, people of all ages and races, without regard to their status, power, or prestige. When Dobby observes others being kind, he befriends them. When they are unkind, he avoids them. This is such a simple criteria, yet in real life we struggle so much with it!

7. Dobby speaks directly to others about what he needs and deserves. He no longer disregards his own needs, as many abuse victims do ("I don't deserve kindness or support; my problems are so trivial; other people are more deserving than I am") and he doesn't use his past victimization to manipulate others with a sense that he is owed special rights. He doesn't make other people tiptoe around his triggers, either. He simply speaks up for what's fair, including what he knows is fair to himself. He doesn't demand more than he's due, but doesn't accept less, either.

8. Dobby slips up, but keeps trying. He doesn't become perfectly healed. *Nobody* becomes "perfectly healed." Healing is a process, not an award that comes all at once at the end of a marathon. Until the day he dies, Dobby is still working to improve himself. When he messes up sometimes—as we all do—he gets back to self-healing work, and doesn't give up.

CHAPTER ELEVEN

Love That Isn't Love: Toxic Obsession

Real love has a paradoxical effect in the *Harry Potter* series. On one hand, it compels someone to protect the person they love from pain. But on the other hand, it can also mean allowing a person to face painful things that they need to face, in order to overcome them and heal. Nurturing, healthy love promotes the well-being of the beloved, and sometimes becoming well means going through a difficult process of recovering from trauma. A truly loving person will allow you to take those steps, as difficult as they are, helping you to build your strength—although they can support you, it is your work to do. Rescuing you from your own necessary struggle is not helpful, because it prevents you from actually developing your inner strength. It feels comforting to have someone to constantly rescue you from unhappiness, but that is neither authentically supportive nor loving. Uncle Vernon and Aunt Petunia have done exactly that for Dudley, ensuring him a life of constant pleasure and ease, but the effect is that Dudley does not develop internal strengths or meaningful relationships. Harry, on the other hand, is guided by his mentors to endure hardships, overcome them, and improve himself with each success, and it promotes real maturity and strength inside of him.

Love That Isn't Love: Toxic Obsession

Many victims of abuse have experienced another toxic form of attachment that might often be labeled "love," but which is actually a form of control and harm. People who inflict abuse on others, especially in close relationships (like parents and children, spouses, and dating partners) often disguise their abusive behavior as "love," claiming that they are too overwhelmed with romantic feelings to be able to control themselves, or are simply maintaining discipline, or are incredibly possessive. In my work with domestic abusers, I never met a single one who ever played hard to get; they were always romantic and grandiose at the beginning of their relationships in order to convince their partners that they were loving, generous, passionate people. As the relationship continued, they would also become more controlling, such as monitoring where their partners went, who their partners spent time with, becoming increasingly paranoid that they were being cheated on, and even using threats and mind games to keep their partners from leaving the relationship. At each step, they would claim that this was all part of "being in love," and even when they used outright violence they would later justify it by insisting they were provoked, or by acting remorseful afterward (with romantic gestures, such as gifts, flattery, and pleading) in order to keep the victim from leaving.

Having an inaccurate view of what love is can make someone more vulnerable to being hurt in a relationship. Relationships in which there is verbal, physical, or sexual abuse are not loving, even though there might be romantic feelings flowing alongside the abuse. One of the first myths we need to throw in the trash is that romance and passion are the same thing as real love. Romantic feelings are not enough to base a healthy relationship on, as we see in the obsession that binds Ron and Lavender together. Lavender is so obsessed by fairy-tale romantic feelings toward him that she is never truly his equal in the relationship. Although there is no actual abuse between them, it is also not a healthy partnership because there is no foundation of equality, deep communication, or freedom. Lavender is so consumed that she values Ron more than she values herself. Ron eats up all the attention, which gives him an appetite for romantic entitlement like a rock star with a fan. At one point, Harry even criticizes their relationship as unhealthy, disagreeing with Lavender that Ron is an interesting boyfriend: "Would you call getting poisoned being interesting?" What has linked Lavender and Ron together is obsession, not love. They have become each other's whole worlds, rather than being equal partners who also have interests, friends, and activities outside the relationship.

The second myth about love that we need to get rid of is that emotion is enough to base a relationship on. Love is a behavior, not (just) a feeling.

There is a dangerous myth that "love is all we need" for a good relationship, and that as long as you "listen to your heart" you will be fine. That is not the case! Love is not a set of pleasant emotions. A healthy relationship is identified by the consistent behaviors that are shown, not the strong feelings that are felt. Many unhealthy relationships are fully soaked with romantic feelings. "But I love him!" isn't actually a basis for continuing a relationship that isn't working. Actually, leaving a toxic relationship can be hard because romantic feelings may still be strong, and some people even have to break free from a relationship with someone they still feel passion for, because they recognize that things are not healthy. Waiting to fall out of love is not the schedule for when to leave a toxic relationship; the time to leave is when you realize the relationship is toxic. Judge a relationship by behaviors, not emotions.

Emotions don't always tell you the truth about something. Many abuse victims feel unlovable, damaged for life, unworthy, and ashamed; these emotions are all absolutely real, but they are not truths. Abusers know this, and will often use your emotions to keep you confused about what you have experienced. The romantic abuser, for example, will begin a relationship with an immediate flood of passion—they've never felt this way before, you're the only person in the world who can understand them, you're instant soul mates—in order to gain quick control over you. As the relationship becomes more unhealthy, though, they will also use romance to keep you with them, such as the "after-abuse apology," in which they give gifts and make grand gestures of passion to you. The goal is to keep you focused on your fantasy of what love *could* be like if you work through the problems, so that you will forgive and accept the abuser.

Abusers of children also use emotional manipulation. Not all child abuse is terrifying and painful at the time because many abusers use gifts, kindness, and special attention to confuse child victims into feeling warmth toward the abuser. Even while the abuse is ongoing, many child victims do not feel traumatized *at the time* because the abuser might be a loved one who also makes the child feel very special. One of the toughest stuck points to work through in therapy is when victims of childhood abuse feel guilty because they felt affection for their abuser, craved their attention, sought time with them, and enjoyed the sense of being special. Not all abusers work this way, but many do, especially in cases where the abuse is committed by a supposed caretaker or authority figure, is ongoing, and where the abuser is trying to avoid being caught. Feeling warmth and affection toward someone who is also abusive because they have been generous with gifts, flattery, and attention toward a child victim is actually perfectly normal. It also shows us, though, that emotions don't always express truth.

Love That Isn't Love: Toxic Obsession

People who are controlling and possessive in relationships tend to repeat their habits in each subsequent relationship they have. I've worked with victims of domestic and dating violence who spent years feeling guilty for being abused, because they thought it was their fault (they were *told* it was their fault), and they constantly wondered, "what did I do to cause this? If I could only figure out how to fix this problem, or change myself in some way, they would finally be happy and stop doing this to me." These feelings of self-blame could last for years. But in reality, we find that abusers bring their patterns of control into each relationship they have. One of the red flags I noticed in my work with abusers is that they would continually talk about previous victims—all of them!—as if the *victims* were always the bad ones in every relationship. In their mind, it was always the other person who was disrespectful, crazy, and to blame for the violence. Even rapists in prison would flat-out deny that they had done anything wrong, insisting that their victims brought it on themselves and then lied about what had happened.

The belief that someone has a right to you, to your body, your feelings, and your devotion, is a product of a distorted view of love. In so many ways, we are taught to think that love is a form of obsessive passion in which we can't help ourselves, because we are swept out of control by our feelings. In reality, that is the opposite of love; true, healthy love *promotes* personal choice, decision-making rights, and the freedom to have a world outside the relationship itself. In healthy love, neither person is idealized as perfect, nor has more power and control than the other person; they do not demand loyalty, do not feel entitled to possess the other person, and do not see the other person as less human if they choose to not continue the relationship.

Dobby the house elf is not able to express healthy love at the beginning of the *Harry Potter* books. He idealizes Harry so much that he develops a warped view of both Harry's worth and his own. The first time he meets Harry, Dobby is awestruck by even being asked to sit, remarking that nobody has ever treated him as an equal before. He sees himself as less worthy than Harry, because that is what he has been taught all his life. Consequently, he over-values Harry, and under-values himself. To Harry's credit, he tries to treat Dobby well (despite becoming angry with him at times), rather than taking advantage of Dobby's sense of inferiority. But Dobby does not have a concept of healthy love, so instead he worships Harry. His obsession even causes him to continually harm himself any time he feels he has let Harry down, despite scheming to manipulate Harry by withholding his letters and tricking him into missing a train to return to Hogwarts.

Love That Isn't Love: Toxic Obsession

I've counseled abuse victims who had similar beliefs about relationships, including over-valuing anyone who treated them with the simple respect they deserved, and harming themselves any time they felt they'd failed someone else. Sometimes, this Dobby-like fantasy even flows from clients toward therapists: "you're the *only one* who can help me, because nobody else understands me like you do!" Often in groups, someone would remain silent and passive because they felt they were undeserving of any care. They would set aside their own needs because they saw others as so much more worthy.

But Dobby is a curious character in that he shows not just traits of an inferior-feeling victim, but traits of a controller as well. His attitude toward Harry is one of obsession not just in the sense that he over-idealizes Harry, but also in that he wants Harry's attention all to himself. He steals Harry's letters, for example, to cause Harry to feel abandoned by his friends in hopes that Harry will decide not to return to school, and he tries to get Harry punished by the Dursleys when his first plan doesn't work. Some attentive readers are rebuking me right now, "but Dobby was only doing that to save Harry from danger!" As a plot point, that seems true. But as an analogy to controlling love, keep in mind that many possessive people also claim that their actions were "for your own good," or "I was just trying to help you," or "you're lucky to have someone like me fix all the stuff you screw up." Dobby may have a far-reaching agenda to protect Harry from Voldemort, but his methods of doing so deny Harry his right to make free choices for himself, and rely on deception and isolation to separate Harry from his friends. He resorts to self-harm to manipulate Harry, sabotages a bludger to intentionally injure Harry, and he blocks Harry from being able to ride the Hogwarts Express back to school (much like the man who takes a spark plug out of a car so his victim can't leave him).

In real-life controlling relationships, we see many of these same traits. In my work with dating and domestic violence, for example, I have encountered situations where one person controls their partner's life in order to keep complete control over them. They regulate where the other person can go, whom they can talk to, what they wear, and how they look. They monitor cell phone calls, sneak into their emails, follow them, have friends report on them, and are constantly suspicious of the other person cheating. Sometimes this is done as clear, direct, unabashed control, but in most cases the controlling person justifies their actions by disguising it as love: "I just want to be with you all the time; you're my whole world; I'm only trying to keep you safe; I can't stand the thought of you being with anyone else; without you I wouldn't want to live; if you left me, I would hurt or kill myself; the thought of you even wanting to do anything without me upsets me..." This type of "I love you/I control you for your own good" thinking is not healthy, but it's exactly how Dobby relates to Harry when we first meet Dobby.

Just to be clear, I adore Dobby. I'm not attacking a beloved character. But I adore him because of who he becomes, not the person he starts as. In his early roles, Dobby is a controlling, possessive character. He expresses "love that isn't love" in the form of obsession that hurts the one it is directed at. Over the next five years, Dobby is able to unlearn many of his attitudes, though, and develops a sense of real respect for Harry and his friends (idealizing someone to the point that either of your real lives is weakened or controlled is not respect). Dobby, then, is an example of a victim who has never learned what healthy love actually is, but is able to change his thinking as he heals from his own abuse. Like many people who grow up only experiencing power, control, and cruelty, he has no other way to possibly understand relationships. Even though he wants to be kind and supportive to Harry, his only experiences are with control and manipulation, so he lacks any better understandings. For many victims of abuse, this is also true, until they begin to form healthier relationships that show them new ways to think and behave toward others. Dobby serves as a symbol of both warning and hope—a warning in the sense that he is at risk for remaining stuck in the unhealthy lessons that he has learned from his experiences, and hope because he shows that we can unlearn those toxic beliefs and become healthy.

How do we unlearn those toxic beliefs and replace them with a clearer understanding of healthy love?

Romantic, Addictive, and Nurturing Relationships

To be clear, when I use the word "love," I am not talking only about romantic love. There are many forms of love in the *Harry Potter* series, as there are in life. There is the kind of love like Harry has for Ron, Hermione, Sirius, Professor Lupin, and Dumbledore, which is the selfless, sacrificing love we have for a cherished friend. We do also see examples of romantic attraction and love, such as what Harry feels for Cho (and later, Ginny), what Snape felt for Lily, and what Ron feels for Lavender (and eventually Hermione). In order to differentiate healthy from toxic forms of love, we have to consider three main types of attraction.

The first type is **Romantic Attachment**, characterized by these beliefs:

- I could never find another person to love the way I love this person.

- No one could ever understand my partner the way I do.

- From the time we first got together, my attraction to my partner was so strong I couldn't control it.

- I try to ignore faults in my partner and see only the best in him/her.

- If we broke up, I would never be able to love again.

- I never let my partner see me without being dressed and made up perfectly. I only want them to see me at my best.

- I don't know why I love my partner, I just do.

- My partner is so much smarter and more capable than I am, and they seem perfect.

- My partner is so special, I don't know why they would be interested in an ordinary person like me.

- Sometimes I think my partner and I took things too fast in the relationship.

Romantic attraction is the "sugar high" form of love. This is Ron and Lavender's relationship. In this kind of bond, people tend to feel controlled by their emotions ("I can't help it, I just feel overwhelmed with passion!") They start relationships quickly, they constantly crave the euphoria they felt in the early stages, and they become bored with their partner when that emotional sugar high wears off. When that happens, they will tend to either jump into a new relationship very quickly, or remain miserable in their current relationship, because either option is seen as a way to (hopefully) get back to that previous happiness.

The risks of romantic relationships are that people don't develop long-term skills or bonds, and they become guided by emotions, seeking pleasure rather than enduring and healthy commitment. If the relationship becomes unhappy or even abusive, there is more likelihood of being emotionally manipulated by the abuser, such as with gifts, flattery, pleading for more chances, and fantasies of "working it out" and "getting back to how it used to be." Romantic attractions also tend to become sexual very quickly, which can expose someone to harm, both emotionally and physically, and make it harder to break free of the relationship later. In this relationship, people also tend to value their partners more than themselves, idealizing them and feeling lucky to have been chosen by them.

While not all Romantic-type attractions are abusive, they do have unequal power and control in them. Romantic attractions do not empower you, they give you bursts of energy while things are happy, but over the long term they diminish your strength by making someone else your whole world. As a result, romantic attraction always changes from its original form into something else…

The second relationship type is **Addictive Attraction**, characterized by these beliefs:

- Without him/her, I have nothing to live for.

- I suppose I should be more interested in other people and activities, but I just want to be with my one partner.

- Whenever I'm a few minutes late or want to be alone, he/she worries that I'm with another person.

- He/she sometimes says or does mean things when they're mad, but when we calm down again he/she promises to change.

- Sometimes I feel better when I'm away from him/her, yet I still call or visit him/her when I know it's not a good idea.

- I feel that I'm nothing without the other person.

- I've thought about leaving my partner before, but I don't think I could make it without him/her

- My partner is afraid that I will change or become different.

- I find myself defending or minimizing his/her actions, even when what they did was wrong.

- My partner loves me so much that he/she becomes jealous and wants to know where I am every minute.

Addictive relationships do indeed function very much like drug dependency. They often start as romantic attraction, but as power and control become more and more imbalanced, one person eventually becomes dominant and the other person is diminished. Many people in addictive relationships still feel romantic attraction to the other person, but the romantic happiness itself has vanished. What's left in its place is a sense of desperation, which leads you to doing things that are unhealthy or harmful so that you can be together. Even when one person has become free of the relationship, the other, still-addicted person may not be willing to let go of their own obsessions.

Not every addictive relationship is abusive, but the risks are highest in this type. In fact, some addictive relationships seem loving and romantic to those who equate addiction with passion: Edward Cullen and Bella Swan in *Twilight* have a relationship that begins as the Romantic type, but becomes Addictive, including full-blown stalking, controlling jealousy, self-injury to manipulate the other person, and risk of emotional and physical harm as a consequence of the relationship.

In the *Harry Potter* books, Severus Snape's obsession for Lily Evans begins as a romantic attraction, but becomes addictive over time. At first, he is enraptured by Lily, and thinks he has found his soul mate and true love. He even feels lucky to have her companionship because he is not popular but she is, and it makes him feel special to have her affection. But Snape is also increasingly possessive toward Lily: he watches her "greedily"; he uses magic to injure those he thinks might threaten his special bond with Lily (such as striking Lily's sister Petunia with a tree limb); he hopes to control which house she will be sorted into ("you'd better be in Slytherin"); and he resents Lily's time spent with anyone else but him. He even rebukes her for forming other friendships, snapping that he "thought we were supposed to be friends...*best* friends?" and tries to regain control over her by telling her he won't let her continue to associate with other people ("Let me? *Let me*?" she replies). Like many controlling people, Snape justifies himself by claiming he is only doing all of this for her own good, to protect her, because he knows what's best for her: "I just don't want to see you made a fool of" (which is a put-down disguised as concern). When his efforts fail, he resorts to a more direct attack against Lily herself, spitefully calling her a Mudblood. He immediately begins apologizing (see #4 above), but Lily refuses to accept the apology. She points out that he constantly resorts to verbal abuse toward anyone he dislikes, and that she knows this is a choice of behaviors he has made, not some tragic flaw he can't help.

Love That Isn't Love: Toxic Obsession

I've probably made some fans upset by casting Severus Snape as an addictive and unhealthy relationship for Lily, but the case is accurate. Snape hurts Lily, wants to keep her dependent on him, forbids her any friendships he hasn't approved, controls where she goes and what she thinks, and lashes out at her whenever she refuses to comply. Snape is obsessed with Lily, but his obsession is more about how Lily fulfills his needs than how committed he is to her well-being. To Snape, though, this *is* love. He feels it deeply. While I fault Snape for his treatment of Lily and for mistaking his own addiction to her as a form of true love, I do recognize that his emotions are absolutely real. He genuinely does feel the pain that we see him feel. His feelings for her are tragic, and Snape may be doing the best he can. He's never had healthy love modeled for him (we learn that he comes from a family where fighting is routine), and Lily represents a form of escape from his misery that he hadn't ever hoped to find before meeting her. He idealizes her as a person, fantasizes about what they should be like together, tries to force the relationship into that arrangement, mistreats anyone else he sees as a threat to his fantasy, and cannot function healthily when Lily chooses not to continue their bond. To Snape, these sincerely are heartbreaking disasters, and he really is hurt. For that, he has my compassion, and I pityingly adore him as a flawed, incomplete man who lives in despair after his own addictive attraction to Lily collapses. When Snape sheds tears for Lily, his grief is real. His remorse at his own role in her death is real. His heroism is real. Snape's emotions *are real*. Even Dumbledore describes them as "the best of" Snape. They're just not healthy love.[1]

Still, we are warned not to confuse obsession with real love. While explaining the Amortentia potion, Professor Slughorn makes sure to explain, "Amortentia doesn't really create love, of course. It is impossible to manufacture or imitate love. No, this will simply cause a powerful infatuation or obsession. It is probably the most dangerous and powerful potion in this room - oh yes…When you have seen as much of life as I have, you will not underestimate the power of obsessive love."[2]

Healthy love, on the other hand, moves you to also uplift the worth of others, and to support others in their own quest for fulfillment. It does not constrain, it frees. It does not wound, it nurtures. These are the traits of **Nurturing Love:**

---

1 J.K. Rowling validates this view of Snape, writing, "Snape is all grey. You can't make him a saint: he was vindictive & bullying. You can't make him a devil: he died to save the wizarding world." Twitter, 27 Nov 2015
2 *Harry Potter and the Half-Blood Prince,* p.186

- I know exactly what it is about him/her I love.

- We help each other explore new possibilities in life.

- Loving my partner makes me feel more loving towards other people.

- I am happy when I am with my partner, but he/she is not my whole world.

- I feel good about myself when I'm with my partner.

- My partner isn't worried that I might change as a person; they even encourage me to.

- My partner is the kind of person I would like my children to be like when they grow up.

- It's wonderful to spend time with my partner having fun together, but I also do these things with other people. I enjoy being by myself or with other friends too.

- When we argue, I feel safe. I'm never scared of my partner's temper—not even a little.

- I like to hear about the good times he/she's had when he/she's been with other people.

Nurturing love wants your loved one to be fulfilled as a person, to become all they can be, and to have huge worlds beyond the relationship itself. Even in the midst of arguments, there is no fear because each person is equal to the other; because power is shared equally, it disappears from the relationship. Neither person controls the other.

In a nurturing relationship, each person can identify exactly what they admire about the other, as well as what flaws they each have. There are no fantasies of being perfect, because each has taken the time to learn about the other person's true self (you would never hear someone describe the "perfect nurturing love" they have with someone they met last week, for example). Respect has been earned over time, which is why nurturing relationships are never sudden. They unfold slowly as people

Love That Isn't Love: Toxic Obsession

discover things about one another, the way Harry, Hermione, and Ron all do in their friendship. Despite the teasing and offended feelings that come with being young and trying to grow into mature friendships, the three friends earn one another's respect over the years. They become more and more committed to not doing things that cause someone else to be hurt. They protect one another, they feel comfortable and safe with each other, and if you were ask them what they admire about the others, they could absolutely tell you. Ron, Hermione, and Harry know more about each other's deepest desires, fears, weaknesses and strengths than any merely-romantic partner could.

This kind of love, then, is knowledge-and respect-based. The love that represents the most powerful magic in *Harry Potter* isn't shallow, sugary crushes, and it's not yearning, obsessive dependence. It's the love that uplifts the worth of the other, which brings happiness and wholeness to each person. Sirius Black, for example, at one point becomes the living person that Harry loves most, because they form a relationship in which there is respect, protection, sacrifice, and wholeness. In fact, Harry's love for Sirius is so powerful that Voldemort is unable to possess Harry because of it; Dumbledore explains that he cannot inhabit a body so overflowing with love. In this parable, we see the lesson that nurturing love is, again, one of the medicines that helps heal trauma.

Take in the important lesson, too, that healing love is not necessarily romantic love. Many victims of abuse crave passionate romantic relationships in hope that such relationships will fulfill them. I think this is because romantic love feels so sweet and joyful at first, and that bliss feels like an antidote to trauma, depression, and grief. As long as we keep up the sugar high of romance, we'll be fine, right? Romantic pleasure is not healing, though. It does not help you form deeper bonds with others who know your true self, including the part of you that is wounded and needs understanding. It does not nudge you toward facing your pain and overcoming it (in fact, it usually does the opposite by giving you flashy, sweet sensations that keep you distracted until they fade, training you to pursue pleasure rather than growth). Healing love, though, happens in many types of relationships. Harry has a loving relationship with both Sirius and Ron, for example. A relationship in which you are safe, supported, valued, encouraged to grow and change, respected, and not put down because of your fears or weaknesses, is a healing, loving relationship, whether it is friendship-based, mentor-based, therapeutic, or romantic.

Kissing Cho Chang is an incredible moment for Harry, but it does not help him actually become stronger or more healed in the long run. Forming nurturing bonds with Sirius, Ron, Hermione, Dumbledore, and Molly and Arthur Weasley does, however. If Harry had joined Draco and the other power-hungry Slytherins, he would never have developed even the potential for nurturing love, since nurturing love by definition forfeits power and seeks equality with loved ones. Likewise, if Harry had continued to be abused, he would not have been able to heal, either. As you are healing, pay attention to the types of relationships you have, because they will impact your progress. Seek allies and companions who offer true understanding and friendship, not just sexy, ecstatic romance, and especially not needy, controlling, confining addiction.

CHAPTER TWELVE

Hogwarts and Equal Rights

"Dumbledore would have been happier than anybody to think
that there was a little more love in the world."[1]

     For a time, I worked with abusers in therapy as part of a court-mandated program they would attend, and sometimes I also conducted groups in prisons. I was able to learn from abusers themselves why they had committed abuse—not just the excuses they give for it, but the real reasons. If you were to ask any abuser why they had committed abuse, they nearly always explain that they were only doing something their victim had provoked or deserved. For example, abusers in a domestic violence group would explain their abusiveness with excuses that invariably began with the words, "because she…"

     Abusers see relationships from a top-down perspective, where having power and control makes someone superior to others. For them, the mere fact that they can abuse is what gives them the right to abuse, in the sense that being stronger and tougher than someone else entitles them to natural dominance. It's important to understand that abuse is not caused by an anger management problem, or by being provoked under stress—it's caused by a mindset. It's their belief system that tells them they have a right to behave this way because they feel their rights are being disrespected, and they are entitled to use force to regain complete control over another.

1 *Harry Potter and the Half-Blood Prince,* p.624

Hogwarts and Equal Rights

Abusers will use nearly any tactic to remain in control; I have worked with abusers who can become extremely romantic, considerate, and sweet to their partners or children as a way to manipulate people into forgiving them, giving them more chances, dropping charges, and appearing good in public. These same abusers become terrifying in private with their victims, using violence and threats. One of the things that often frustrates victims of abuse is how people outside the abusive relationships never see what's really happening, and pressure them to "give him another chance" or "forgive her, because she just made a mistake; she's really such a good person!"

I've also seen abusers fault their victims for the abuse. In fact, this is perhaps one of the most evident traits of an abuser: someone who hurts, mistreats, and humiliates you, and then tells you that what they did is your fault. Whether it's a rapist who blames you for causing them to rape, or a batterer who insists you provoked them to violence, abusers always hand their guilt to their victims to bear. Even when an abuser is begging and pleading for forgiveness to keep a victim from leaving them, the tactic is only temporary until they need to wield power and control again.

Abusiveness is a learned behavior, drawn from many sources. Draco Malfoy would not have been such a bully had he not been indoctrinated into a belief in his superiority over others by his father. Crabbe and Goyle, as well, were recruited by Draco and indoctrinated by him, too, as well as by their own death eater fathers. One of the tactics abusers learn is to be publicly charming; Lucius Malfoy is extremely skilled at keeping himself under control when others are watching, he gives generously to charities, and seems to always be in control of his temper. His abusiveness is very cunning. This is why I say that abusers don't have anger management problems (or, at least that's not what causes them to be abusive); most are very good at hiding their abuse in public, which would not be the case if they were out of control. Far from it; abusers are very much *in* control of what they do, which is why they tend to abuse in places and ways where they will not be easily caught. Some of the most important warning signs of a potential abuser include:

- disrespect toward former victims/partners,
- disrespect toward you (including disrespect disguised as teasing or "for your own good"),
- offering to forgive *you* if you only try harder to fix what they have done,
- jealous and possessive behavior,
- justifying their abusive behavior toward their victims,

- intimidating people into submitting to them,
- the belief that certain types of people are inferior,
- idolizing other bullies and power-holding authoritarians as "real men" and "just what the world needs to get us back on track."

In the *Harry Potter* books, we see all of these traits in each abusive character, whether it's Voldemort demanding complete loyalty and service from his followers and inflicting harm on them if they have failed, to the Dursleys insulting and neglecting Harry because they feel he deserves it. Throughout the books, the belief that certain kinds of people are inferior is one of the main traits we see in villain characters, too: the Dursleys believe having magical powers is shameful and disgusting, and try to deny to themselves that such things even exist. The death eaters see Muggles and non-pureblood Wizards as inferior people who deserve to be oppressed and even tortured.

I've seen similar attitudes in the abusers I've encountered in my anti-violence work, too. Many of the abusers who have spoken with me believe that they have superiority over others, such as their certainty that women are inferior to men, gay and lesbian people deserve to be picked on and denied equality, other races are subordinate to their own, and tough people run the world. Even more telling, most of the abusers also told me that they think that everyone else secretly believes the same things too, but are too shy or "politically correct" to admit it. Men who rape, for example, often believe that what they've done is something any other man would probably do too, if given the chance, and that they simply got unfairly caught doing it. All of these beliefs are learned, and abusers use them to maintain a worldview in which they are supreme above others. Even some people who publicly take an anti-abuse stance revert to abusive actions against those they think deserve it, such as men who use vulgar terms for women with whom they disagree, people who cheer/mock the prospect of someone being raped in prison, and using feminine terms to describe weakness—all of which J.K. Rowling has publicly called out.[2]

Social scientists call this an "authoritarian" mindset. An authoritarian person demands strict obedience at the expense of personal freedom, and does not offer genuine warmth or acceptance in return. They tend to over-punish, mock sensitivity or vulnerability as weak, treat women as inferior to men, believe they are entitled to sex, and think that being tough is an

---

2 See for example, Rowling's tweets on 7 June 2017 about the use of misogynist vulgarities toward women by men who otherwise consider themselves non-abusive: "Every woman I know who has dared express an opinion publically has endured this kind of abuse at least once, rooted in an apparent determination to humiliate or intimidate her on the basis that she is female."

important virtue. Children who are raised by authoritarian parents tend to be very good at following rules, but not as good at understanding other peoples' points of view or experiences. They—both the authoritarian parent and the child—tend to associate love with obedience, and to have very rigid gender roles, such as men being tough and in control, while women are emotional and submissive. Top-down beliefs about relationships go hand-in-hand with abusiveness: they don't *always* lead to abuse, but abusers *always* have these beliefs.

In your own healing journey, you will find that it becomes important not just to mend the emotional wounds inside of you, but to work to diminish these abusive mindsets in the world itself. However, surviving abuse can make it difficult to challenge some of these ideas, particularly if you have bought into the idea that if *you* were also tougher and superior, you would not have been abused. Many abuse victims do, for a while, adopt the idea that toughness is the antidote to being abused, and that if they could become a fiercer person, they'd finally be safe. Unfortunately, becoming controlling and tough in order to be superior to others increases the amount of abusive thinking in the world, rather than reducing it. Plus, the idea that toughness is protective can lead to additional inner shame, because it suggests that people are abused because they are weak. If you adopt this Draco Malfoy-like philosophy of strength, your actual inner shame may increase because it means you've accepted the myth that strong people rule weak people, and if you've ever been abused it must mean you were weak.

Instead, the goal is to reduce the total rate of abusive thinking in the world, which means rejecting superficial toughness as a form of strength, and developing a different type of strength that makes room for others to be your equal, that protects yourself from traumatic shame, that uplifts those around you who need allies, and that respects the needs of others as part of true friendships. Fortunately, the world of *Harry Potter* offers us examples and role models, both of what to do and what not to do, to affirm this deeper, more healing type of strength.

The friendship of Ron, Harry and Hermione gives us a good model for what abuse-free equality can actually look like. Hermione, who as a girl is the minority member of the trio, is seldom treated as if she belongs less than the two guys. The ease with which Ron and Harry relate to her as an essential, valued, equal member of the group shows that this kind of relationship can be natural. Let me be clear: I am not applauding the two guys for being cool enough to accept her, since that would still be a sexist nod to Ron and Harry as actually being the ones who are entitled to make the choice whether to accept a girl sidekick. Rather, what I am saying is that all three members of the friendship *choose the other two* as their friends, which means Hermione is not an accessory that the two boys bring along. Hermione is absolutely comfortable challenging them, setting boundaries with them, and insisting that they treat her in respectful ways, which they don't always do. The two guys don't accept her as an equal right away; early on, Hermione is teased and treated as a lesser partner by Harry and Ron, and when Harry rescues her with Ron's help, it creates a hierarchy in their minds that Hermione spends years undoing.

Hermione's gifts save the other two repeatedly, and not just because she was luckily endowed with amazing magical powers. It is she who is able to use logic, math, and unconventional thinking to solve riddles, and she who acts quickly when the others are dumbstruck with indecision. She does not wait for other people to come rescue her when she is in danger, and when she has been insulted she does not act as if someone else ought to take up for her. She responds personally and directly. Hermione is also more insightful than her friends about relationships, and is usually the one to explain nuanced feelings to the others, such as helping Harry understand why Ron has become jealous of him, or why Cho is upset by her conflicted attraction to Harry after the death of Cedric Diggory.

If I have one critique of her character at all, it's that she is presented as being so completely *different* from the other girls in these ways, when in fact I have found that smart, strong, independent, capable girls are quite common, and make terrific friends. We can strive for a world in which girls like Hermione are not treated as unusually rare, but rather how the world helps all girls, everywhere, to be. The Hermione we come to know in the books, however, is more useful to us in our healing than the Hermione in the films; "book" Hermione often forgets her own strengths and abilities, and has to be reminded of them at times ("Are you a witch or not?" demands Ron, when Hermione forgets her own skills). "Book" Hermione's hands shake with fear at times, and she doesn't always get spells right, or know the right thing to say, or have the courage to face what frightens her. "Movie" Hermione, however, suffers none of these faults. In your healing, remember to allow yourself to be more like "book" Hermione: imperfect, occasionally afraid, and accepting the support and encouragement of others. Whether you are female or male, you can find healing lessons in Hermione's strengths *and* weaknesses; a healthy person draws wisdom from both female and male role models.

One of the ways J.K. Rowling helps us understand the importance of equality is by showing us examples of people who just *don't* get it. Even characters who mature to respect others often err in their acceptance of sexist ideas along the way. For example, Ron repeatedly berates his sister

Hogwarts and Equal Rights

Ginny for dating a couple of guys during her fourth year: "D'you think I want people saying my sister's a—"

"A what?" shouted Ginny, drawing her wand. A *what*, exactly?"

Ron is lashing out at her, shaming her for exercising her own choice of who her romantic interests will be, which is a controlling attitude by Ron. Ginny, rebukes him for his sexism: "let's get this straight once and for all. It is none of your business who I go out with or what I do with them, Ron…" And she's 100% right. Part of being a free person is having the right to spend time with whomever you like, and not being controlled, shamed, or accused for it. Ron eventually matures into a man who not only accepts but embraces his equality with others, but until that happens he does have an attitude of judgmental superiority toward the girls in his life.

In *Goblet of Fire*, scandal journalist Rita Skeeter writes a smear piece in which she portrays Hermione as a scheming temptress who has broken Harry's heart, even though nothing of the sort is true. Hermione is certain this is just nonsense that nobody would possibly care about, but Molly Weasley actually becomes angry with Hermione over it. To Molly, Hermione's not just wrong for allegedly hurting Harry, but for doing what any girl ought to be free to do at any time: choosing who she dates, when she breaks up with him, and who she dates afterward. Even if it were true, there would be no cause for Molly to resent Hermione for it. Molly's mind doesn't change on the matter until Harry, not Hermione, puts it right for her. It takes a male's input to settle the matter for Molly, which diminishes Hermione's status in the situation even further. I adore Molly Weasley, but even good people can have "blind spots" when it comes to subconscious beliefs about men's and women's roles. Someone who understands full equality would have realized that anyone, male or female, has the right to choose their partners, including the right to end the relationship. Denying this right to a girl and considering her to be scandalous for exercising her rights in a relationship is a form of inequality.

Throughout the books there are many other examples of characters failing to grasp the importance of equality. Ron resents Hermione for dating Victor Krum, but is perfectly happy to have Lavender Brown fawn all over him. Clearly, Ron has immature attitudes toward women and relationships, and it takes a lot for him to outgrow his stance that men ought to be in control, and his actions have consequences (we remember Lavender from her lowest moments in the book as a "girlfriend prop" for Ron, while her later bravery and death during the Battle of Hogwarts are barely celebrated). Attitudes that foster inequality cause harm because they reduce others to mere accessories to someone else's more important ambitions.

So that my point is not missed, let me clarify that I am not claiming that the *Harry Potter* series is sexist, or that J.K. Rowling had sexist attitudes that she wrote into her characters. I think the opposite is true. I think J.K. Rowling intentionally wrote sexism into her characters at times in order to demonstrate what sexist attitudes look like, and even more importantly, how we outgrow them as we mature. J.K. Rowling herself has said that "the Potter books are a prolonged argument for tolerance, a prolonged plea for the end of bigotry," and researchers agree. In one study, young readers of the *Harry Potter* books showed diminished prejudices against other races, LGBT people, and racial minorities.[3]

As counterpoints to her characters' sexism, she also offers role models for equality and respect, such as Albus Dumbledore and Minerva McGonagall, who work together closely and with complete respect for one another. Arthur Weasley clearly adores and respects his wife Molly, and treats her with complete equality. Ron and Harry exhibit misguided attitudes toward girls and dating, and suffer the consequences when their dates become utterly disinterested in them and choose to leave the relationship.

J.K. Rowling has revealed that Albus Dumbledore is a gay man, a fact that is never an issue during any detail in the books except when Rita Skeeter makes innuendos that Dumbledore's relationship with Harry is somehow unnatural and unhealthy. Skeeter never elaborates to the point of specifically citing Dumbledore's sexuality, but she is referencing a homophobic myth about gay men and children. In writing Rita Skeeter this way, Rowling is showing us that acceptance of prejudices against non-heterosexual people is a trait shared with the likes of Skeeter, a character who has no regard for facts or the damage her bigotry causes. The characters we admire reject Skeeter-like thinking, and want no part in her brand of narrow-mindedness. Rowling has repeatedly affirmed that every person, of any age, gender, and race, gay or straight, should find a place in which to truly belong: "If Harry Potter has taught us anything, it's that no one should live in a closet."[4]

When Hermione learns that her food at Hogwarts was prepared by house elves, she refuses it because she has seen how elves are treated during the Quidditch World Cup. She wants no part of a system in which others are mistreated or regarded as having lesser worth. Ron and Harry are at best indifferent to the matter, until Hermione forms the group S.P.E.W. ("Society for the Promotion of Elfish Welfare"), and some students join,

3 Vezzali, L., Stathi, S., Giovannini, D., Capozza, D. and Trifiletti, E. (2015), The Greatest Magic of Harry Potter: Reducing Prejudice. *J Appl Soc Psychol*, 45: 105–121. doi:10.1111/jasp.12279. Online at http://onlinelibrary.wiley.com/doi/10.1111/jasp.12279/abstract
4 Twitter, @jk_rowling, December 16, 2014

although mostly to stop Hermione from badgering them about her cause. Ron even mocks the group as S.P.U.G., "Society for the Protection of Ugly Goblins," itself a demeaning slur disguised as a joke.

It's not until the others really form affection for Dobby, and are heartbroken by the sacrifice of his life for them, that they truly begin to see house elves as something more than servants. During the Battle of Hogwarts, they suddenly realize that the Elves themselves will be annihilated by the death eaters if they are not protected as well. At last, the lives of Elves have meaning to Ron and Harry, as they have had to Hermione for years. Little by little, the characters grow away from their younger indifference toward inequality, and become more committed to it.

I am not claiming that every attitude of inequality is full-blown abuse. I am, however, claiming that without exception, and even by definition, abusers see other people as less worthy than themselves. They arrange their relationships into hierarchies where they deserve the most privilege, and others deserve less. This hierarchy allows them to think that they are entitled to mistreat others, and their victims deserve the mistreatment. In relationships where abuse is ongoing, many victims try to cope by frantically wondering what more they can do to avoid provoking the abuser, how they can please the abuser more, and how they can change themselves to become less abused—all of which amounts to offering more power and control to the abuser. Abusers do not think of their victims as being equal to themselves, and despite blaming their victims ("if you'd only...! I told you not to...! It's your fault; you make me do this to you!"), they cannot actually conceive of a possibility that their victims will truly ever deserve equality.

As you are healing from your abuse, you will need to identify and reject the attitudes your abuser held. It's impossible to heal from abuse if you also hold the same beliefs that your perpetrator had, because those beliefs serve to justify their actions against you. Victims who still believe "I deserved it; I caused it; it's my fault" are subconsciously maintaining a belief that they are inferior, and that the abuser was justified by a superior motive and a superior position over them. As long as you look inwardly to find what was wrong, you cannot see yourself as someone who deserves equality, because seeing wrongness inside of you is what your perpetrator did, too. Albus Dumbledore, when speaking to the students after the tragedy of the Triwizard Championship, reminded them (as us):

> ...We are only as strong as we are united, as weak as we are di-
> vided. Lord Voldemort's gift for spreading discord and enmity
> is very great. We can fight it only by showing an equally strong

bond of friendship and trust. Differences of habit and language are nothing at all if our aims are identical and our hearts are open.[5]

In order to overcome self-blame for your traumas, one thing that becomes necessary is the absolute rejection of inequality between types of people. *Actions* can change how much respect someone deserves (for example, your abuser is less worthy of it than you are), but until someone removes themselves from the human community through their own abusive behaviors, we remain as equals. Ron and Harry begin their lives with certain attitudes that are sexist, but they are able to grow into the realization that men and women are equals, and they develop a respect for women (not just Hermione) they did not originally have. When they see Voldemort exhibiting prejudice against Muggles and non-purebred Wizards, they reject his racism and actively defend those he wants to harm. Harry never lets any issue of Albus' identity as a gay man affect his respect and adoration of him as a mentor, and names his son after him.

Not every character in the series grows and matures as a person, but those who do *always* grow toward an increased sense of equality and kinship with others. It is the death eaters, after all, who want to impose rules and laws that revoke rights from those they see as less worthy, and their justification is that seizing those rights from lesser-valued people will uplift the wizarding world to its deserved glory. They envision a world in which they are entitled to supreme power and privilege, and others who they consider inferior deserve to be hurt. This is not the world that *Harry Potter* shows us: "What did my books preach against throughout? Bigotry, violence, struggles for power, no matter what," said J.K. Rowling.[6] Or, as Kingsley Shacklebolt put it, "We are all human, aren't we? Every human life is worth the same, and worth saving."[7]

Masculinity and Femininity in *Harry Potter*

In addition to sorting people into "superior vs. less deserving" categories, another trait of people who commit abuse is their belief in very strict, stereotypical gender roles. Men are meant to be tough, dominant, in control, and invulnerable; women are meant to be subservient, frail,

---

5 *Harry Potter and the Goblet of Fire*, p.723
6 *TIME Magazine*, Dec. 19, 2007. http://content.time.com/time/specials/2007/person-oftheyear/article/0,28804,1690753_1695388_1695436,00.html
7 *Harry Potter and The Deathly Hallows*, p.440

emotional, and devoted to the needs of the man. Repeatedly in my work as a counselor, I encountered men and women whose abuse was a direct result of the abuser's enforcement of these roles. For example, many men I worked with could talk at length about their own difficulties, such as losing jobs, being addicted, having affairs, etc. But what brought them to tears was being asked to talk about their relationships with their own fathers. They would tell me about dads who yelled at them to be tougher, to be "a real man," to walk-off pain, to "stop crying like a girl," to go back outside and finish the fight with the bully they had avoided. If they grew up with physical abuse, it was often directed by their fathers against mothers or against themselves as children, for failing to meet the father's expectations. Women, likewise, told me about what it was like to be forced into subservient roles all their lives. They were expected to defer to the needs of others as more important than their own, and to exhaust themselves taking care of other people. Compliments directed at young girls were limited: "you're cute, you're sweet, you're nice, you're cute, you're pretty, you're sweet..." without any broader values ("you're a strong leader, you're smart, you're creative, you're thoughtful, you're brilliant...").

All of these rigid roles compress gender into very narrow, stereo-type forms. "Gender," of course, means the identity and behaviors associated with masculinity and femininity; it is not the same as "sex," which is the biological state of maleness or femaleness. By "stereotypical gender," I mean the performance of toughness and invulnerability (male), or daintiness and weakness (female); these are taught-and-learned attributes, not naturally innate ones. The world of *Harry Potter* shows us a much broader, more robust, stronger, freer, and more sophisticated concept of gender than many people learned in their own lives.

Already, some readers are uncomfortable with the very notion of gender being expressed more broadly than the rigid masculine/feminine duality. Perhaps that is because we are conditioned to fear gender overlap by social pressures, media, and political agents who intentionally use fear to rein-in the expansion of human development, suggesting that gender which outgrows masculine/feminine confines results in confused sex roles, bathroom controversies, weakening of boys, and coarsening of girls. None of this is what is meant by the suggestion that we progress beyond the confinements of rigid gender, nor am I putting forth the idea that masculinity or femininity are inherently toxic or bad. Rather, I am suggesting that men and women be free to develop their *entire* personality, not just the half of it that conforms to the tough guy/nurturing girl stereotypes.

One of my former clients, Eric, was a tall, broad man who epitomized the "tough guy" archetype. Biker jackets, unshaved stubble, huge muscles, buzz cut hair, military tattoos, and a conservative view of masculinity—he was the epitome of the badass. As one of only two men in an eight-member therapy group, Eric was faced daily with the grief and trauma of others, mostly women, who had suffered abuse by the hands and words of others. It caused him to see himself reflected in their stories of being controlled and hurt by tough men. As his insight grew, so did his misery: he began to realize that he was a product of his father's "tough guy" parenting style. Beaten daily by his father and forced to watch his father's violence against his mother, Eric was raised to be a gladiator. His father was a biker and drug dealer who instructed the children to serve as "lookouts" for police during drug deals. At age eight, Eric was entered into knife fight tournaments with other boys: they were confined into a circle, surrounded by adults who bet on fight winners, and forced to slash and stab one another until one gave up. The loser was beaten, and the winner rewarded with a beer and a marijuana joint. Eric's body was covered in scars from childhood gashes and stab wounds, and he still had nightmares about the circles of screaming adults forcing him into deadly combat. I thought of my own son, also eight years old, swinging from tree limbs and laughing freely in our home.

At times, Eric was punished by being whipped with electrical cords. Once, he was duct-taped naked to a tree in the snow for several hours while his father teased him about his nudity and threw rocks and darts at him. Eric was unable to withhold his tears as he divulged these stories to me, one at a time. He became able to finally tell me the secret his masculine strength had forbidden him to ever share: that he hated himself.

One day, while watching a film about child abuse, we came upon a scene in which gang members forced younger boys to fight in street battles to prove their toughness. The boys in the scene were terrified, tears in their eyes, but they tried to act tough so they would be seen as "real men" by the older gang members. Watching this, Eric began to sob. He finally saw himself not as a tough guy, but as a wounded person. For once he saw his own innocence as an abused child. After group was over, Eric approached me and told me, somewhat sheepishly, "Matt, there's something I've never done before, but I feel like I need to do it before I can heal. I want to ask you to do something for me in our group tomorrow." He left the request unspecified, and left my office.

The next day as Eric returned to his seat among all eight clients, I often glanced toward him, wondering when he would bring up his unusually-vague request. He shifted uncomfortably as he gathered up his courage, and then he spoke. Eric explained that he had never felt loved, never been cared for by his father, and never allowed himself to be vulnerable or gentle. He had always been vicious, tough, and cruel—a war veteran, both in the military and in the wars of his childhood. Eric said that he knew that before he could heal he would need to allow other emotions to become valid in his life, and to accept that he could both give and receive care. Eric asked me, very nervously, if it would be okay if he received a hug from me. It was significant that he asked to receive one, not give one.

I rose and walked to Eric, both of us standing eye to eye, both of us well over six feet tall. I put out my arms and pulled him into a hug, and Eric clung to me and held tight. There was no embarrassment, no macho resistance or fear of seeming "gay," no typical clumsy "guy hug" (hug, pat, pat, done!), no withholding of vulnerability. Eric, the veteran gladiator, held me and cried. It was a long time before he finally backed away and sat down, dabbing his eyes. The group was stunned. "Eric," I finally said, "when you were a child you were forced to stand in a circle, face another guy, and do battle. And it was terrifying." Eric saw where I was going with this and he finished for me: "Today," he said, "I stood in another circle, scared to death, facing yet another man, and had to fight. Only today, I wasn't fighting him for control. Today, I fought *myself*, my past. Today I won. I don't have to stand in a circle and fight myself anymore. I don't have to hurt anyone to feel control and power anymore."

He left therapy with me after that, and I occasionally heard from his social worker that he had moved back home, and had become a loving father with his boy. It turns out, his boy was a sensitive kid with giant glasses, a love for Harry Potter, and a fondness for tiny animals—exactly the kind of little boy who needs a gentle, thoughtful daddy, not a drill sergeant.

Eric dropped by my office once, a month later, smiling more warmly than ever. He told me that he had gone back to work and apologized to his coworkers for his bullying, and they had been awestruck. One of them had told him, "You're so nice now! You're fun to be around!" Eric was amused by that feedback and told me, "Matt, I had no idea what a beast I must have been! It's so nice to have friends who want to be around me now!"

He then presented me with a rolled up paper bag and said, "I brought this to you as a gift." I opened it, and inside was a black leather jacket, ripped to bits and nearly falling apart. The fabric lining of the tattered leather was faded and had obviously bred outbreaks by types of mildew science has not yet categorized. Eric told me, "That was the actual jacket I wore when I was eight, when I was forced into those fights. It was the only thing my dad ever gave me." I looked closer at the decrepit leather and saw that it was covered in stab holes, slashes, and rips—the battle scars of a wounded child. "I want you to have it."

To anyone lacking imagination, that would have been nothing more than a rotting piece of garbage hat should have been burned years

164

ago. But to Eric, it was the giving up of a tragic history, the symbol of his woundedness. To me, it was a priceless symbol for a man's healing. It was the symbol of a man overcoming the limits of what he'd always thought being a "real man" meant. He had become *more* than a tough guy; he had become a whole man.

Notice that outgrowing his traditional concept of gender did not mean that Eric had become feminine. It meant that he had grown to include skills and qualities in his own life that he had previously thought were off-limits to men, such as loving and caring for his child, kissing his little boy's head, snuggling with him during story time at night, roughhousing with him, holding his son while his son cried (instead of barking at him to "walk it off! be tough!"), and talking thoughtfully with his boy about life. Before therapy, Eric had associated all of those acts with femininity; it's women's work to care for kids and soothe hurt feelings. Men, he believed, were meant to work on engines, bring in income, and win fights. Eric found that his life was more complete when he embraced the emotions of fatherhood, of gentleness, and of acceptance. In fact, assimilating qualities he had previously discarded as "sissy" helped him gain the strength to overcome his own traumas. By choosing to readjust his understanding of what it means to be a man, Eric became more of a man, not less of one.

Throughout her writings, J.K. Rowling also helps us see a broader concept of gender than the "action hero tough guy gets the girl as a prize" cliché. While so many fantasy stories treat men as the determiners of action and women as the sidekick rewards that men achieve for victory, Rowling's work departs from those formulas. The *Harry Potter* books do not pivot around a girl's obsession with whether or not a boy obsesses over her, or whether the girl can change and sacrifice enough of her life to become compatible with her magical boy idol. Nor does Rowling treat men as universally thick-headed, unfeeling, superficial warriors. Men and women in her work have a variety of skills and flaws, and each person's qualities or failures are a result of their own specific choices, rather than being attributed to their genders.

For example, Harry might seem to typify the traditional hero, being a humble nobody in a modest life who is suddenly called to action. But unlike most other heroes, Harry's journey does not call on him to become increasingly tougher. He does not succeed at his quest because he becomes well-armed, macho, and fierce. His success comes from him *rejecting* those attributes, and instead embracing friendships, loyalty, thoughtfulness, wisdom, and ultimately, humility. Had he rejected a single one of those qualities, he would have failed completely. Harry is no Thor, no Wolverine, no Katniss with a bow leading an army. He cries. He worries. He apologizes.

He struggles internally with his anger specifically to *keep* himself from hurting others. He rejects the temptation to see himself as entitled to service from others based on a belief that his own suffering warrants it. In fact, Harry chooses to be cooperative rather than competitive, such as when he costs himself his own victory in the second task to help free other champions' captives, and when he offers to share the Triwizard winnings with Cedric. Harry sees himself as improved, not diminished, by helping others gain what he could have for himself.

When we see Harry years after the Battle of Hogwarts at the train station with his own children, he kneels down to his young son, consoles his son's worries, reminding the little boy of all the good within him and of his father's pride. He is tender with his child, rather than scolding him to "toughen up" and "quit being such a little chicken." Harry is able to empathize with his own scared child, remembering his own childhood fears, and he uses his feelings to connect with little Albus Severus Potter. Harry is, simply put, nurturing. Imagine if an adult had knelt down to you during your abuse, told you how much good you had in you, how lucky anyone would be to have you as a friend, and how much they understood the fear you felt because they had once felt it too. That is what Harry does for his little boy, and boys need gentle, loving, safe men to reach out to them and support them. That is what you can do for others who feel just as scared as Albus Potter feels, or as scared as *you* felt.

Hermione has a slightly tougher time of it, probably because of her gender. Despite being the intellectual and magical superior of both Ron and Harry, she is rejected by both of them as first. They are annoyed by her (which she doesn't deserve; they interpret her confidence as arrogance—a scenario many confident women can relate to[8]), and as a result they treat her as an optional third wheel rather than an equal. Hermione has to do *more* work than they do, and do it better than they can, just to achieve belonging in the trio. Initially, the friendship is structured as a Ron-And-Harry boys' club with Hermione as an appendage to it, and Ron and Harry have to mature to the point of seeing her as their equal, and even their better. Hermione, in fact, seldom mentions having friendships outside

8 Although, we can wonder whether Ron and Harry would have resented her as much if she had been stereotypically feminine: she is described as having bushy hair, giant teeth, and being somewhat awkward. Hermione, not conforming to the superficial "pretty girl" role, presents qualities that are actually deeper and more meaningful than appearance, but Ron and Harry have not yet recognized that those qualities matter more than the appeal of looks in traditional gender roles. In fact, at first even Hermione herself does not yet realize she can offer more than an appeal to boys' approval; being rejected by Ron results in her crying in the bathroom. It is later that she gains the confidence to realize that being rejected by Ron is not a tragedy and does not diminish her *actual* worth, which comes from within.

their trio. She does not talk to other girls very often, and her friendship with Viktor Krum is treated resentfully by a jealous Ron, and her friendship with Harry as assumed by Rita Skeeter to be a scandalous liaison. These are common misinterpretations of healthy male-female friendships by people who subscribe to outmoded gender assumptions.

Ron and Harry begin their friendship with Hermione steeped in those myths about masculinity and femininity, which they have to later outgrow. They fail to value Hermione's qualities at first, and even find them annoying (perhaps because Hermione's qualities infringe on their concept of themselves as the rightful superiors in the trio). It is not until Hermione is in danger of being killed by a rogue troll, which allows them to save her like traditional action heroes, that they fully accept her into the friendship, because in their minds she has taken the "proper" role as a girl who is vulnerable and needs rescuing. When Hermione exhibits intelligence and outspokenness, Ron and Harry are disinterested. They are unaware of their own acceptance of gender role myths, which cast them as the superior, stronger heroes and Hermione as the girl to be saved. It take countless instances of the reverse being true—Hermione saving each of *them* with her skills—that they begin to unravel their own gender beliefs. In real life, women and men who remain stuck in the notion that a woman needs to be completed by a man to fulfill her potential value, and a man needs to be in control in order to dispense importance to the woman he selects, will also tend to find their relationships becoming unequal, needy, and energy-draining rather than healthy and happy. Those are sexist gender concepts, and replacing them with a view of men and women as equal will benefit both, including helping to heal gender-based stuck points caused by trauma. Hermione, for example, epitomizes the truth that healthy relationships are about selecting friends and partners who meet your own standards, as opposed to hoping to appeal to someone else so that they will select *you*.

What strengthens Hermione's place in the friendship is her growing confidence and her refusal to be treated as an inferior. She slips beyond traditional girl's gender roles and speaks up to the boys, setting limits with them and confronting them when they are unfair to her. We never see Hermione resort to coy flirting, pretending to be less intelligent than she is, or feeling disallowed from expressing what she will and won't accept from others. Hermione does not spend her life waiting for a prince to complete her; she is not hoping to be chosen by someone else in order to feel complete. Perhaps most important of all is that these traits are not treated by Rowling as remarkable or exceptional, but simply the qualities and rights she (like any girl) ought to have, naturally (the only characters to ever question Hermione's fortitude is Draco Malfoy and his Slytherin cohorts). Some critics have accused that Hermione remains second to Harry, using her skills only to help him. There is some truth to that, but it is not because Hermione weakly sees Harry's needs as superior to her own. Rather, it is because she chooses to align herself with the overall quest to thwart Voldemort, and her joining with Harry is a result of their shared values. It is like women and men working as allies in the effort to end abuse, rather than either side turning the work into a misguided "us only, they're not welcome!" disunion.

Throughout the series, we see that male characters who are more nurturing, emotional, and sensitive turn out to be the stronger, more healthy men as well. Male characters who subscribe to the view of manhood as violent, controlling, superior, and unfeeling become abusive (as in real life), and never develop the inner strength to bring good to the lives of others. It is men who are thoughtful and kind who become the happiest, and it is men who regard themselves as equal with others who form the most fulfilling relationships. Arthur and Molly, Ron and Hermione, Harry and Ginny all form lasting, contented relationships because each person values the other as an equal, rather than falling back into the "man in control, woman as submissive helper" structure. Among Ron, Hermione, and Harry, all three show their vulnerability to one another at times, becoming afraid, anxious, heartbroken, and openly tearful, and as the characters grow over time, they each become more able to help console and nurture one another during those moments.

How does this apply to healing from abuse? Not all abuse has a gender aspect to it, but *nearly* all of it does, and domestic violence, sexual assault, human trafficking, dating violence, and anti-LGBT violence *always* do. It is important to think about what false lessons about gender your abuse carried with it. This task can be uncomfortable because it asks you to intentionally try to think from your abuser's mindset: what did your abuser believe about gender (their own and yours) that might underlie their treatment of you? Eric's father abused Eric because he thought violence made men more powerful, so he intentionally broke apart Eric's childhood. Draco Malfoy continually invokes his father, not his mother, as the source of his strength when he is challenged. Men face higher rates of criminal violence than women overall, but violence specifically committed by an aggressor in a relationship affects women *far* more often, which is why abuse like rape, domestic violence, molestation, and emotional cruelty clearly have a gender aspect to them.[9]

---

9 Even abuse that occurs in the other direction, by female aggressors against male victims, still carries gender implications, rather than nullifying the point. For example,

While unraveling the false lessons about gender that your abuse brought with it, it is also important to question the beliefs you might still carry as well. For example, many abused women I have worked with have sought approval from men as a way to soothe their own feelings of worthlessness: "I'm not actually unlovable if I have a lover." Victims of domestic violence sometimes spend years of their lives trying to figure out how to finally placate their abuser: "if I can just figure out what I'm doing wrong, he'll be happy and stop what he does to me." Teens I counseled who had been molested as children often enter into unhealthy sexual relationships with older partners: "See? Someone who can take care of me loves me!" In each case, acceptance by another person, rather than someone's own health and freedom, becomes the priority. It's like Bella from *Twilight* intentionally hurting herself or putting herself at risk to manipulate Edward into returning to rescue her: "if I sacrifice myself enough, he'll *have* to accept me!" Those are self-limiting gender roles, and you'd never catch Hermione doing anything of the sort.

I've thought about Eric many times over the years. I don't know where he is now; I don't even remember his last name. Yes, I still have that leather jacket after all this time. I had never thought of it until now, but Eric and Dumbledore share a lot in common. Dumbledore, too, grew up with the idea that "might makes right," that having the power to hurt someone else gave him the right to do so. Dumbledore and Grindelwald played with the idea of forcing all the Muggles to do their will, which might not have been based on their gender, but did arise from a belief in being superior to others. It was when Albus Dumbledore's and Gellert Grindelwald's violence caused the death of Ariana Dumbledore that Albus suddenly realized what his hunger for power had cost him. Albus Dumbledore's belief in his own strength and supremacy over others resulted in his loneliness and broken heart, something he had to spend his lifetime mending. Somehow over the years, Albus learned to forfeit his own might and ferocity to become the gentle, affable Wizard who jokes with children and takes delight in the successes of others, and yet can become absolutely serious when he

male victims of female abuse face unhelpful reactions and blame by society, law enforcement, media, and others that is directly targeted at the male victim's gender: "If you can't stop an abusive woman from hurting you, turn in your man card!; A man who is raped by a woman isn't a victim, he's *lucky!*; boys who are abused are just being taught how to be tougher…" Men who are abused by other men are also disparaged on the basis of gender, too: "I was whipped by my dad, and I turned out fine!; This generation of men is so weak, they're all so-called victims, but back in the day we just got stronger from whatever didn't kill us!; Don't drop the soap in prison! (casual acceptance of justified rape)", and so on. Gender clearly plays a role in most abuse, and whether the victim *or* abuser is male or female doesn't remove gender from the matter, it only changes which sets of victim-blaming rhetoric is used in disparagement.

is needed to help protect someone from harm. Albus departs from his "power makes power" mindset to the more moral "knowledge makes power" attitude of his later years; this is why he can still fight Voldemort, even though Voldemort had powers that Dumbledore could, but wouldn't, use. He has transformed from a young man who believes toxic "power is good!" ideas into a man that people can feel safe around.

Harry shows us another way to be masculine, instead of playing the role of a man who remains coolly detached from women, sees sex as an emotionless pastime, relies on stoic toughness and invulnerability, and conceals any hint of nurturing traits. Harry is strong and confident in his beliefs, but he also connects with others. He doesn't treat women selfishly. He respects his children's feelings, including their fears, and does not mock them for them. Harry is able to have close friends like Hermione without sexualizing the friendship, even to the point of spending weeks alone with her while hunting Horcruxes, and never once violating her boundaries.

Unlike some guys who pretend at being nice to girls only for the purpose of persuading girls to have sex with them,[10] Harry relates to Hermione with genuine respect. In fact, when he is presented with a book on how to charm girls as a gift from Fred and George, he rejects its girl-manipulating agenda and uses the book purely to improve his genuine understanding of girls' experiences and feelings. He stands up to other guys who make sexist, racist, and cruel jokes at others' expense. His entire model of masculinity is both strong and anti-abusive.

Likewise, Hermione shows us a creative model of a strong woman. She craves knowledge, enriches herself at every opportunity, and locates her strength within herself rather than waiting for a male partner to complete her. She does not believe that her value comes from what others think of her, but from her own successes and abilities. When men disrespect her, she refuses to accept the disrespect; she speaks up, sets limits, and refuses to feel guilty. She also makes choices without checking to see whether Ron or Harry agree first. Nor does she conceal her skills in order to spare her male peers' egos, and she does not dumb herself down to make Ron and Harry more comfortable around her.

---

10 This would be the so-called "nice guy" or "white knight" who uses niceness as a sexual ploy, and then complains at being "friend zoned" when he isn't rewarded with the sex he feels he deserves. It's not genuinely nice when the real agenda comes from a sense of entitlement to girls' bodies as a payoff for fake manners.

Departing from *Harry Potter* for a moment: the Case of Newt Scamander

One of the finest examples of creative maladjustment and healthy masculinity in all of J.K. Rowling's works is the character of Newt Scamander, first revealed in the film *Fantastic Beasts and Where to Find Them*. Newt is not always comfortable around people, but he does not let his shyness suppress his deep sense of gentle empathy either. Famously, Newt is especially empathetic with magical animals, but it's easy to miss how often he is also able to sense humans' needs and feelings too, not from some magical skill, but simply because he is in tune with what other people are experiencing. Newt is shown being entranced by beasts that are misunderstood by others, his love for them giving him an unusual patience with them. When other wizards resort to very typical judgments toward non-magical people, Newt defends them ("who's going to marry *him?*" asks Tina about Kowalski, an uncool, overweight non-magical man; Newt befriends Kowalski and cares for him). Unlike other hero wizards who are made great by their magical strength, Newt is made great by his empathy, his kindness, his gentleness, even referring to himself as "mum" while speaking soothingly to the animals he loves. He does not become weak or less of a man by crossing this gender boundary, but rather adds rare skills. He is enhanced, as opposed to being limited by tough guy rules.

Newt's character was criticized by some viewers for not being tough and macho enough; viewers raised on images of Thor and Wolverine have expectations for what a tough leading man is supposed to be like. These beliefs carry over into our real-world lives, too, which is why men who have been abused often have a particularly difficult healing journey; they are constrained by the myth that men are supposed to be unabusable, unmolestable, emotionally and physically muscular, and fierce in the face of pain. Women who have been abused by men can also carry certain gender beliefs as well, having experienced masculinity's potential to wound, to humiliate, and to exploit. Even though these are painful experiences, they do carry the implicit lesson that masculinity is about power, and the unfortunate result is a belief by both men and women who have been abused that "real men" are tough bad boys. I am arguing that these views of masculinity are both the cause and the result of abusiveness, and that truly working for an abuse-free world will mean rejecting such gender expectations. It's no wonder Newt Scamander was criticized for not being traditionally masculine; he wasn't. He was something far better.

Newt's personality contrasts with the traditional masculine hero in a lot of ways, and when we start seeing the differences we realize just how much we've become used to traditional violent masculinity being normal. Newt is not a glorious "chosen one" who is destined to battle and vanquish a foe using weapons and muscle, but is instead a healer, a nurturer, a protector. These traits are not seen as departures from heroic strength, but as a different way of *being* strong. It's not as if Newt Scamander represents a too-naïve idea that being kind and gentle somehow insulates a person from the real traumas of the world; in a deleted scene from the film, Newt is shown shirtless, covered in all the scars he's received from the work he's done.[11] And yet he still loves his life, and loves the creatures he's able to understand. Rather than being too innocent a character to possibly apply to your life as a role model for overcoming abuse, Newt Scamander is actually a superb role model for you on your healing journey; he has genuinely suffered from his experiences and has the scars to prove it, yet he carries on without fail, never fails to be kind and protective toward others, and is enthralled with the beauty of what he continues to discover about the world.

Newt isn't obsessed with being sexy or cool, and he doesn't vainly try to impress people with his outward performances. Indeed, he even shies from eye contact at times. In any interaction, it seems his intention is to uplift the worth of others, to make sure innocent lives are protected, that the misunderstood are accepted and have a safe place to be. This makes him the kind of man I had always hoped to be like, and which I hope I've raised my sons to be like. He carries with him the qualities that I've personally seen save abused peoples' lives when they shed their fear of not being tough and finally grasp the importance of connection, empathy, and kindness—even in the face of being teased for it.

It is in the film *Fantastic Beasts and Where to Find Them* that we first encounter the concept of an *Obscurus*, the displaced power of a wizard or witch who suppresses their own magic.[12] A child who made to be ashamed of what she is, for example, might crush down her own magic out of a fear of being punished or despised for what she truly is. At some point, the compressed, hidden magic within her finally begins to consume her. In my past work as a therapist, I wish I had had this concept from J.K. Rowling! It would have helped express the despair and self-loathing that so many abuse and rape victims go through for so many years, as well as the depression that I encountered in young LGBT clients whose families had rejected them, or the helplessness that I saw in young boys who grew up afraid of their fathers. All of the individuality, the freedom, the childlike

---

11 http://www.imdb.com/title/tt3183660/trivia?ref_=tt_trv_trv
12 An '*Obscurial*' is person who suppresses their own magical power; the '*Obscurus*' is the power they have suppressed.

potential joy within them had been squashed down by their traumas. You may, in a sense, have been an Obscurus for much of your life as well, feeling as if you were not allowed (or able) to experience pleasure, joy, or hope. Your trauma just crushed and crushed those feelings into a hardened core until you couldn't hold any more of your grief and pain inside, and after years of appearing numb and fine it all started to erupt out again. Perhaps you were even terrified when this happened: "why am I suddenly falling apart after all these years? Am I crazy? Am I weak?"

In the wizarding world, an *Obscurial* is usually treated much the way abuse victims are treated in our real world: shut him down, quiet him, banish him yet again. The very pain that is evident in someone's life as a result of them feeling banished and unwanted is treated with more banishment! But this is why creative maladjustment is such a life-saving personality. It refuses to accept the notion that being healthy comes from faking strength. Newt Scamander sees the Obscurial for what it really is: the wounded, exiled or a hurt person who has not yet accepted themself.

Some obscurials, sadly, explode outward and hurt still more people, much like someone who embraces the abuser's mindset and carries on the habit of deriving power from inflicting harm on others. Others, like you, do the hard work to un-suppress their own power, which sets yourself free and allows you to balance the internal pressure between your trauma feelings and your true potential. That is why it takes a more mature and wise concept of yourself as a man or as a woman to achieve this balance. A woman or man who still accepts the myths about women's and men's places in the world aren't able to fully realize their entire true selves, because they have to conceal any parts that don't conform to the women-as-emotional-damsels or men-as-tough-warriors attitudes. Adhering to rigid mindsets will cause you to further compress your true, complete emotional and spiritual self, which is the opposite of healing your obscurus. Like Newt, Harry, and Hermione, you have to form a sense of awe for the wonder of life around you, and a willingness to be gentle with your own spirit, and with the lives of those around you who also need kindness and understanding to heal.

CHAPTER THIRTEEN

Rita Skeeter, Draco Malfoy, and Other Adversaries

Hermione was furious.

Scandal-tabloid writer Rita Skeeter had just outed the lovable, gentle Hagrid as a half-giant in the *Daily Prophet* newspaper, calling Hagrid a "giant mistake." Wizards have a prejudice against giants as violent beasts, and aurors had hunted down and killed most of them years ago. Even Ron accepted this bias, explaining to Harry that "they're not very nice… no wonder he keeps it quiet."[1] Exposing Hagrid's background is a disgrace against Hagrid, which sent him into hiding because he was so ashamed.

Just before Hagrid was exposed as half-giant by Skeeter, he had timidly disclosed this fact about himself to Madame Maxime, a similarly-gigantic woman Hagrid had formed romantic feelings toward. He was hopeful that opening himself up to her about his own past would form a bond between them, finding her to be a kindred spirit. Instead, it backfired horribly when Madame Maxime became insulted by Hagrid's implication that she, too, is part giant, and she angrily rebuffed Hagrid. She insisted she simply has "big bones," and rejected the very notion that she herself is also a half-giant person.

---

1 *Harry Potter and the Goblet of Fire,* p.430

Rita Skeeter, Draco Malfoy, and Other Adversaries

Hermione was astonished that anyone would use Hagrid's past against him in such a hurtful way, and she lead Harry and Ron storming down to Hagrid's cabin to assure him of their love and support for him. Hagrid refused to answer the door, but to their surprise, Dumbledore was also visiting the hut, and he invited them inside where they found Hagrid crying. Hagrid had not only been rejected by someone he adored over her rejection of his past, but his past had been used as a slur against him.

You will face similar moments of rejection in your own life, and someone at some point will use your past against you. While most people are compassionate and gentle toward victims of abuse, there are some truly awful people out there who lack decency and will make cruel statements about what you have endured. You may have even read all of this book to this point and found hope in the idea that relationships and allies are antidotes to trauma, only to come to this story, where Hagrid's own kindred spirit rejects him for the very same thing that is true for her own life. If someone who shares the same past as you might also reject you for it, where is the hope?

It is true that forming healthy relationships is an essential part of trauma recovery, and that connecting with others who understand you is part of the remedy for the wounds you have carried. It is also true that not everyone—*even others who have also been through trauma, too*—are capable of being the source of that love, and may even cause more hurt. While most people genuinely want to be understanding and kind, you will face bullies, gossips, and victim-blamers. Fortunately, J.K. Rowling teaches us some ways to deal with them...and shows us some examples of what *doesn't* help, too.

Types of Rejection You Might Face

Previously in this book, I have described successful clients of mine who started therapy, began to understand how their traumas had affected them, and developed ways to overcome their pasts. Gradually, their nightmares, panic attacks, substance use, self-harm, and other symptoms of trauma subsided, and they formed new, healthy relationships in which they were loved and respected. Like Dobby, they were able to become free of their abusers and create their own lives and identities. They found they were able to accept and return love, to care for themselves, and to set self-protective limits with those who did not show them respect. In some cases, that meant detaching from abusive family systems, marriages, or past friendships.

Many times, they were also rejected by their abusers, including their families, as well. Families that continue generational cycles of abuse tend to protect their habits and beliefs from being challenged, which means they will defend the abuser's actions. Even victims of the abuse may sometimes rally to their abuser to protect them, and thus the family itself, from being portrayed as dysfunctional. When one person frees himself from that sickness, the remaining family may turn against him as well, targeting him as a betrayer, a liar, an exaggerator. Clients of mine who went through this told me about being cast out by their former abusive families! Even brothers and sisters who had also gone through the same abuse would reject the one sibling who was becoming healthy and was now speaking out against the abuse. Those who were still traumatized would internally deny that they had even been abused, or downplay the effects of the abuse ("Dad had to use the belt on us; we were difficult, and it taught us discipline" or "we weren't molested; it was just playing around"). When someone becomes honest about what was actually happening, it pierces the denial that the rest of the victims rely on to protect themselves from reality. As a result, when you speak out about what you endured, your honesty and courage are a threat to those who want the traumas to stay buried. *You* become their enemy, rather than the abuser. When Hagrid opens up about his half-giant past, it stings Madame Maxime because she is ashamed of her own family, and rather than seeing Hagrid as a companion, she turns against him to keep him from bringing up things she wants to deny about herself. Remember, too, how Rufus Scrimgeour presses Harry to join in the pretense that the Ministry of Magic is admirable and effective, and becomes hostile to Harry when Harry refuses. Harry's refusal to comply with the public lie ("I don't want to be used") makes him the moral, honest one, but it also results in Scrimgeour's unpleasant regard for Harry as a result. This is *exactly* what many abuse victims face when their abusers (and their abuser's allies) pressure them to keep silent about those secrets, and how the victims are rejected and labeled for refusing to cooperate with the abusive secrecy any longer. If that happens to you, you have not gone astray; you have become more like Harry Potter.

Other victims, even when they have gone through the same thing you have too, may turn against you so they can inwardly deny their own abuse even happened. For example, I have found that people who were enduring domestic violence could often be the loudest victim-blaming voices in groups and seminars of mine. Why would they do such a thing? In their minds, convincing themselves that "victims" were very different people from themselves helped them maintain an illusion that they were not also victims, too. They would adopt the most primitive myths about victims—"they're stupid, weak, and they like being abused!"—so they could distance themselves from those stereotypes. By creating false differences between themselves and other victims, they could pretend they hadn't been abused, raped, beaten, or molested too. Madame Maxime could swear that she is just "big boned" and that she has nothing in her family history that would link her to something she would feel embarrassed by. Cornelius Fudge refused to believe Voldemort had returned, even when Harry shared his own personal experience with Voldemort that same night. Like someone who rejects a victim's report of being abused in order to maintain the family's false image, Fudge says, "It seems to me that you are all determined to start a panic that will destabilize everything we have worked for!"

Victims who blame other victims are doing so as a way to protect themselves from the truth of their own traumas. It allows them to continue their made-up image of everything being okay, as long as you don't rock the boat. The blame has nothing to do with you, but with their own inability to (yet) face their life's truths. They are essentially dumping off their own shame onto other victims to carry for them. Dumbledore could not convince Fudge to see the truth, and had to simply part ways and continue doing what he knew was right. Likewise, you may not be able to convince people of the truth of your abuse, especially if they depend on denying it to preserve their own fairy tale beliefs. This is not your failure, and like Dumbledore, you may have to simply stop trying to convince them. What you know to be true is enough to move on with your life, doing the things you know are important. Dumbledore checks with his allies to be sure he can count on them, and together they undertake the important work of opposing Voldemort. He is not flustered by the fact that some people naively oppose his efforts to warn and protect others.

In some unhealthy families, a person might be the opposite of abused; they are over-entitled as little princes and princesses. A family abuser might defend their own bullying on the basis that "we're just better than other people," raising offspring who feel supreme. They don't feel shame like abuse victims do, they become narcissists who are incapable of empathy or mercy. Lucius Malfoy is such an abuser. His abuse is directed at victims outside the family, not at family members. He degrades people on the basis of their race, their status and income, and whether they serve his own arrogance. Draco learns these values from his father, and becomes an abuser-in-training. He believes that he, too, is superior to others, which he has learned by being spoiled. Any time Draco's status is challenged, he reverts to the same power source: "Wait until my father..!"

(Notice that he defers to his father, not his mother, as the source of his power; like many abusers, Draco also buys into male privilege.)

Real-life Draco Malfoys abound. You'll find them in internet comments sections, for example, where they poison any story about child abuse, rape, human trafficking, LGBT civil rights, feminism, and racism with callous remarks. They'll be the ones sneering at victims, venomously attacking them for "deserving" to be hurt, mocking their traumas, lashing out at victims as "snowflakes" who simply need to be tougher and smarter. They'll be attracted to (and exhibit) macho, authoritarian personalities, and regard nuance, sensitivity, or Hermione-like sophistication as nonsense. Their mindset is that if people were just tough like they were, if society hadn't become so wimpy, if people simply knew their places, then all the problems with abuse, trauma, and emotional pain could be dispensed with. Despite seeing themselves as tough, they'll become apoplectic with rage if they are disagreed with. These are not your allies. They will blame you, ridicule you, and see no personal gain in showing you compassion or solidarity. They might not even *believe* you.

Finally, you will face people who don't mean to be hurtful, but simply don't understand the right way to respond to your traumas, or to the issues of child abuse and rape in our culture. They blurt out the exact wrong thing without realizing that what they're saying is completely wrong: "Why didn't you fight back? Why did you put yourself in that position? What did you do to provoke them? Couldn't you have told someone?" They may not mean to, but they are actually supporting abusers, not victims, by implying that it is up to you, the victim, to make your own abuse stop.

Because people lack good information, many still believe outdated myths about abuse, such as:

- Abuse is caused by alcohol or anger management problems;
- Rape is caused by libido (horniness) that someone people simply can't control;
- Abusers who apologize will stop abusing;
- Abuse happens because victims provoke their abusers;
- Most women who report rape are lying;
- Back in the good old days, we didn't call it "child abuse," we called it "discipline";
- Some people just like being abused, which is why they stay.

ABUSE APOLOGIST BINGO

"Well how are you defining abuse?"	"He feels awful about it, hasn't he suffered enough?"	"I don't know what to believe"	"You're being over dramatic & making too much of it"	"take the high road" "be the bigger person" "holding onto anger is like holding onto hot coal"
"He's not that kind of person"	"It's not his fault. He's struggling too"	"Well he said..." "Consider his side of things"	"You're ruining his life!"	"He's not like that anymore."
"It's not like it was REAL abuse, though"	"I understand you're hurt by what he did, but..."	FREE "I've never seen that side of him"	"You're lying for attention!"	"He made a mistake. What's done is done. Let it go."
"So why didn't you bring this up sooner, then?"	"You should have..."	"misunderstanding"	"You make it harder for REAL victims"	"Forgive him. Not because he deserves it but because he needs it/ because it will help you heal"
Asks for details so they can judge your story	"There's two sides to every story. You just remember things differently."	"I'm not taking sides."	"false rape claims"	"I think you were just toxic for each other"

When people downplay ("you should be over it by now"), deny ("you're lying"), or misunderstand ("are you sure it was even that bad?") your abuse, it can cause you to feel deeply betrayed. It denies the core truth of what you have experienced, and treats your pain as something that you shouldn't feel. One of the ways these responses can hurt is by increasing your feelings of loneliness, because it feels like nobody can really understand the very thing you probably have the strongest feelings about in your entire life. Every person who reacts badly to your trauma creates a new layer of separation between what you desperately need people to understand, and what they seem incapable of ever understanding. In some cases, victims even fault themselves for other peoples' failures to respond helpfully, believing that they are the ones with the defective thoughts: "they're right, I should be over this by now; why can't I move on? What's wrong with me? Am I *that* messed up?"

2 This image has circulated online without attribution to an original source. It's fantastic, but I acknowledge the issue with its one-sided use of "he/him" pronouns for abusers, who in real life can be male or female.

Rita Skeeter, Draco Malfoy, and Other Adversaries

Remember that having incorrect information about abuse isn't entirely that person's fault. Actually, I'd be amazed if most people didn't have some defective beliefs about abuse, rape, and exploitation because most of our education on the subject comes from garbage sources: movies, romance novels, TV dramas, gossip, advertising, and porn. It's not fair, but it's true, that being a survivor gives you a new job to do: you become a source of information for other people, and hopefully that information is correct. Otherwise, people's knowledge about trauma remains a blank bulletin board to be filled by whatever images are carelessly tossed out from media. People who read Rita Skeeter's exposé against Hagrid might simply assume that it's accurate to judge and reject him, just like people who see stereotypes about LGBT people, rape victims, child abuse victims, and other races and cultures may never question whether those messages are even true.

In the case of Hagrid, we see several examples of how to react. Ron inadvertently shares the beliefs of Rita Skeeter at first, putting forth his belief that giants are predisposed to badness. He adopts the "Hagrid ought to hide that part of his past" position. In his mind, Hagrid is one of the good ones, but people like Hagrid in general ought to keep themselves—or at least a specific aspect of their pasts—hidden, so as to appear normal. When Ron says "no wonder he keeps it quiet," he's agreeing with the premise that being half-giant is indeed something that ought to be concealed. He sees Hagrid as a single exception to the belief that giants are just vicious—"it's in their natures…everyone knows that"[3]—rather than changing his views of giants in general. Although Ron begins with an immature understanding of the matter, he actually shows us a lot of hope by demonstrating how much someone can change their thinking when exposed to new facts and relationships.

When you are insulted by others as a result of your abuse, such as being mocked, treated as an outcast, blamed, or scolded for being a victim, you might at first respond the way Hagrid does when his life is similarly devalued. Hagrid becomes a recluse. He stops teaching his classes and shuts himself inside his hut with his grief:

> Hagrid was sitting at his table, where there were two large mugs of tea. He looked a real mess. His face was blotchy, his eyes swollen, and he had gone to the other extreme where his hair was concerned; far from trying to make it behave, it now looked like a wig of tangled wire.[4]

---

3 *Harry Potter and the Goblet of Fire,* p.430
4 *Harry Potter and the Goblet of Fire,* p.452

Tears trickle down his cheeks. He cannot imagine anyone could still care about him, knowing his secret past now. It was the one secret about himself he had hidden, and when he had finally shared it with someone, he had been rejected for it. It hurts to be rejected, and Hagrid's feelings are absolutely appropriate. They're normal. You'll feel them, too, and when you do, you'll believe there is no other possible way to see yourself than as a pitiful outcast.

Harry, however, does not see Hagrid's and Madame Maxime's secrets as something shameful. In fact, he's surprised this is even an issue at all, because to him their status as a half-giant is just self-evidently true. To Harry, there's never been a reason to have any objection to it at all, and it's news to him that this would even be a scandal. He reasons that if Hagrid is a half-giant, nobody could doubt that Madame Maxime is, too. For Harry, there are things that are simply true about some lives, and they're not good or bad, they're just facts.

To carry it over to your life, the "Harry response" would be that some people are survivors of abuse, sexual assault, and other forms of violence, and none of those facts are value judgments about the people themselves who have been through those things. In fact, Harry helps Hagrid understand how someone's past has nothing to do with their worth as persons: "Hagrid, look what I've got for relatives!" Harry said furiously. "Look at the Dursleys!"[5] The "Harry response" is a very healthy one. Harry knows there are bullies in the world, but he adopts a mindset that is different from theirs. He simply accepts that there are things in some peoples' pasts that are difficult to cope with, but they don't affect the worth of those people. His response is the "yeah, so what?" response. Harry has been abused by the Dursleys—yeah? And how does that make Harry a bad person? It doesn't. Harry learns that Hagrid is part giant—yeah? And how does that make Hagrid a bad person? It doesn't. Harry judges people by their treatment of others, not by their pasts or their status. He supports Hagrid, pointing out to him that they both share things in their private family histories that are sometimes judged. Hagrid is able to recognize this, and to see that someone's past should not be held against them. Hagrid, realizing that he loves Harry, can finally understand how people could still love him despite the secret he is hiding, too.

Dumbledore picks up Harry's point and helps drive it home by revealing his own family "scandal" as well, involving his brother Aberforth's violation of an embarrassing magical statute. Each person who gathers around Hagrid and supports him has a background that some people

---

5 *Harry Potter and the Goblet of Fire*, p.454

would mock. Ron's family is famously poor. Dumbledore is ashamed of his own part in the battle with Grindelwald that caused the death of Dumbledore's sister, and he has a brother who has run afoul of the law. (We also don't know if Hagrid is aware that Dumbledore himself is also gay, another attribute that some people also judge and reject) Hermione is a Muggleborn. Harry was abused for years by a Muggle family that remains ashamed of his very existence. Each person carries a fact that some might judge. What they find, though, is that the very things that cause some people to reject them are the parts of their lives that help bring them closer to others who truly understand and accept them.

J.K. Rowling's storytelling does not give us a way to vanish all the jerks in our world. She does not show us how to simply make people stop being arrogant, judgmental, or prejudiced. What her storytelling does show us, though, is that being rejected by such people does not impact our worth, and that avoiding the world out of fear of being judged for your past is not a way to become stronger. When Draco hurls the "Mudblood" epithet at Hermione, it does not diminish Hermione, it shows us what kind of person Draco is. When Rita Skeeter uses Hagrid's race against him, it does not make Hagrid a less-lovable person, it shows us that Rita Skeeter is a racist who takes delight in hurting others. What you can learn from J.K. Rowling's writing, then, is to be discerning about whose opinions of you, you let matter. This takes practice. It's easier said than done, but it's no less true.

For example, Hermione and Harry confront Rita Skeeter in a Hogsmeade pub about the hurt she has caused, publicly accusing her of intentionally trying to ruin Hagrid's life. To them, the real offense is someone being unkind to a person like Hagrid, who has caused no harm at all to anyone. They are able to correctly interpret what has happened, and they put the shame on the person who has been unkind, rather than on the victim. Then they help Hagrid do the same thing. We learn from Hagrid that Dumbledore has always been this sort of ally to him, too: "Dumbledore was the one who stuck up for me after Dad went. Got me the gamekeeper job," said Hagrid. "…trusts people, he does. Gives 'em second chances… tha's what sets him apar' from other heads, see. He'll accept anyone…"[6]

When you encounter people who reject or judge you because of your abuse, your rape, or any other trauma you have endured, keep the examples of Harry, Hermione, Hagrid, Ron, and Dumbledore in mind. At first, you will probably respond like Hagrid does. He absorbs all the shame, and isolates in humiliation. His heart is broken. He feels like the private thing he most sensitive about has been hurled against him, and

---

6 *Harry Potter and the Goblet of Fire*, p.455

that his entire worth as a person is demolished. He is convinced nobody will want him around now that they know his big personal secret. But he is able to hear the messages of love and support that his friends offer to him, and draw strength from them. He even begins to realize that all of his friends also have things in their own lives that are hard for them too, and yet they are still worthwhile. Finally, he recognizes that people like Harry and Dumbledore are also wounded people who have shown the sort of acceptance and kindness for others that he, Hagrid, most admires and needs. Hagrid is able to move from "I'm no good; nobody wants me now that they know my past!" to "I have good friends who love me, and I love them, and they're right—having something in your past doesn't make you a bad person. I'm hurt, but not 'damaged goods.' I can recover from this."

Be like Dumbledore, who is willing to share his own difficult family past with someone else for the *other* person's sake. Rather than making it about himself, Dumbledore simply mentions his own family issues to show Hagrid that a person's past does not determine their value. Hagrid realizes this, too: "[Dumbledore] knows people can turn out okay even if their families weren'…well…all tha' respectable. But some don understand that. There's some who'd always hold it against yeh…"[7]

Be like Hermione, who sticks up for her friends when she sees their pasts used to hurt them. Hermione confronts the victim-blaming abusiveness of Rita Skeeter, making it known that picking on innocent victims is not okay. Hermione is not the type who would laugh emptily at jokes made about rape victims, abuse victims, or people of other races or lifestyles. She isn't afraid to speak up and make it clear that cruelty isn't just a type of amusement. She also goes out of her way to show someone who has been hurt that she is there to support them.

Be like Harry, who has learned that his own past is not something to be ashamed of, either. He knows there will always be people like Draco who are cruel to others, but he doesn't let Draco's attitudes change his, Harry's, values and decisions. In fact, Harry seems to find direction in his determination to be very different from Draco. When Draco taunts Harry, Harry is bothered by it but uses his feelings to empower his drive to do better. When you encounter someone who is unkind to you about your past, don't absorb the shame. It's not yours to carry. Instead, follow Harry's example and use their torment as a way to guide yourself into becoming even more unlike them. Recognize your tormentors as ideological landmarks that steer you away from their kind of thinking.

There's one more surprising role model in this mess who deserves praise, too: Madame Maxime herself.

---

7 *Harry Potter and the Goblet of Fire, p.455*

Maxime is self-rejecting at first, denying that she is even part giant like Hagrid. She is unable to come to terms with her family's past, and simply denies it all with a flimsy excuse. She is like many abuse and rape victims who also deny their own experiences; I have worked with clients who praise their abusers as "simply being tough and strict," who cannot even say the word "rape" and refer only to "the R-word," and people who hide their pasts (including some clients who, because they were men, could not identify themselves as victims of rape or molestation). Their insistence that they were never abused is the equivalent of Madame Maxime falsely saying "I'm not half-giant, I'm just big boned!" It's impossible to be a whole, healed person while still denying that a major chunk of your past is even true.

But let's look at what happens with Madame Maxime. As her character evolves, she becomes softer to Hagrid about her past, and approaches him again to revive their friendship (Hagrid is cold toward the idea at first, understandably). But most remarkably, she not only finally comes to terms with her identity as a half-giant, but accompanies Hagrid as special ambassador from Albus Dumbledore to reach out to other giants!

She reminds me of a client I once had who, upon meeting me, flatly told me that she would absolutely *not* be speaking during my therapy groups. The fact that I am a male was part of the reason, but the heart of it was that she had been so traumatized by a lifetime of physical and sexual abuse that she simply could not bear the truth of that part of her life. To cope, she simply denied any of it had happened at all, and swore that the only reason she needed therapy was for job stress. Day after day, she nestled back into a corner of the group room, actually concealing herself beneath a blanket, listening. It took about two weeks' worth of daily sessions before she began to interact at all. Once she finally began to open to the group, the truth of her years of trauma flooded out—painfully so—and she was able to burst those Horcruxes one-by-one until she was free.

Where is she now? She remains in contact with me so many years later. She freed herself from an unhealthy marriage and found her own Hagrid-like soulmate, someone who was able to truly know her, past and all, and adore her. She has become a public speaker on the topic of sexual assault and child abuse, and has shared her story and her therapy writings publicly[8] as a way to reach out to other victims. Like Madame Maxime, she went from "this is absolutely not true about my life, and I *will not* talk about this with you!" to being a special ambassador to others who are like her. In fact, she even allowed me to be present when she finally got a tattoo of the word "Survivor." She had come from being ashamed to feeling confident

---

8 See *Resurrection After Rape*, RAR Books, 2017

Rita Skeeter, Draco Malfoy, and Other Adversaries

and valuable, and seeing her past not as a disgrace but as something that could connect her to others who shared the same experiences. Today, if someone were to make unkind remarks about her past—and some people have!—rather than being destroyed by them, she sees them as examples of why her voice is so needed in this world, and why supporting other victims is so important to do. She sees the Rita Skeeters and Draco Malfoys of the world as reasons why her work is so important, because there are still so many Hagrids crying alone in so many cabins without anyone telling them they matter.

CHAPTER FOURTEEN

Forgiveness

As you heal, you may be given a lot of advice by people who mean well, but don't have all the insights into trauma recovery that they ought to. For example, being told to simply "focus on positive thinking" and "stop dwelling on the past" and "pray it away" and "take St. John's Wort and vitamins to cure your depression" and "balance your energy with crystals." But the trickiest, most potentially dangerous advice of all is the one you might even hear the most: "you have to forgive your abuser to move on."

The "forgive them to move on" advice is usually born out of a misunderstanding of trauma that sees it as a burden you are carrying, which you can let go and be free of all at once if you simply make a certain choice. Your resentment toward your abusers is the burden, and it's holding you back, they believe, and ending that resentment is like dropping the rocks you are hauling. "Forgiving" them is how you unload that burden and free yourself from your own resentments. By now, you can probably see all the things that are wrong with this notion.

For one thing, trauma is not a burden you are carrying just because you haven't yet made the choice to be free of it. Trauma itself is, by definition, not a choice, and the effects of post-traumatic stress are caused by many impacts of your experiences on how your brain functions. It is not based on your personality, your faith, your toughness, or your heroism; it is based on how specific parts of your brain respond to stimuli. The notion that forgiving someone cures this is like saying letting bad drivers cut you off will cure diabetes. If anything, the fact that trauma is a function of the physical brain means that the person you ought to forgive is yourself, for how long it takes you to recover.

Abuse trauma is caused by one person betraying their relationship with another. Whether your abuser was a family member, a relationship partner, or a stranger, they removed themselves from the normal and healthy bonds of human relationships in order to inflict intentional harm on you. Consequently, *they* are the ones who are displaced from normal relationship patterns, not you. You, then, are not even capable of restoring them to a right relationship, and it certainly does not become your job to try, and no victim should ever feel it is their job to rehabilitate their own abuser. If creating Horcruxes damages and fragments a wizard's soul, abuse is the real-life method of doing the same thing, and it is the abuser's or rapist's soul that is damaged and broken by what they have done. Trauma affects your relationships by making you feel alone, as if everyone can tell exactly how worthless you are, and yet you also feel that nobody can ever really know the full you. So yes, you do have work to do to reintegrate yourself into the "web of life" with others. But that does not include renewing a "clean slate" relationship with your abusers. In fact, trying to do so would be a form of connecting yourself to someone who does not have healthy relationships in the first place, which has no healing power for you. It would be like Harry trying to overcome his traumas by joining the death eaters.

Another reason the "forgive them to move on" advice can be dangerous is that people who suggest it often have other motives. Many times, they simply mean well and they think that forgiveness is a virtuous choice, a holy practice, something good people do, so they think it's the right choice for your situation. It's like someone who knows nothing about medicine or psychology thinking to themselves, "Hmm, vegetables are healthy, so surely it's good advice to tell someone with post-traumatic stress to eat vegetables to heal themselves." Eating vegetables, like the word "forgiveness," has healthy connotations, but it's totally mismatched advice to the specific situation. Positive-sounding advice that uses positive-sounding words seems like it should be obviously positive, when in fact it's little more than a "deepity," an attractive inspirational meme that sounds good, but really carries no effective wisdom at all. It is false depth. It is a mosaic of words that seem profound, but don't actually convey anything helpful. For example, "what you put out into the universe comes back to you," or "everything happens for a reason," or "your heart expresses infinite wisdom" are deepities. People who say this stuff, or share it ad nauseum on the internet, feel they have contributed something profound to the cosmos, but the phrases are sheer fake wisdom. Clumping together a lot of positive words doesn't mean the sentiment itself can bear weight. "You have to forgive them to move on" is another example. People fall back on deepities when they want to seem insightful, but don't actually have a grain of understanding of a complex issue.

Another agenda behind the "forgive them to move on" advice can be more sinister. Some people want to help cloak the abuser's actions because they are invested in maintaining the relationships around the abuser. Family members sometimes discourage victims from ever speaking up against abuse they endured at the hands of a parent, for example. If you begin to deal with the abuse, others might actively discourage you by excluding you as "the crazy one," minimizing the abuse ("It wasn't that bad; stop being dramatic!"), faulting you ("Dad was doing the best he could do deal with the problems you caused"), denying it altogether ("that never happened! What are you even talking about?"), shaming you for being wounded ("Hey, we're fine; you're the one still carrying this on after all these years. When are you going to get over it?"), actually praising the abuser ("I got whipped my whole childhood and I'm better for it. It made me a stronger person"), and giving you advice that helps the family keep the abuse secret ("you need to just forgive him and move on with your life").

My own approach to the issue of forgiveness is more about your needs, not about how forgiveness makes someone else feel about you or your abusers. Put simply, what it comes down to is you: if you feel you would heal by forgiving, then forgive. If you feel that someone doesn't deserve forgiveness, don't forgive them. The choice should be based on your needs, not anyone else's. This is one time when being a victim actually does entitle you to personal privileges and status: you, and you alone, get to make this choice based entirely on your own needs.

If you do choose to forgive, though, think carefully about what the word "forgive" means in you situation. There are three major concepts of forgiveness to sort through, and in my opinion, only one ought to apply.

Sometimes, forgiveness simply means repairing a minor or temporary rift in an otherwise-healthy friendship. When Ron is angry with Harry for Harry's selection in the Triwizard Championship, he begins to shun Harry. Part of Ron's resentment is justified, because he sees Harry always getting glory, and part of it is immature, because he assumes Harry has intentionally put himself at the center of attention. Their friendship, though, is strong and the rift is only temporary. Ron approaches Harry and apologizes for judging him, and Harry and Ron forgive each other. In this case, "forgiveness" means that they set aside their past hurt feelings and continue their relationship with a fresh start. They truly do "forgive to move on." There is no lasting damage that needs to be healed; they can continue together without their friendship being significantly harmed. Forgiveness, in this instance, is the classic "wipe the slate clean and move on with their lives"-type. Because Harry and Ron have an otherwise-healthy relationship based on love and support, this low point is just a brief immature pout. Forgiving one another brings no harm and all gain. Plus, they both become more mature as a result, learning not only to trust one another more, but to muster the strength to reconcile for the sake of a valued friendship. The "Harry and Ron" type of forgiveness is healthy, and should be one of the skills you can easily practice in your life, too, in both directions (apologizing when you are wrong, and being gracious to others who sincerely apologize to you). When a relationship was previously happy and healthy, the "forgive, clean the slate, and resume the connection" form of forgiveness is perfectly suitable.

The second type of forgiveness is harmful, though, because it applies the "Harry and Ron" type to a situation that does not deserve it. Wiping the slate clean and reconnecting the relationship works when the relationship is otherwise healthy and loving, like Ron and Harry's, but it's not a good plan when the relationship was abusive or toxic. The problem I have with the idea of forgiving a rapist or abuser is that "forgiveness" clears the offender of their consequences and guilt, letting them off the hook. It bulldozes over the righteous outrage of the victim, replacing it with a false serenity. It allows violence to continue. And it suggests that after "forgiveness," you aren't supposed to ever feel any of your former emotions about the trauma, which simply isn't realistic. It may even keep you from completing therapy by making certain feelings out-of-bounds for discussion: after all, you've forgiven them, right? So those feelings are supposed to be gone, right? It has come to describe the act of letting someone else off the hook, wiping the slate clean, cancelling the accountability or consequences deserved by another person, and granting an emotional truce with an offender. I call these the "false serenity" definition of forgiveness.

You owe your abusers none of these things. When someone tells you to forgive your abuser, you have every right to refuse to do this, as long as "forgiveness" means pardoning them for their offenses. In all my years of work with trauma victims, I never saw a single case where doing this earned any actual benefit for the victim. The expectation of being freed and unburdened ("closure") never came. Some people felt a slight alleviation of religious guilt because their theology told them they had to forgive, but actual healing from trauma? Nope.

There is, however, a third way of understanding forgiveness that truly can benefit you, and it can be a bit shocking. It completely reverses the understanding of the second type, so that instead of letting the abuser off the hook or wiping their slate clean, you let *yourself* off the hook of the pain they have caused you. You are not pardoning them for anything, you are purging them from your life. You "forgive" them, which means expunging them from your feelings. Forgiveness, then, isn't a form of recovering a relationship; it is a form of being emancipated from it. In this sense, you don't treat forgiveness as a way to drop a burden of resentment; you treat the abuser's impact on you as a presence in your life that you are evicting. Instead of the word "forgive," substitute words like "purge" and "cleanse." When we think of forgiveness as a way of purging someone from our lives, cleansing ourselves of their effects, we're approaching a more useful, healthy, and enlightened concept that applies to trauma.

While Harry Potter never uses the word "forgive" in this way, his actual experiences with Voldemort give us a symbolic example of how it works. For all his life, Harry has felt that he carries the presence of Voldemort within himself. Voldemort has been impactful on Harry's life, causing Harry ongoing torment and depression. Harry's quest is not just to defeat Voldemort outwardly, but to cleanse himself of the effects of Voldemort's actions that Harry still carries within himself. His years-long process of learning to face his fears, find trustworthy mentors, form healthy relationships, and extract all the painful remains of his traumas from within himself are mirrors of the therapeutic healing journey you are on. His last steps are also your last steps: facing the worst aspects of the trauma still inside him, exposing them, and facing them so they can finally be released. For Harry, this means walking into the Forbidden Forest where Voldemort is waiting for him. For you, it means sharing your story with someone who can hear it sympathetically, until every detail has finally been overcome. In both of these cases, you and Harry both must let your guard down and feel temporarily overwhelmed in order to become victorious in the end.

When you finally reveal your story to someone else, you may feel emotionally flooded at first, because you are finally allowing all of the horror, with no details left out, to erupt out of hiding. You are releasing the Boggart from its hiding place, and facing it at its full strength. By facing it, you allow the emotions you have to be fully expressed, which reduces their intensity inside you. By allowing those emotions to finally "speak," they don't have to use as much force to percolate inside of you in search of release. Those emotions are not healed by pity, so looking for special soothing or pitying care from others will not strengthen you, and will teach

Forgiveness

others to only relate to you as a constant victim. Instead, healing comes from opening yourself so that the pressure of your emotions can be settled. Once that happens, you begin to purge the effects of your abuser/rapist/betrayer from your life, once and for all. You have to understand your emotions, not hide from them, to become healed. Or as Dumbledore said, "Understanding is the first step to acceptance, and only with acceptance can there be recovery."[1]

When Harry faces Voldemort in the Forbidden Forest, he goes in defenselessly, prepared to be overpowered. He is terrified, but knows it is a necessary step. In fact, he expects to lose the battle entirely, and sees this as a final self-sacrifice. What actually happens, of course, is that he and Voldemort are both struck down by Voldemort's attack, and find themselves in an afterlife experience. Harry is conscious and whole. Voldemort, however, has taken the form of a frail, trembling carcass. Harry clothes himself in clean robes, while the naked carcass on the floor is "something furtive, shameful."[2] Harry meets the spirit of Dumbledore, who explains what has happened:

"So the part of his soul that was in me…"
Dumbledore nodded still more enthusiastically, urging Harry onward, a broad smile of encouragement on his face.
"…has it gone?"
"Oh yes!" said Dumbledore. "Yes, he destroyed it. Your soul is whole, and completely your own, Harry."[3]

Harry, by opening himself, letting his guard down, and facing his ultimate trauma, finally purges the remnant of Voldemort from within himself. For the first time, Harry sees the real difference between himself—whole, cleansed, and alive—and his abuser—frail, maimed, and shameful. Achieving this is painful to Harry. It doesn't come easy. He has to becoming willing to endure that pain, and not flee from it. Dumbledore says to him, "I think we can agree that you are not dead – though, of course…I do not minimize your sufferings, which I am sure were severe."[4]

By purging out the remains of Voldemort's affects on his life, Harry has completed the third understanding of forgiveness. He has not pardoned Voldemort, and he has not reconciled with him or let him off the hook or absolved him of his wrongdoing. In fact, if anything, Harry has completely

1 *Harry Potter and the Goblet of Fire,* p.680
2 *Harry Potter and the Deathly Hallows,* p.706
3 *Harry Potter and the Deathly Hallows,* p.708
4 *Harry Potter and the Deathly Hallows,* p.712

and utterly rejected Voldemort entirely, separating himself from him so thoroughly that Harry is completely freed. This type of cleansing benefits the victim, not the abuser. It restores the victim to a sense of wholeness, prioritizing your needs and keeping the abuser's needs irrelevant, as they should be. By doing this, you can reclaim a sense of control, independence, and wholeness. As Luna Lovegood put it, "Things we lose have a way of coming back to us in the end, if not always in the way we expect."[5]

One woman who applied this method of forgiveness, wrote to me about what happened as a result:

> I chose to forgive.
> We didn't get to choose whether we would be raped or not, but we do get to choose how we respond to it... just like anything else in life. I didn't want to spend my life eaten up with vengeance, hatred and bitterness.
> For me and my understanding of forgiveness, it was a matter of fully acknowledging what they did and what it cost me, what it's still costing me today. This places the blame and responsibility exactly where it belongs: on them. As I went over my 'list' of the costs, I took those things and acknowledged that they were now mine to live with and work on, but I gave up my need for vengeance. (I am not talking about not pressing charges. This is a legal matter and is what our laws and government are for). I gave up my hatred of them.
> What I didn't expect were the benefits. It cut the bond/tie/cord between them and me. The fear began to dissipate and I gained peace. The panic attacks subsided and I was able to leave my house again.
> Forgiving did absolutely nothing for them and they still stand accused, but it empowered me and brought me a large measure of peace. It brought me to the place where they were no longer the issue... I was. My healing, my wellbeing, my life, to do with as I choose.
> As far as forgiving AND forgetting: the forgetting part isn't going to happen this side of heaven. That's just life and to think otherwise is pretty much denial of reality.

Ashley, a 22-year-old survivor, said, "I needed to forgive them in order to move on. It might not be right for everyone, but it was for me. I've forgiven those who have hurt me. That doesn't mean I've forgotten. It

---

5 *Harry Potter and the Order of the Phoenix,* film adaptation

just means that I'm starting to move on. I just refuse to let it rule my life anymore."

Kara, 24, also made this decision for similar reasons. She said, "He completely consumed my life; I had so much anger built up that it was scary. I couldn't live my life like that anymore. I'm not excusing him in ANY way for what he did, but I had to forgive him to move on. Rapists are all about control, and after forgiving him and releasing him from my life, I feel like I have the power and control back."

Jessica, 19, added, "I needed to forgive, because I hated too strongly. The hate I felt towards my attacker consumed my life, so for me, forgiveness had to be part of my process of moving on."

Notice that all of these experiences are about purging one's self of dark, toxic emotions, leaving themselves free to live happily. Not one involved any gesture toward their offender; in fact, these acts of forgiveness set the victims farther apart from their abusers. That liberating disconnection from trauma, after all, is the whole purpose of real forgiveness. It is self-made justice.

If you re-define "forgiveness" as "purging my abuser from my life," you return control to yourself and prioritize your needs, not theirs. When someone tells you "you need for give and move on," instead of being offended by their bad advice you'll be able to honestly reply, "that's right, because I need them completely gone from my life." Additionally, you won't have to endure myths about forgiveness, like the idea that you should never have tender feelings about your abuse afterward, or that you should be suddenly and completely healed afterward (Harry still has battles and difficulties ahead of him, even after he purges Voldemort out).

Casting your abusers out of your thoughts, your soul, your life, is the strongest way you can overcome them. Because abusers are self-absorbed and feel that their own interests are supreme, eradicating them from your life is a powerful way to repudiate them. Even if they don't particularly seem to care—I can't imagine the Dursleys being stung by Harry never interacting with them again—it is, for *you*, a way of being stronger than they are. As Dumbledore explained,

> "Voldemort himself created his worst enemy, just as tyrants everywhere do! Have you any idea how much tyrants fear the people they oppress? All of them realize that, one day, amongst their many victims, there is sure to be one who rises against them and strikes back!"[6]

---

6 *Harry Potter and the Half-Blood Prince*, p.510

CHAPTER FIFTEEN

Final Work

Harry Potter learned that healing cannot come by simply waiting for it. It is not a birthright that will flow to you. It does not come by pleading with other people to make you happy by saying what you want to hear. Each of us is responsible to choose to seek it, knowing that the process can be painful at times. I know many, many wounded people who stumble with the burden of their traumas, year after year, because they are used to the weight and they say, "I just don't see the point in going back over all that stuff and opening it up again." They become calloused to the burdens they bear. There is a fear that facing your pain will be more painful that letting it persist, and many refuse.

When you doubt your own value, you lose your sense of place in the world. Putting yourself down is living your abuser's lie. You cannot simultaneously discredit yourself and feel connected to all life. Your sense of self-value cannot come to you from any external source, and yet this is precisely where you are conditioned to seek it; media, advertising, and success myths all misdirect us toward external answers for internal crises, like Gilderoy Lockhart, who looks for happiness in the adoration of others. But deep within, wounded people share a feeling of being homesick no matter where they are.

Final Work

Betrayal trauma wounded you in more than one way. It demolished your beliefs and assumptions about yourself and the world (or, if you were very young, it prevented such beliefs from ever forming at all). Your senses of safety, trust, and invulnerability were, for a time, shattered, which can make the world seem very dangerous and confusing. It can also drain your self-image, causing you to feel stupid, weak, childish, ugly, and alone. This will make it difficult to accept help from others, to trust, and even to see yourself as a good and worthy person. Harry Potter, after all, felt that his role at home was to remain hidden and as quiet as if he was not even there.

Another way you have been hurt is one of the most difficult to overcome. This is what I call the "second trauma," and it describes the daily re-injuring you receive from peoples' insensitivity, lack of support, and flat-out rudeness about your trauma. A person who reports their rape to a hospital or police may have experienced this secondary wounding during a rape evidence exam, or by having to constantly repeat their story to a detective or social worker. People may be telling you that your trauma wasn't "real" because your perpetrator was a parent or a partner, or the abuse was emotional rather than physical. You may have even been blamed for your trauma with suggestions that it was *your* fault (when it wasn't): if only you had behaved properly, been responsible, minded rules, prayed more, and made more effort to please others, you would not have been mistreated. Ridicule at school, smirks on the face of your abuser, rumors and gossip, and jokes about your abuse are all forms of re-injury. Harry, for example, thinks he has escaped the abuse of the Dursleys when he leaves their home, only to find that he faces constant taunts and insults by Draco Malfoy, who repeats the themes of Harry being worthless, stupid, and unwelcome. Simply being free of the Dursleys does not also free Harry from the pain inflicted by others' cruelty. He has to learn to overcome much more than just the original abuses he'd suffered. In response to these traumas, you may even find yourself doubting your own memory ("Did I imagine that? Did I misunderstand? Am I crazy? Are my feelings exaggerated?"), joining with your critics against yourself ("I know, I was stupid!" and "It was my fault. I put myself in that position" and "It's no big deal").

But the worst way in which your traumas have affected you is by causing you to feel you were ruined and worthless. Even worse than when other people say these things about you, is when *you* say them about yourself. When you constantly put yourself down for your looks or body, fail to nurture yourself physically, harm yourself like Winky (or Dobby, before he changed his own habits), drop out of society, or just generally feel insignificant, you reiterate to yourself the same things your abuser thought about you. Joining your abuser's view is not fighting trauma.

In my therapy groups, people would often apologize to me for crying or raging while working through their abuse, as if they feared being judged for "attention-seeking" or "taking up too much time in the group" to focus on their own needs (traumatized people, incidentally, often begin to forego self-care and will apologize for taking any time for themselves; many times they would also tell me they were considering leaving therapy because they were convinced their treatment issues were insignificant in contrast to others', and they felt unworthy to take time away from their more-deserving peers in group therapy). They were embarrassed by their own natural reactions to the pain of trauma, and devalued their own emotions: "Who am I to even deserve to feel feelings about what was done to hollow, little me?"

All of this shame leads to feelings of loneliness. Even victims of abuse who have many friends tell me they still feel alone, as if nobody can ever truly understand them. The fear is constant that someone will discover that they are frauds: "If you really knew my secret, knew how much pain and anger and brokenness I feel inside—and if you knew *why* I feel those things—you would reject me. You only accept me because you don't know the truth, which means nobody actually accepts the real me."

What I have found, though, is that people who begin to open up about their true inner selves tend to draw others in as allies, rather than alienating them. There are always people like Draco Malfoy or Pansy Parkinson who will reject others in need, and you will encounter them. But vulnerability actually strengthens good relationships rather than dissolving them. By "vulnerability," I do not mean becoming constantly pitiful, or using your traumas to suck the sympathetic energy out of others for your own attention—some victims do that, and become "Moaning Myrtles," or worse, "pity Dementors" who simply drain energy from others around them—but being open and thoughtful. Neither pity-seeking nor fake toughness attracts warm relationships like Harry, Hermione, and Ron's friendships. What does draw people in is the discovery, "You feel those things, too? I thought I was the only one!"

When rape victims in therapy came to the point of telling their trauma stories to others, they were always terrified. It meant disclosing what they had been through at the worst moments of their lives, in every detail, in order to burst open their "trauma Horcrux" and finally destroy it. Many of them were afraid that they would be overwhelmed by their own emotions, but by far the worst fear of all, every time, was "what if the person who hears it becomes horrified and rejects me? I would be completely crushed by the remembrance of the rape itself, plus the humiliation of knowing I am stranded alone with those feelings!" But when they actually took the step, they were never abandoned. They were always uplifted, grieved with (and for), accepted, and affirmed.

Remus Lupin felt the same fear that you might feel about how others would treat him if they discovered his secret. To Lupin, the fact that he was secretly a werewolf was something to be ashamed of, and he was sure others would reject him if they ever knew. He thus concealed his secret, never telling anyone of the injury in his youth that had caused him to become something that even he hated about himself. But the time eventually came for him to tell his closest friends what he had been struggling with: "I was terrified they would desert me the moment they found out what I was. But of course, they, like you, Hermione, worked out the truth ... And they didn't desert me at all."[1]

Lupin's fear of being exposed is a lot like the fear that abuse and rape victims have of their secrets becoming known, too. Frankly, not all people are accepting, and I have seen people rejected by friends, and even known a few instances of husbands who have left marriages when they lacked the maturity to be their wife's allies in her healing from rape. But by far, most people want to be compassionate and supportive. People who do not value kindness are not your allies. Those who do, though, will tend to be the kind of friends Remus Lupin was able to find: "I was happier than I had ever been in my life. For the first time ever, I had friends, three great friends. Sirius Black ... Peter Pettigrew ... and, of course, your father, Harry – James Potter." Healing does not require that everyone accept you. Popularity is not a remedy for trauma. Companionship, trust, and gentleness with feelings are the aspects of relationships that do help you heal.

Like Hagrid said (and which I've quoted previously), "I am what I am, an' I'm not ashamed. 'Never be ashamed,' my ol' dad used ter say, 'there's some who'll hold it against you, but they're not worth botherin' with."[2] Being able to identify as a victim of abuse is not a negative or self-shaming thing, any more than Harry stating directly to people, "Voldemort killed my parents" makes him weaker for saying it. In fact, Harry is able to transform the meaning of that statement from something tragic he has to confess about himself, to something he says defiantly to those who doubt him. It becomes his way of saying, "Someone did his worst to me, but I wasn't destroyed. Now I'm stronger than them, and I'm using my strength to resist them." Being brave about who you are is strength, and it will attract the people who are most able to value and understand you. Hanging your head low, always needing pity, and feeling entitled to special treatment

1 *Harry Potter and the Prisoner of Azkaban*, p.354
2 *Harry Potter and the Goblet of Fire*, p.455

because of your abuse are the habits that will repel people and leave your isolated; they don't defy your victimhood, they reinforce it. Harry hated the very idea of people treating him like a victim, or that his own victimization would ever cause others to suffer. He sought to develop his inner strength so that he would be able to show others that he valued them just as they did him, thus becoming equals.

That kind of transformation is a rite of passage. When you are traumatized, you have no idea that there is an entire invisible world of other people like you right in front of you every day, but hidden, and that you are welcome to be part of it. If the worst wound of trauma is loneliness and disconnection, healing from trauma brings a sense of reconnection and belonging with others who understand you. All around you are hidden victims, going about their day like normal Muggles, but endowed with insights and openness to others who have also endured what they, too, have endured.

I learned from years of working with victims of trauma that they are like a "tribe" of kindred spirits who can recognize each other. Members of Dumbledore's Army carried charmed coins that would carry a signal to alert them to action. Only members of the group had this invitation, or were even aware of one another's belonging in the group. In real life, I have been amazed to see that survivors can detect other survivors in groups, as if their "DA" galleon had become warm. To someone else who has also healed, you are a member of the tribe, the "Dumbledore's Army" of survivors, people who struggle together against the dark, who learn from one another, guide one another, and share knowledge about what works and who to trust. To anyone outside the tribe, the entire movement seems nearly invisible, like Muggles who can't see a port key or a hidden castle. You carry a special membership, and it's not open to everyone.

As a result, many people won't ever notice your inner transformations, or know how amazing it is that you've overcome such hurdles. After all, most people who see Harry on the street only see a normal, skinny man with an insignificant scar, and have no idea that he'd fought not only for himself, but fought to help overcome something in order to improve *their* lives, too—without them even knowing it. They simply hurry past him on the street, like they will do to you, too. Your transformation will not make you glow, and it will not announce itself. It's inward. It's something others in your tribe can recognize and honor, like how Harry notices people who specifically recognize him, wave to him and smile at him, because they *know*. They spot one of their own. The fact that nothing special is recognized by Muggles is a form of protection, not a failure of Harry to radiate his glory.

Final Work

The best way to fuel your flickering spark of recovery is to connect with others who share that spark. Your recovery is not meant to turn you into a "normal" or "ordinary" person, it is meant to imbue you with power. I do not suggest that survivors necessarily start crusading to become therapists and victim's advocates, which can be extremely traumatic and disturbing work, but I do believe that becoming a survivor is a process, not an event. Many of the people who finish their work with me commemorate it with a ceremony: a tattoo, cutting hair, burning old journals or social work case records, etc. But this is not an end of a process; it signals the start of a new life.

The final growth of healing is to begin reaching out to others in need who are not yet as far along as you. If survivors of abuse are like a tribe, then you are becoming one of the tribe's elders. For too long, people have had to endure the effects of trauma alone, which is a shame because there is such a remarkable community of survivors just waiting to become interconnected. While I don't think this means every survivor should feel led into careers related to trauma work or writing a memoir of their traumas, I do think there are some amazing opportunities for survivors to pass along hope to victims that they are not alone, and that there is a way out of these feelings. In my therapy groups, I would have clients prepare to leave by writing a "letter to survivors" that they would leave behind, so that those just starting therapy could receive wisdom and courage from those who had succeeded; I eventually compiled some of those letters into the book *Letters To Survivors*.

Other former clients of mine have gone on to do public speaking about the realities of rape, child abuse, human trafficking, and LGBT rights. Some work with colleges as class speakers, and as consultants for campus counseling centers, fraternities, and sororities. Other friends and former clients have gone into social work. Some have gone into political work, defending the rights of children, funding for domestic violence and rape crisis centers, and the civil rights of minorities. Many of them are nurses.

When Harry follows Hagrid though the streets of London for the first time, he is amazed at the hidden world of people like himself that he never knew were all around him. For all of his life, he thought he'd been alone, just a useless, abused boy with no hope and no real family. He had no idea that others were ready for him to come forth and join them, be one of them, belong among them. Certainly, not everyone in his new world would be safe or healthy; he would face wizards every bit as abusive as any Muggle. Some would bully him. Others were vain and sought glory. Some regarded themselves as more important than others. Likewise, not everyone in the community of survivors is healthy, either. There are those who create crises to force others to serve their needs. Some are resentful and unwelcoming of the opposite gender, even when they share experiences that ought to be the basis for alliance. You'll still encounter bitterness, elitism, and bias, even among those who were hurt by abusers who practiced bitterness, elitism, and bias.

But Harry is able to sort through this mix of good and bad, and find what he needs. For him, learning that people in his new world aren't always perfect isn't a disappointment. He's able to accept that. Instead, he finds that this new, special community has wonderful complexity in it, and he is able to accept that not everyone accepts him. Having a Gilderoy Lockhart-like need to be cherished by everyone is not part of healing, and Harry instead focuses on the close group of friends who truly do know and love him. What matters most, though, is his discovery that he is part of a living whole, and not as alone as he had always believed.

When Dumbledore was killed by Snape at the end of the film, "*Harry Potter and the Half-Blood Prince*", the grim image of the Dark Mark loomed ominously in the clouds over Hogwarts. The symbol of hope and safety the students and professors had depended on had been shattered; surely all was lost. As they gathered around the body of Dumbledore, they grieved and felt defeated, as if some flicker of life within each of them had been snuffed out, too. In that moment, it seemed that evil had won. Nothing would ever be the same.

But one by one, they lifted their wands skyward, sending pinpoints of light into the dark. Each wand's luminescence joined with that of the others, until a warmth of light expands. The reverential, holy brightness of each person joining together evaporates the image of the Dark Mark over them. By sharing one another's grief, they have also found the way to share one another's hope, and in that communion they overcome the darkness that seemed to have defeated them.

At a healing retreat for survivors of sexual assault, I stood in a circle of women who were celebrating the steps they had taken to reclaim their voices, their power, and their lives. We all stood around the embers of a fire, which we had built next to a lake in a wooded, secluded, beautiful place. Each woman took a turn approaching the fire and laying something symbolic upon it.

"These were the jeans I was wearing the night I was raped. I had loved them—they were my favorite pair—but they were turned into something connected to the worst memory of my life. I leave them behind now."

"This is a folder of the medical records from when I was abused. All my test results and the notes about my injuries are in here, and photographs that were taken of me. I'm no longer that person, so I'm burning them tonight."

"These are the poems I wrote for years about how much I hated myself after what happened. I don't hate myself anymore."

"This is the suicide note I wrote the night I tried to overdose."

As each offering was made to the fire, the woman would return to the circle and be enveloped in hugs and acceptance. Their artifacts of trauma curled and smoked and caught fire, and the soft light of the flames brightened the circle, and all of our faces emerged from the dark. One by one, each woman shed her shame and added her light, and little by little the Dark Mark of defeat that had hung over them began to vanish. What each of them had lost was precious, but as we each lifted our lights upward again with tears on our faces, we found that we were all undefeated.

As you shed the cocoon of your despair and loneliness, and as you make progress in your own battles against Dementors and Horcruxes, you will also make your way into the community of other survivors that is waiting for you. The more you begin to speak up about your past, present, and future, the more you will find people connecting to it. At church, in therapy groups, online, while volunteering at a crisis center, and during marches, you will find others all around you that you never knew were also survivors, coming forward out of hiding and saying, "You too? I thought I was the only one!"

Taking those steps will be terrifying at first, and joyful as you learn and achieve more. Right now, even the very idea of taking those steps to find and join your new community might feel dreadful.

It will also help you heal your scar.

CHAPTER SIXTEEN

Scars and Post-Traumatic Growth

"You are protected, in short, by your ability to love!"
-Albus Dumbledore, *Half-Blood Prince*

Throughout this book, I have assured you that you can heal from your traumas. I have assured you that *you* should be the one who defines what it means to heal. I have assured you that you are not damaged for the rest of your life, and that you can grow larger than your pain. I have assured you that you are confined to the limitations that your abusers have placed on you.

But what does that actually mean? I once asked a group of abuse survivors what it means to them to become healed. Here are some of their answers:

- When you can face the thoughts of trauma rather than having to avoid them;
- When you understand the connection between your current self-concept and your abuse, so that when you feel down on yourself you won't accept that as a permanent "truth" of who you are;
- When you no longer engage in self-harming behaviors (including substance abuse) to manage emotions and memories;
- When flashbacks have diminished to the point they either

no longer happen, or no longer interfere with your life and emotions;
- When you can appropriately respond to people's ignorant attitudes about abuse or rape, rather than withdrawing from them and wilting in lonely shame;
- When you have begun to offer support to other survivors;
- When you have begun to view your body as a valuable thing and not as a betrayer or curse, and you take care of its needs;
- When you learn to recognize the warning signs of abusers and avoid them, no matter how charming they appear to be;
- When abusers no longer have control over your opinions of yourself;
- When you make your own choices whether to disclose your abuse to someone because of something you need to say, not something you need to hear, for you to make progress;
- When you no longer feel guilty for asking for help, or for having rough days, or for taking the length of time needed for growth.

This sounds like a difficult list, but you don't have to achieve all of these at once. You will have some breakthrough "a-ha!" moments that bring success to several of these at once, too, like a domino effect. Improvements in one area will tend to bring improvements in many other areas too. If you continue through your therapy, and with this book, you will find yourself accomplishing most (or all) of this list.

Because it is important for people to define healing for themselves, I listened to a group of survivors sharing what the word meant to them. One person responded:

> Healing and Recovery from trauma is truly the sum of so many little things that you do on this path every day. It is consistently being willing to work on yourself and look at yourself over and over again. However, those words mean to me that I can recognize the difference between that something that happened to me, or thinking that I was bad and responsible for that trauma. What happened to me is in the past. I can't change the past, but I can live in the present...
>
> Healing and Recovery is being able to say the words that you could not previously say. It means that I live more connected to the world versus focused on protecting myself and having the walls up. I can look inward and see me. I am

able to forgive myself and all younger versions of myself. I am grateful in knowing that I did what I could in those moments to survive, instead of hating myself. Moving toward knowing that my perpetrators don't need space in my life. I don't have to forgive them…

It means knowing that I may be triggered and that I will have to deal with it, but I can see and deal with it quicker. Knowing that I do have PTSD. Instead of being angry about it, I know that I have it and need to live with keeping my nervous system calm every day.

The early days are so horrific. That is the beginning of healing and recovery. I must say that I could not see that for a very long time.

Another friend told me,

> Healing can be distilled into a single word: Freedom.
>
> I find "recovery" to be the liberated fruits of my labor, while "healing" is the actual messy, painful, sorrowful, seemingly hopeless work that must be done to get there. And one can't be had without the other.
>
> Inner freedom has always been my ultimate goal, and I have no doubts about full recovery from past, finite trauma. I happen to be pretty close now.
>
> How do I know? My peace of mind, knowing deeply and emotionally that rejection has nothing to do with my self worth, present pain doesn't overwhelm me, other people's opinions have no effect on my joy or choices, and my personal power is about my personal acts of will based on my values, passion and needs.
>
> And my vulnerability is not a threat or a weakness, but a prerequisite for connection, both internal and external, and also, surprisingly, an important part of my self-confidence. I feel light, and often times gloriously free. It's so much more than being free of PTSD symptoms. It's so much more than accepting oneself and ones limitations. It's so much more than compassion and empathy. It's a powerful and secure feeling. A zest for life. It's living. It won't protect me from the storms of life, but I will act differently through them now. I am free to do so.
>
> I also know I still have a few things to do, and I have no

intention of stopping until I'm completely free. I recently worked through a stuck point and it's the first time any stuck point work has lasted for months on end. It took me almost as long to realize it was a stuck point. But the fact that I had the strength to work through the extreme, rock-bottom emotions is another indication of where I am in my healing. A year ago I wouldn't have been able to stand it. I was feeling exceptionally raw and lonely through most of it, too. In those times it's good to remind myself that darkness is a powerful liar and that the hardest emotions are potent echoes of my past. At the time, I had no idea I'd eventually come out of it into this new state of being, or freedom, which I'm in now.

Internal freedom is not an on/off switch, but a gradual progression. In the beginning of my healing, feeling better usually meant a few seconds of well-being, but as I progressed, these moments became more frequent and eventually came to stay. Every sense of relief or fragile happiness, transient or no, is a good indication that one is going in the right direction.

We all matter, no matter what. Not because I, or someone else says so, but because it's our birthright.

For my friend Lucinda, healing meant becoming able to attend a public anti-violence march as a survivor of abuse, carrying a sign and wearing a dress decorated with teal ribbons bearing the names of other women who had been raped, and who had allowed her to represent them by name.

Another survivor, Tara, told me:

Healing/recovery for me right now is about challenging the people who want to distort my reality and challenging the internal distortions. When I was fighting the notion of incest by dad, in a really short space of time I was cycling between reality and denial, and I was paying for it in the highest way. Denial would lie to me and pretend I felt better, but I was actively suicidal and losing control. It was a terrifying time. Thankfully, I came to the conclusion that stopping the denial was much less painful than keeping it. And I was done sacrificing myself for him (and others).

For me, recovery looks like no longer being held down by victimized thinking or behaviors. It looks like believing my worth with such depth that I no longer even contemplate selling myself to others or engaging in psychologically damaging behaviors.

Recovery looks like honesty and openness. I'm getting better at this. But having the confidence to talk to safe people...recovery would look like the opposite of my isolation now. I'd let people into my vulnerabilities and I'd reach out.

Elizabeth said,

I was thinking about some of what has happened to me, and I wasn't freaking out. I wasn't triggered or disassociating, my heart rate didn't skyrocket and I wasn't gasping for breath or feeling lightheaded. (Now that's not to say that those things never happen, or that I am never upset or emotional about it, but they happen with much less frequency than they used to.) I realized that I can choose to think of my experiences and my reactions to those experiences without always having panic set in. Furthermore, I thought about it for a bit, and then moved on to something else. That's a big deal.

I see healing in myself at the fact that I can stand to not drink. And while there have been some days that I've thought a drink sounded nice, it's not hurting my feelings to not drink. In fact, I'm thinking I like not drinking so much that I'm just going to keep it up...That is a BIG DEAL.

The fact that feeding myself an appropriate amount of nourishing food is no longer a daily battle... I rest when I am tired. I have found compassion and forgiveness for myself. Not completely, and maybe not all the time with every single thing, but self-compassion and forgiveness used to be completely foreign to me, and they're kind of my bag now.

I realize now that I don't hold any blame for the things that were done to me. I think I held onto blame for a long time because it felt like a safety mechanism. Like, if it had been my fault before, then that made it possible for me to make sure that it would never happen again. But it wasn't my fault. That was a tough truth to accept, because it's scary.

I'm still here. I made it to the other side. It did not kill me. Nor did it ruin me. I deserve to be happy, and healthy, and free, and have peace and joy...I was lost for a long, long time. I despaired and lost hope, and did not want to go on. But I did. And now, it's okay. I am this amazingly strong and resilient woman who MADE IT. I made it to the other side of all that darkness.

Notice that these responses all have a couple of things in common: 1) becoming capable of dealing with old feelings, and 2) becoming connected with others again.

I also asked survivors of abuse and rape what they had learned that helped them recover.

A teen girl suggested,

Recognizing what you yourself have done! Recognizing the little steps and big steps alike, and seeing yourself grow from a victim into a survivor. I feel like we all need this, because many of us forget how far we have come, we forget the obstacles we have overcome, when we should be realizing them and bubbling over with pride about them!

Judy responded,

Honesty. Honesty with yourself. Sitting back and recognizing progress and honestly seeing it for yourself. Writing the facts as they present themselves....not just the ones we are willing to disclose because we are afraid of having to hash them out in session…And patience with ourselves...that sometimes we progress with ease and sometimes sessions are just awful. Patience with our progress...it goes no faster or slower than it has to. Patience with the person trying to help guide us, they don't know what's in our heads...unless we tell them. Patience with our significant others when they are unable to be what we need them to be at a moment, but take stock in them as a whole. Mine is worth it! Oh and they don't know what's in our heads either...unless we tell them, they can't do any different than they do.

Andrea added,

Hope for brighter days, especially when you are in the depth of depression each and every day. Hope that you will truly love who you are as a person. Hope that you can see your worth as a human being. Hope that you can make others lives better, because of who you are…Learning to love the person that we are now. Loving ourselves enough to realize that we are just as important as any other person in this world. And knowing that we deserve to be loved with respect! We deserve to be loved, unconditionally. Being able to love someone unconditionally, realizing that they have faults. Loving what we can accomplish as a survivor of rape or sexual abuse. Loving who we were at the time. Because, that girl or guy deserves love despite the circumstances.

Stephanie said,

I think positive music has been a huge part of recovery for me. It calms me down when I'm upset. Lifts me up when I'm down. And it's something I can blast in my car and sing along to on the highway to both drive away my fears of 18 wheelers and chase away tiredness. Music is something that has gotten me through a lot of hard times in my life. I don't know what I would do without it.

...We need to admit when it is we need help, when we are struggling, when it gets too big for us. We need to take action when this happens, because depression is never far away, and it can swoop down on us, and swallow us up if we fail to admit our feelings, to ourselves, and to others who want to help us—if they only knew when we need them most.

I suggested,

Mercy. Remember to be merciful to yourself, rather than sifting through the mistakes of your past and condemning yourself for them. You are not wicked, and you are not without value. You may find it hard to believe at times, but there are people who will know your story and yet look you in the eyes with pure respect and acceptance. Do not forget to do that for yourself, AND for others you meet along the way who may have also stumbled. Survivorhood is built from a never-ending process of forming linkages between merciful people who see one another as humans, not as person-shaped collections of flaws.

In your recovery, it is important to change the language that you might use. I have found that trauma victims can be very cruel to themselves and recycle awful self-criticisms in their own minds. For example, "I'm scarred for life." A person in recovery will reconsider what "scarred" truly means: a scar is a healed place, a marker and reminder of what was formerly a wound but is now a protected and useful (and even useable) growth. While we cannot lose our memories of the wound that caused the scar, we carry the evidence of our healing as the scar. Harry's scar is the evidence of what he has survived, not the evidence that he is weak or ruined. As he works through his battles with Voldemort, his scar stings with supernatural symbolism, just like doing therapeutic trauma work will cause you to feel many older pains returning. But when Harry has won, his scar no longer hurts. It simply represents what he has overcome. In fact, Harry's scar marks him as a victor over trauma, hate, and violence.

Examine the self-talk you use:
- Do you continually degrade yourself, criticize yourself, and expect rejection?
- Have you begun to believe that because of your abuse, you no longer have anything worthy inside to contribute to another person's life?
- Does it feel like you have "hurt me" printed right on your forehead, like Harry's scar?
- Do you find yourself accepting all of peoples' criticisms, but none of their praise?
- Do you continually produce art or writing obsessed with images of defeat, injury, or despair?
- Do you pick fights with people, or have a "chip on your shoulder," and then criticize others for failing you when the conflict starts?
- Do you behave in ways that you think will cause people to reject you because you believe "they'll reject me anyway, so let's get it over with"?
- Do you tell yourself that nobody can love you now?
- Do you warn people who love you that you are no good, and suggest that they abandon you?
- Do you deliberately provoke people who love you in an effort to drive them away to "save" them from you?
- Do you find yourself asking permission to speak, apologizing for seeking help, or feeling undeserving of time?
- Do you make comments like, "you would be better off without me" or "I'm sorry to be such a burden on you" to people who try to support you?

Recovery is absolutely possible, and many people do recover from this trauma. The ones who do not recover are those who commit suicide, who remain in abusive relationships, who continually choose alcohol or self-injury over the difficult work of recovery, or cannot find competent support and help from others. I simply can't imagine how anyone would recover from this if, at the same time, she were also beating herself up with negativity.

Harry is able to achieve healing from his trauma. He evolves from a person who has nightmares, feels despair and anger, becomes easily triggered into arguments, and feels contaminated by his traumas, and becomes someone who rejects power over others, is able to empathize with others, can apologize for what he does wrong, and sees himself as a generally good person. He is able to form close friendships and a healthy marriage, become a good father, see other points of view, accept others in spite of their flaws, and find ways to be strong that aren't just "tough guy" masculine clichés.

In therapy, we call this "post-traumatic growth," and it contrasts with post-traumatic stress disorder. In a disorder, your symptoms cause you distress and interference with your normal life. But when you confront your traumas and become stronger than your symptoms, the disorder can actually recede and allow growth in those newly-opened areas of your mind, heart, and soul. There is the kind of struggle that produces little change, like spinning tires in mud. This unproductive type of struggle happens when someone:

- tries to force their feelings about abuse back into hiding,
- avoids thoughts or examination of their own traumas, cannot endure discomfort in therapy,
- self-harms to manage emotions,
- seeks tough-type power as a way to feel strong,
- seeks pity or feels entitled to special rights or privileges because of their victim status,
- rejects others as "betrayers" simply for having flaws or making mistakes,
- treats their abuse as "no big deal" in the past.

Struggle can actually produce positive change, though, when it happens as you challenge your traumas in order to actually overcome them. Harry's own struggles shows us five ways to accomplish this.

First, he becomes open to the new opportunities and possibilities that he had not experiences before. He changes from being a person who lives in a dark, dusty closet under the stairs who must always be silent, to someone who explores his world. He summons the courage to ride hippogriffs and dragons, explore secret chambers, and perhaps most bravely, date and kiss a girl he likes. In your real life there won't be any chances to ride dragons or explore magical castles, but you have many ways to try things that are challenging to you. For example, many of the abuse survivors I've worked with in therapy and friendship alliances have embarked on careers in nursing and social work, they do public speaking about rape and abuse, they volunteer at crisis centers, they work with victims of human trafficking, and many of them have bravely escaped relationships that were violent.

Second, his relationships with others change. Harry is finally able to trust that people who love him will actually be dependable and kind to him. At first, he falters in his trust in his friends. When he doesn't receive their letters, he becomes resentful and cold to them. He's still stuck in the mindset that if he *feels* disappointed by a friend, it proves they have *actually* betrayed him. Many people remain stuck in this false belief, but Harry is able to outgrow it. He eventually is able to trust his closest friends with his secret fears, hopes, despair, happiness, and love. He doesn't expect others to make his life easy for him—he knows this is his work to do—yet he doesn't adopt a macho "tough guy" posture that makes him hard to be close to. Harry has learned from his own abuse that simply having power over someone else does not make someone morally right. How we *use* power matters more than whether we have it at all; Dumbledore is an authority figure who supports and loves Harry. Umbridge, however, wields the same official authority as Headmaster, too, but uses her power to hurt people. Simply having power does not make one good. Harry, then, learns to use the power he develops very carefully, and becomes willing to sacrifice for those he loves, rather than trying to become powerful, too, such as discarding the elder wand and resurrection stone. Even though he is sometimes made fun of for his mistakes, he remains emotionally open to those he loves.

Third, he develops a new sense of his own strength: "If I can face Voldemort, I can face anything." Harry's views of what it means to be strong is different than a superhero view. He doesn't become a stoic, emotionless, muscular badger of a man. He's not the kind of person who believes "might makes right," or that controlling other people is how to be strong and safe. Even when others doubt him, tease him, reject him, and bully him, he tries to still just do what is right. Harry is able to reject abusiveness, never repeating the patterns of behavior that he grew up with. He is an example of why growing up experiencing abuse does *not* make someone destined to become abusive, too. Being neglected, molested, and hurt does not mean you have become a "Voldemort Horcrux" who could easily be sorted into a life of committing abuse against others, too. Harry shows us that it is your choices, not your experiences, which make you who you are. He shows that he is stronger than his abusers by rejecting their lifestyles and becoming a non-abusive, thoughtful person instead.

Fourth, he begins to have a greater appreciation for life in general. In 2015, J.K. Rowling responded to someone who asked her what she would say to someone who feels lost and wants to give up. "I'd say, the world is full of wonderful things you haven't seen yet. Don't ever give up on the chance of seeing them," she replied.[1] Harry truly comes to see the wonder and beauty in the world around him, even though he is beset by evil, violence, and horror by the bad people in it. Knowing that there is bad in the world does not strip the world of its beauty, too, and Harry becomes the kind of person who sees qualities in people who are very different from him. While entering his trial in *Order of the* Phoenix, Harry sees the fountain inside the Ministry of Magic headquarters, into which coins have been tossed. The fountain has a sign that says "ALL PROCEEDS FROM THE FOUNTAIN OF MAGICAL BRETHREN WILL BE GIVEN TO ST MUNGO'S HOSPITAL FOR MAGICAL MALADIES AND INJURIES."[2] He pledges to himself that if he is able to return, he will contribute ten galleons of solid gold; he does indeed return, and instead donates his entire bag of money. Harry sees the needs of others as personal priorities, and chooses to support others who have been hurt, in addition to learning to care for himself. We learn from the sorting hat that we become the kind of person we choose to be, not the kind of person someone else tells us we are.

Fifth, he grows spiritually. He comes to realize that just because we grow and heal does not mean we will not still sometimes suffer, but that suffering is not the limits of our lives, and does not define us. Harry also learns that being "cool" is not important; being kind is, which is why he doesn't carry his resentments against people like Draco forward through his entire life. He sets a boundary that keeps unkind people out of his relationships, but he does not remain bitter, either. He becomes someone who people can feel safe and comfortable around, rather than someone who repels, intimidates, or uses people. For Harry, the "spirit" of another person becomes more important than their status, their blood, or their popularity. One way to apply that lesson in your own life is to remember that family can mean blood relationship, but it doesn't have to mean that; Harry finds a bond with others who make him feel safe, loved, and supported, and they

1 Twitter, @jk_rowling, May 4, 2015
2 *Harry Potter and the Order of the Phoenix,* p.127

become his new family. It is their souls, not their blood, that make them complete.

Why is it that Harry is able to grow as a person after his trauma, but someone like, say, Draco pretty much remains stuck in his points of view no matter what he experiences? Researchers say that there are a couple of reasons why some people are able to achieve post-traumatic growth, and others aren't. Those two traits seem to be openness to new experiences, and a willingness to seek connection with others.[3] I have seen this borne out in my work as a therapist, too; clients who become curious about the causes and effects of trauma, connect with others (even those who haven't had the same experiences), are comfortable with people of other races, gender, sexual orientations, and lifestyles, and who see their lives as still being created rather than stuck in past traumas, tend to do very well compared to those who remain emotionally numb and isolated.

Draco was raised to see himself as above everyone else, and as a result has the seed of an abusive mindset planted within him from birth; Harry, on the other hand, was raised to see everyone as better than him, but grows to see that he is equally as important to others, and others are equally as important to him. This contrast between Harry and Draco is critical because it shows us that victims of abuse actually have a greater chance of healing than abusers do. It is more possible to grow into a sense of self-worth and equality after feeling low, than to sacrifice a view of one's self as superior and entitled in order to become equal to others. That means you have more potential to become whole and healed than your abusers, rapists, or betrayers do. For example, Harry, Ron and Hermione have a conversation about Horcruxes:

> "Isn't there any way of putting yourself back together?" Ron asked.
> "Yes," said Hermione with a hollow smile, "but it would be excruciatingly painful."
> "Why? How do you do it?" asked Harry.
> "Remorse," said Hermione. "You've got to really feel what you've done…Apparently the pain of it can destroy you. I can't see Voldemort attempting it somehow, can you?"

Harry later actually confronts Voldemort with this, urging him to repent of his evil:

---

3 Collier, Lorna. "Growth after trauma"; http://www.apa.org/monitor/2016/11/growth-trauma.aspx

"…before you try to kill me, I'd advise you think what you've done . . . . Think, and try for some remorse, Riddle. . . ."

"What is this?" Of all the things that Harry had said to him, beyond any revelation or taunt, nothing had socked Voldemort like this. Harry saw is pupils contract to thin slits, saw the skin around his eyes whiten.

"It's your one last chance," said Harry, "it's all you've got left. . . . I've seen what you'll be otherwise. . . .Be a man. . . try. . . Try for some remorse. . . ."

"You dare --- ?" said Voldemort again.

"Yes, I dare," said Harry…

Harry is so thoroughly un-abusive that he is actually brought to tears by the very idea that anyone would ever be hurt for him, or even die for him. Unlike Harry, Voldemort is unable to feel humility or debt for the effects he has had on others. As an abuser, Voldemort feels superior to those he hurts, using power for his own sake and not as a means of making lives better. The very act of challenging his actions feels like a taunt to him. As a result, he is not able to grow or heal, because he regards even the suggestion that he *could* be better—let alone that he owes it to anyone else to change at all—as an insult to his superiority. Someone who feels they owe nothing to others is not able to heal from their own actions. But someone who has been hurt can heal, because healing by definition means reconnecting with others in healthy relationships, which is a form of self-empowerment. Healing from abuse does not mean needing to repent, because being abused or raped or mistreated are not failures by the victims. This is why seeking remorse from your abuser is usually a dead end; confronting abusers almost never brings closure for victims, because abusers typically do not acknowledge that that they'd done is wrong. Rather, they tend to repeat their excuses that "you made me do that; it was your fault; you're crazy; that never happened; what about all the stuff *you* did to *me*?" Like any other abuser, Voldemort feels free to hurt others, but when he feels hurt, let down, or failed by anyone else, he becomes irate—it's always their fault.

These are the differences that set you apart from your abusers. In their minds, whatever they have done to you is *your* fault, which prevents them from showing remorse or growing spiritually. But you have the chance to heal, because the shame and guilt you have felt are not what you really deserve to suffer, which means you are allowed—and able—to rid yourself of them. Abusers need to feel something they cannot feel before they can grow, which is why they almost never do heal from being abusive. But victims need to feel *less* of something you don't deserve to feel, and becoming free of those feelings also sets you free to become a healed person. That makes you very, very much *un*like an abuser, and in fact, better. Hagrid expressed this point of view when he said, "I am what I am an' I'm not ashamed. 'Never be ashamed,' my ol' dad used ter say, 'there's some who'll hold it against you, but they're not worth bothern' with.'"[4]

Research into post-traumatic growth shows that not only can you be injured by your traumas, but you can also change in positive ways as you work to overcome those injuries. This does not mean that traumas are good; I have never liked the phrase "what doesn't kill you makes you stronger." Rape, molestation, abuse, and neglect do not make anyone stronger; they are not things that carry silver linings. Rather, *recovering* from what has harmed you makes you stronger, and that slight change of wording makes a huge difference. Trauma causes depression, anxiety, broken relationships, and physical illness. But healing from it brings new insights, empathy, and rejection of false forms of strength and power. What you have lived through cannot be undone. Healing does not mean becoming someone who was never abused, and in fact acknowledging your abuse is a real step toward healing. Harry cannot hide his scar; everyone who sees him knows this part of his past. But he is able to transform its meaning from "this is from when I was hurt" to "this is what I have overcome." He is "the boy who lived," and not "the boy who was abused."

One of the ways people are transformed by post-traumatic growth is in their need to tell stories. Interviews with survivors of concentration camps during the holocaust found that many of them were sustained by an inner promise to help preserve the truth of what had happened to them, so that their suffering would never become meaningless. It was important to them that others know what happened, so that the ideas that caused the horror could be recognized again, and overcome. Ette Hillesum, a victim of the Nazi concentration camps, wrote about the importance of facing our sadness and accepting our wounds without seeing ourselves as worthless people. She said,

> You must be able to bear your sorrow; even if it seems to crush you, you will be able to stand up again, for human beings are so strong, and your sorrow must become an integral part of yourself; you mustn't run away from it. Do not relieve your feelings through hatred, do not seek to be avenged on all Germans, for they, too, sorrow at this moment. Give your

---

4 *Harry Potter and the Goblet of Fire*, p.455

sorrow all the space and shelter in yourself that is its due, for if everyone bears grief honestly and courageously, the sorrow that now fills the world will abate. But if you do instead reserve most of the space inside you for hatred and thoughts of revenge—for which new sorrows will be born for others— then sorrow will never cease in this world. And if you have given sorrow the space it demands, then you may truly say: life is beautiful and so rich. So beautiful and so rich that it makes you want to believe in God.

Additionally, each holocaust survivor felt a bond not just with other survivors, but with those victims who didn't make it, so that their lives would be uplifted as precious, and not silently left in the disrespect that had been put on them by their tormentors. In my work with abuse victims, one trait I have noticed is growth from "I can't even talk about it, let alone use the word 'rape' or 'abuse'" to "I have to tell my story; I have to write it down, or speak, or share my words with others who are going through this, too." As Dumbledore said, "We must try not to sink beneath our anguish, Harry, but battle on."[5]

Even just this one change shows so much about healing. It represents someone ridding themselves of shame ("I have no voice; I have no right to speak, to occupy anyone else's time or space with my meager, useless needs; I deserve nothing") and becoming more confident and equal ("I have to let others know that they deserve the healing I've found; I have to help end this kind of trauma for others!"). This personal growth, this enlargement of your spirit, can free you of the ways you've coped with trauma until now. Drinking or getting high, cutting, reckless sex, suicide attempts—these are all ways of remaining smaller than your true self. Picking on others, bullying LGBT people, treating women as less worthy than men—these are all ways of creating fake empowerment, and they keep you from forming the equal bonds with others that helps you truly heal.

I once polled a group of trauma survivors as to *their* needs in recovery, and the overwhelming first answer was, "We need a way to come together socially with other survivors and just enjoy group activity. Not constant therapy, not constant attention to trauma, but a time to joke, tease, laugh, play, eat, have coffee, plan, and find out what it's like to fully belong in a 'tribe' of survivors. We've never had that." Another woman answered, "I know this sounds weird, but I feel like what's missing is a place where we can just sit on the floor together, sing, eat pizza, pray, do art, read our poems…a kind of 'Wounded Peoples' Coffeehouse.' But no therapist I've

5 *Harry Potter and the Half-Blood Prince,* p.357

ever found will do it!" I asked why she thought that was, and she said, "I think they're afraid of seeming weird, or getting in trouble if someone questions why they're inviting us 'crazy people' to have fun with them. But we need it. We *really* need it!"

When Harry is still feeling hurt by his traumas, he exhibits many of the same feelings you may have felt: he thinks negatively about his future, sees no meaning to his life, has no reason to see himself as a good person, lacks happiness, and has no positive relationships. He is simply "the boy under the stairs." But as he grows, he values his life more, which actually helps him fear death less. He cherishes his relationships, becomes more understanding and tolerant, defends others who are also being hurt, and refuses to become tough and hard. In order to grow like Harry grew, you have to also muster the courage to face your Boggarts, and not hide from them. No skipping therapy sessions or "forgetting" your journaling because it's too hard, no getting intoxicated to avoid triggers instead of enduring them and learning what causes them and how to overcome them, and no more punishing yourself for what someone else did. If you don't treat yourself like someone who deserves to be healed, how can you heal?

Another way to begin challenging your older beliefs about trauma is to reconsider the language you use about yourself. Try to gradually stop using dark, catastrophic words to describe yourself; many victims believe they are broken, unlovable, dirty, wounded for life, etc. In truth, you are none of those things—you are *hurt*. Transform your "abuse language" from one of being bad to one of being injured but recovering. Avoid using terms like "Weak" to describe yourself.

Use language that evokes strength and determination. Harry, for example, defiantly uses the name "Voldemort" when others are so timid they can only refer to "he who must be named." The name has a taboo curse on it, which Voldemort uses to track those who utter it, including Harry himself. Likewise, there are certain words associated with your trauma that will also evoke discomfort, and you may be temped to avoid them out of fear. For example, many of the rape victims I have worked with in therapy resist using the word "rape." In their writings (both online and in journals), they use clever ways to avoid the word that frightens them: "I was R'ed... My r---, I was hurt..." all to avoid the direct language of their experience. But avoidance is a symptom of post-traumatic stress, not a remedy for it. Engaging in the symptoms does not resist those symptoms. As Dumbledore said, "Always use the proper name for things. Fear of a name increases fear of the thing itself."[6] Face the taboo, and defy it. Use language that reflects the fact that you are in charge, not your victimization. "I was raped...I was

---

6 *Harry Potter and the Sorcerer's Stone*, p.298

abused, molested, tortured…" as the truth may be. "…And I am a survivor of it. I was not weak then, and I am not crazy now. Being wounded by it does not mean I am weak, only giving up my fight would. I have the scars from my battles, both lost and won, and like Harry I will do this, even when I am afraid."

Seek love, not pity. Share your story with those who have earned hearing it, not as a way to move people into treating you differently. Accept the help of others, while still knowing that this is your work to do for yourself. And above all, forgive yourself when you slip up or fail. Harry alternates between moment of victory, such as winning Quidditch and earning the adoration of all, to failure, such as costing Griffindor a loss of points that puts them in last place. Yet he persisted. Hermione is strong and confident, knows the answers and is eager to share them, but others reject her sometimes, and she retreats to the bathroom in tears. Yet she persisted. Persistence, not perfection, is what works. Use honest language, don't avoid saying things that are true—if you were raped, say the words; if you were beaten, say the words; if you were molested, or trafficked, or tortured, or verbally abused, say it. Remember that saying things that are true also means being positive toward yourself—if you are creative, say it; if you are proud of something you achieve, say it; if you are able to speak out in behalf of other victims, say so.

I have seen many people's journals, collages, poems, and works of art where they describe themselves in images that are very weak, defeated, distorted, and ugly. Online support forums for rape survivors, for example, are full of self-hating statements by women, and many of them use photographs of very sad, morose, helpless figures as avatars to represent themselves. In TV commercials, movies, and advertisements about sexual assault, women are often presented as isolated people, heads down, huddled into a small posture, and with very dark and ominous shadows over the images. YouTube is home to countless videos made by rape and abuse victims of slideshows set to music, but which depict image after image of injury, darkness, dread, defeat, blood, shadow, and grief— not a single image of empowerment or hope. They are in the Azkaban of their own beliefs about themselves, inviting the Dementors to keep them empty.

Many victims of rape and abuse have told me that they feel "scarred for life" by what they've endured. Maybe you are. But that's not a cruel thing to say. A person in recovery will reconsider what "scarred" truly means: a scar is a healed place, a marker and reminder of what was formerly a wound but is now a protected growth. While you cannot lose our memories of the wound that caused the scar, you carry the evidence of your healing as the scar. Don't allow yourself to think of abuse victims as dark images of broken, faceless figures in shadows. No more poems about blood, holes, and unholy souls. You cannot simultaneously crave the triumph of a sanctified survivor while branding yourself with the imagery of defeat and weakness (I once had a client with the word BROKEN tattooed boldly cross her chest. It was years before she added the word NOT in front of it).

Remember when Bill Weasley was disfigured by the attack of Fenrir Greyback? As he lay, helpless, in the Hogwarts hospital, Molly sobbed at the sight of his scars. "…and he was g-going to be married!", she cried out. Fleur, Bill's fiancée, responds at once, challenging Molly's belief that a scarred man is no longer loveable. "You think, because of these bites, he will not love me? …All these scars show is that my husband is brave!"[7] You will face some people who do not understand the scars, physical and emotional, that you bear from your past, and they will indeed see you as flawed. There is nothing you can do to force other people to repair their own faulty beliefs. But their thoughts are not your truths. Your truth is reflected in the attitude of allies like Fleur, who understand that scars that have been received through struggles against the cruelty of others are evidence of your goodness and your bravery. In Bill's life, it is likely that many who saw his scarred face would never know the true cause of them, and might unkindly turn away from him. That will happen to you at times, too, and that rejection is not a true indicator of your bravery or worth, only of some peoples' inability to understand your battles. But those who know Bill and his story will see his scars as honorable things, not degradations, and will offer him respect and affection. In your life, not all people will honor you as a survivor, and the failure of some to extend respect to you is not a problem in your life that you need to fix. Being misunderstood by others is not an issue you have to work to fix! Their thoughts are not your flowerbed to weed.

I have known people who feel defeated every day by their encounters with unkind or thoughtless people in the world, as if there was still some inward flaw they needed to fix in order to change how other people respond. The solution is actually far simpler: change how *you* feel about your wounds and the bravery they represent, rather than making the inner beliefs of *other* people your priority. Bill's own mother failed to understand the noble symbolism of Bill's scars at first; it was Fleur who correctly reinterpreted them. Fleur recognizes that Bill's traumatic wounds represent Bill's heroism and goodness, and his scars represent qualities she loves about him. Likewise, your scars can either represent something

7 *Harry Potter and the Half-Blood Prince*, adapted to colloquial English wording

you despise about yourself and want others to pity about you, or they can represent battles you faced and your choice to reject and resist the evil you have endured. Whether they are external and visual or internal and emotional, your scars can represent an undeniable truth that you have made cruelty your enemy, and that you stand as an ally to others who are also hurting and need support. In that sense, your scars are positive signals to those who respect your story, regardless of the offensive attitudes of others who do not understand those signals. In the story, once Fleur reinterprets Bill's scars, Molly is suddenly able to also recognize them as something wonderful about her son as well, and she and Fleur embrace with a newly-shared love. Fleur's ability to reinterpret Bill's trauma wounds endows Bill with honor his own mother had not initially recognized. [8]

Declare an intellectual war against the images of abused people as targets, objects, tools, things, fallen angels, or broken toys. Remember, you are battling your own inner beliefs here: you are fighting against the tendency to see yourself as lost, alone, ripped, and ashamed. You are not a hollow straw-filled person with a dry voice, quiet and meaningless. This kind of transformation is possible, but you have to fight for it to happen, not wait for it to happen. In your artwork, poems, journaling, and thoughts, give careful attention to the words, ideas, and images you choose to represent yourself. It saddens me to see people—who for once get to choose the emblem of their identity, their "selves" as humans and survivors—opt for images of defeat and emptiness. Wouldn't it help future young survivors if they found role models such as you displaying monuments of fortitude, victory, and unbrokenness? For once, you get to choose the face of your survival. Choose wisely. Choose triumphantly.

What does it mean to begin to cry/grieve more as you experience memories of your abuse during recovery? Should you go ahead and cry, or hold back the tears, when you talk about your trauma in therapy? Some clients in therapy avoid crying, and they describe these events with stoic detachment: "Yeah, I was gang-raped at college when I was twenty," but in the same tone of voice as "Yeah, I recorded this show on TV last night, but I haven't watched it yet." What I have learned is that people who "flatten"

8 So yes, people *can* change their attitudes toward traumas and scars when the reinterpretation is presented to them. I am reminded of the story of Yvette Cade, a woman who was set on fire by her abuser. Her entire body was scarred, including her face, which became unrecognizable, and she endured PTSD and chronic physical pain. Those who did not know her story may have looked with judgment on her appearance, but instead of wilting beneath those judgments she chose to become a public figure in the fight against domestic violence, speaking publicly on television and workshops nationwide. Those who learned her story were transformed, and rather than rejecting her, have found her to be inspirational and have honored her with dozens of awards: http://www.yvettecadefund.org/

their emotions when they describe their abuse are often doing so because they think this is how a recovered survivor is supposed to sound. They say to themselves, "I should be over this; crying is weakness; if I show emotions, then it means I haven't dealt with this yet and that's bad; this is my way of showing that I am strong."

This is called "alexithymia," which is a fancy way to describe the state of being emotionally shut down, robot-like, with little connection between thoughts and feelings. But let me state this as clearly as I can: people who have recovered and overcome their traumatic abuse do still have some tender emotions about their experiences, and they do not bury or deny those feelings. It is possible to transform your emotions from the suffocating, flooding despair you might feel now, to a sadness that reflects the hurt you have suffered which doesn't overcome you, drown you, and terrify you.

Stuffing your feelings down is not actually a form of being in control of them. It's not a form of strength to be solid stone when it comes to your grief. Being healthy means being able to express all of your states of being-physical, spiritual, and emotional. It does not mean having a mask of continual happiness. By crying for your trauma, you are beginning to accept it as a real loss, and not merely "some disgusting thing done to little-old disgusting me." Grieving, as opposed to merely being moody and weepy, is a sign of change for you because it means you are starting to see yourself as a worthy person who was wronged. You are seeing that you are a *hurt* person, not a *bad* person, and that you were hurt by someone who never saw your worth. You will also grieve the lost time when you could not see your own worth, and buried it in whatever lifestyle came after your abuse.

By grieving, you are changing your attitude toward abuse itself, not as something horrible done to a person who was somehow damaged, unlovable, and awful, but as a form of THEFT from which you are not only recovering but resurrecting. By grieving, you are recognizing that your abusers have honored fewer and fewer of your gifts, and offered you less and less choice about who you will be. Abuse steals away your very sense of power and security in the world. Grieving is a healthy way to recognize that you live in a world that has limited who you, as a person, can be. Recovering is your way of fighting back against those standards.

As one client of mine realized in therapy, "There are some pieces of me I just won't ever get back. I have to accept that they are gone. And for years I felt hopeless because of that, as if the core of me was stolen and I had to live out my days like a hollow tin man with no heart inside. But what I realize now is that I don't need those old pieces to re-grow. Those were pieces of a person I'm not like anymore. They were pieces of a hurt and broken me, and they can have 'em. I'm growing someone new."

Scars have significance, both in *Harry Potter* and in your life. Some survivors of abuse have actual physical scars; for many others, the scars are within. Harry's scar represents not just his literal injury from a trauma, but his unhealed sense of connection to his ultimate abuser, Voldemort. For Harry, part of his healing is to break the bond he feels between himself and his abuse/abuser, in order to become free. The scar represents not just a physical wound, but Harry's ongoing struggle to free himself from the legacy of the man who inflicted it. In fact, although J.K. Rowling has never confirmed this, the lightning design may even represent the *Eihwaz* rune, a zigzag line that represents the yew tree— the very wood that comprises Voldemort's wand. It is clear, though, that Harry's scar is meant to represent more than a simple injury from childhood. It represents Harry's unhealed emotional self, the part of him that is still linked to the one who hurt him. As he heals, the scar will remain, but the meaning of it will completely change.

Harry is not the only one who bears scars from his experiences. Ron Weasley's arms are scarred with welts caused by the tentacles of a brain-like creature in the Ministry of Magic. They seize Ron, who cannot free himself from their grip. What is most significant, though, is Madam Pomfrey's explanation for the scars:

> There were still deep welts on his forearms where the brain's tentacles had wrapped around him. According to Madam Pomfrey, thoughts could leave deeper scarring than almost anything else...[9]

The tentacle-brains, then, clearly have symbolic meaning. Ron carries physical scars on his arms that are caused by the brain's control over him. I have worked with people who also had physical scars on their arms, too, which were also caused by the effects of thoughts they could not be free of. Madam Pomfrey is wise to note that our thoughts often cause us more pain than any other injury.

Hermione is also scarred by her abuse at the hands of Bellatrix Lestrange. Bellatrix tortures Hermione, cutting her with a knife and leaving marks. In the film adaptation, Bellatrix goes even further, carving the word "Mudblood" into Hermione's arm. This detail isn't actually that far a departure from the significance of the scars in the books, though:

---

9 *Harry Potter and the Order of the Phoenix,* p.847

> "Why shouldn't I [call myself a Mudblood]?" said Hermione. "Mudblood, and proud of it! I've got no higher position under this new order than you have, Griphook! It was me they chose to torture, back at the Malfoys!"
> As she spoke, she pulled aside the neck of the dressing gown to reveal the thin cut Bellatrix had made, scarlet against her throat.[10]

Hermione shows what it means to transform from a victim into a survivor. She identifies herself as someone who has been abused, and feels no shame about her trauma. In fact, she names it, and claims it with pride. It is her version of saying, "I am proud to be a rape survivor" or "I am proud to be an abuse survivor," knowing that the rape and abuse are not shameful things to have endured, and recovering from them is something to be proud of because it takes immense strength and courage. One way that you know you have transformed from a victim into a survivor is when you are no longer ashamed to have ever been a victim at all, because you fully embrace the truth that being abused, raped, molested, or neglected are not failures within *you*. Recovering from them, though, does show strength within you. Hermione's approach to her cuts and scars is a model for what a healed victim is like: "I am proud of what I am. I have nothing to hide. In fact, I will share my truth in order to inform and guide others."

Harry bears the scars of his abuse by Dolores Umbridge. As headmistress, Umbridge is unable to enter the actual Headmaster's tower because the tower refuses to recognize her authority, and seals itself off from her. Even that little detail is a good lesson for victims of abuse: just because someone has power over you does not mean they are legitimately your superior. Many people I know have cut ties with their former abusers and perpetrators when they are able to, refusing to recognize them as having any ongoing place in their lives. There are times when you can't always resist what a powerful person does to you, but that does make their power valid. Despite not recognizing Umbridge's right to have power over him, Harry must still endure what she does. He cannot physically resist, and so he must comply. Compliance is not a form of consent, and obeying what he is forced to do by Umbridge it does not make Harry guilty of "putting himself in that position" or failing to stick up for himself. Instead, his resistance is in his mind: he can't save himself from what Umbridge is doing to him, but he refuses to accept it as right. He endures what happens, while not allowing his moral personality to be ruined by it. In fact, he reverses the significance of his abuse—scars that read, "I must not tell lies"—into something he later uses as a way to show his

---

10 *Harry Potter and the Deathly Hallows*, p.489

superiority to Umbridge. Likewise, you can use your own scars as symbols of being greater than your abuser, rather than symbols of weakness: "These are no longer who I am, but they do represent what I endured. I no longer deserve them, but I bear them because they testify that I am not like you. I will not harm others (or myself) as you harmed me, and therefore I am your superior."

In the books, there is one way to heal a wound so completely that it leaves no scar at all, and that is through the magical medicine of phoenix's tears. When Harry's arm is gashed by the fang of a basilisk, the wound itself should be inevitably fatal, let alone causing a scar. But Fawkes sheds tears for Harry, and that simple act of empathetic grief gives Harry the healing he needs. These tears, though, carry more than simple magical symbolism. They show you that those who truly value you will join with you in grieving for what you have suffered, and their empathy with you is also healing. I remember several instances during my past work as a therapist when women who had been raped would finally trust me enough to tell me their entire trauma stories. They would read, out loud, their own hand-written diaries, complete with every detail of every sensation they remembered, tears streaming down their faces. When they were finished, they would look up, and often see others in the group (including me) with tears on our faces, too. They were always genuine. I wondered sometimes if my own tears were embarrassing to them, or if my clients felt the tears were somehow inappropriate, but I still couldn't help shedding them. One of the women told me, though, that seeing them was healing to her. Instead of seeing shame or judgment or disgust, they saw other people crying with them. All those years of solitary pain and suffering had led to that moment, and for the first time they had opened up completely. Seeing others grieve beside them made them feel valued, not pitied, and those tears were healing to them. If a phoenix symbolizes rebirth after being destroyed, its tears represent that companionship in your painful journey. Harry felt the same way, too, about his grief at Dumbledore's death:

> "Somewhere out in the darkness, a phoenix was singing in a way Harry had never heard before: a stricken lament of terrible beauty. And Harry felt, as he had felt about phoenix song before, that the music was inside him, not without: It was his own grief turned magically to song..."[11]

Be proud of your scars, then, and don't add to them. Let them be symbols of what you have endured. If you have physical scars, realize that they show the history of what you faced, but have become stronger than.

---

11 *Harry Potter and the Half-Blood Prince*, p.614

Scars and Post-Traumatic Growth

Instead of seeing them as ugly, remember that Harry, too, was self-conscious about his own scar, and often felt like it was the only thing people noticed when they saw him. But Harry was able to create a whole new legacy for himself, and instead of the scar representing a tragedy that he was always identified with, it represented a triumph he had achieved. By transforming what his scar meant to himself, he also transformed how people saw him. The scar, rather than being a disfiguration, became a symbol of his inner goodness, his love for himself and others, and his new life story. Once a scar means that, it's no longer something to hide.

You already know the stories in your life that you don't want to be bound to. What will you choose as the story for your life now?

What will you choose for your scars to mean?

Also Available:

Resurrection After Rape is a workbook-sized guide for women who are recovering from rape. Useful for both clients and therapists during the healing process, "RAR" (as it is affectionately known by readers) includes dozens of examples of journals and "homework" from therapy that women have consented to share for publication, illustrating how other real-life survivors handled difficulties with PTSD, sexuality, anger, self-blame, conflicts with therapists, and more. "RAR" is used as the primary treatment guide in many rape crisis centers, and is even used as a textbook for training therapists in some universities.

Letters To Survivors: Words of Comfort for Women Recovering From Rape is an award-winning full-color book that contains the hand-witten collected wisdom of women ages 16-70 from around the world who are recovering from rape. Each writer shares what she has learned about handling difficult aspects of recovery, such as coping with people who criticize your efforts to heal, dealing with self-harm and intense shame, handling setbacks, and what to do when friends fail to understand your recovery needs. Every letter has been turned into a full-color work of art, making *Letters To Survivors* a gorgeous book of hope and encouragement. Suitable for readers from adolescence to elder, Letters To Survivors is positive without being superficial, and does not include upsetting or triggering content.

For more information or to request bulk purchase discounts:
resurrectionafterrape.org
letterstosurvivors.com
expectoptronumbook.com

About The Author

Matt Atkinson is a Domestic and Sexual Violence Response Professional. He has worked in crisis services as a staff director with the YWCA in prevention of domestic and sexual violence, where he developed and implemented programs with women's prisons, university sports teams, churches, and Indian tribes. Matt has also worked with youth at an in-patient treatment hospital, and with adults at an intensive outpatient day treatment group.

In 2004, he became the first male given the National Award for Outstanding Advocacy and Community Work in Ending Sexual Violence by the National Sexual Violence Resource Center.

In 2005 he was awarded "Most Therapeutic" by his professional peers.

In 2006 he began to teach college courses on domestic violence and crisis intervention as an adjunct professor.

From 2009-2012 he worked as the director of a program to help establish crisis centers to serve rural and remote victims, including training of counseling staff, victims' advocates, nurses, and law enforcement.

In addition to a career in fine art (mattatkinsonart.com), he regularly presents trainings at workshops and conferences on topics ranging from myths about false rape reports, sexism in media, special considerations for men working with female survivors in therapy, understanding Native American survivors' needs, presenting tough topics to resistant groups, and using *Harry Potter* in trauma recovery.

Matt has three Bachelor's and a Master's Degree in Art/Human Physiology, Behavioral Science, and Social Work. He is very happily married to the most amazing woman in the world, and has two incredible sons who live in and explore the Rocky Mountains of Colorado with him.